96 – Rogin + McCa

116 – Kansas vagrancy controversy

127 – – Pop. agenda (congressional) + C's argument

159 – Bryan's enemies = Pop's enemies

POPULISM

The Humane Preference in America, 1890–1900

SOCIAL MOVEMENTS PAST AND PRESENT

Irwin T. Sanders, Editor

POPULISM

The Humane Preference in America, 1890–1900

Gene Clanton

TWAYNE PUBLISHERS • BOSTON
A Division of G. K. Hall & Co.

Populism: The Humane Preference in America, 1890–1900
Gene Clanton

Copyright 1991 by Orval Gene Clanton.
All rights reserved.
Published by Twayne Publishers
A division of G. K. Hall & Co.
70 Lincoln Street
Boston, Massachusetts 02111

Copyediting supervised by Barbara Sutton.
Book production by Janet Z. Reynolds.
Typeset by Compset, Inc., Beverly, Massachusetts.

10 9 8 7 6 5 4 3 2 1 (hc)
10 9 8 7 6 5 4 3 2 1 (pb)

Printed and bound in the United States of America.

Library of Congress Cataloging-in-Publication Data

Clanton, Gene.
    Populism : the humane preference in America, 1890–1900 / Gene
Clanton.
        p.   cm.—(Social movements past and present)
    Includes bibliographical references and index.
    ISBN 0-8057-9743-2 (hc).—ISBN 0-8057-9744-0 (pb)
    1. Populism—United States—History—19th century.   2. Populist
Party (U.S.)—History.   3. United States—Politics and
government—1865–1900.   I. Title.   II. Series.
E661.C56   1991
324.2732'7—dc20   90-49798
                                                                                 CIP

For
Kayla Ann and Ashley Diane

Contents

viii
Contents

Acknowledgments

My sincere appreciation to those who sacrificed life's most precious gift—time—in order to read all or part of an earlier version of this study. Extra-special thanks are owed to an old friend and colleague, Richard L. Hume, who despite chairmanship responsibilities read the entire manuscript, improving it greatly. My thanks also to LeRoy Ashby, another splendid colleague and next-door neighbor by virtue of office assignments, for his reading of several chapters. This he did despite a heavy teaching load, extensive research commitments, and a much more ambitious writing agenda than mine. More importantly, Professor Ashby graciously allowed me to bounce an occasional idea his way—no matter how ludicrous.

Of course, the outstanding editors at Twayne Publishers—Irwin Sanders, Athenaide Dallett, John Martin, and especially Barbara Sutton, manuscript editors *extraordinaire*—are to be commended to the limit, for they devoted more time to the manuscript than others and improved it enormously.

My thanks—and my apologies—to many students over the years who were subjected to much of the material included herein. Among them, I owe a special debt of gratitude to Sara Dant, who ably assisted me during the fall semester of 1989, assuming an unusual share of the load in a section of an entry-level course; likewise to Dagmar (Daggie) Weiler, whose interest in this topic has long been a source of inspiration.

My thanks as well to an artificial person called Washington State University—more specifically, the Department of History, the College of Sciences and Arts, and ultimately the unsung citizens of the Evergreen State. Had it not been for a professional leave during the 1988–89 academic year, my work for this book and the completion of the research for another would not have been possible.

But the greatest debt of all is owed to Jane Ann Buffington, my dearest friend, the love of my life, and my closest companion for more than thirty years. In addition to all those wonderful qualities, she helped me to make a long-overdue transition to a personal computer.

Introduction

Populism was the popular name for a predominantly agrarian and decidedly democratic, social-political movement of the 1890s that was formally known as the People's Party of America. Perhaps the most instructive way to introduce that movement would be to recall a scene from what most genuine Populists surely would have considered their last noble cause. To do that, one must direct the spotlight to the congressional stage at the turn of the century and highlight the person who was the last Populist congressman. His name was William Neville. The man no doubt sensed that he and his political kind were on the verge of being added to the endangered species list, along with the buffaloes and the first Americans (that is, the "Indians"), those magnificent and more symbiotic inhabitants of the Great Plains, which had since become Neville's temporary homeland.

It was early February 1900 when the newly elected congressman from North Platte, Nebraska, stood before the House of Representatives to deliver his first formal address. Populism had been in near total eclipse since the outbreak of the Spanish-American War early in 1898. The great debate over empire set in motion by that war—already more than a year in the making—had reached a new level of intensity as casualties and appropriations escalated on yet another killing field. This was no "splendid little war," as the 1898 conflict had been popularly adjudged; rather, it was a brutal and controversial guerrilla struggle in the Philippines, ten thousand miles to the west of the nation's capital. Pretense removed, the Republican administration of William McKinley was using deadly force to suppress the Filipino independence movement in order to dominate the Pacific archipelago; ironically, Filipinos were fighting to preserve Asia's first republic, which had been inspired in part by the American example.

This was the issue that prompted Neville's speech. From his perspective, the war was simply "imperialism attempted under the cloak of expansion."

Even though the current of reform had been muddied considerably, this Illinois native, Civil War veteran, lawyer, and former judge managed, with his speech, to tap an original, undiluted Populist vein. He announced at the outset that he wanted to approach the topic from a different angle than had hitherto been advanced in the debate—"human rights." He said he was proud to "belong to a party which believe[d] . . . the declaration of principles upon which the American people passed from the condition of colonial dependencies to the enjoyment of human liberty and national greatness [was] still as sound as the day it was written." Consequently, it was "a real consolation to believe in the common brotherhood of the human family; to believe that when God made man and woman as the source of human development, class distinction was not decreed." Human rights were transcendent and universal: "classes, royalty, kings, monarchs, lackeys, valets, serfs, tramps, and slaves are all attributes resulting from man-made law and rule of conduct."

As the congressman continued, echoes could be heard reminiscent of Abraham Lincoln's immortal words concerning a nation "conceived in liberty and dedicated to the proposition that all men are created equal." The prairie Populist reminded his colleagues: "No government can claim the dignity of being a government by the people when a portion of its people are subjects not having equal rights before the law." He did not ask what had become of Lincoln's dream of government "of the people, by the people, for the people," but he was sufficiently committed to the Lincoln ideal to be able to expose several outrageous contradictions that were prominently on display among Democrats and Republicans. Since the words of this long-forgotten Populist congressman are included in that part of U.S. history "lost, strayed, or stolen," perhaps he should be given a rare opportunity to speak to his posterity, briefly and without interruption:

[Facing the Democrats] It is amazing to a Populist to hear members upon this side of the House declare that "this is a white man's government," and justify a property and educational qualification to exclude the black man from the right of suffrage and at the same time denounce the Republican party for trying to govern the brown man without his consent. . . .

. . . [Turning to face the Republicans] As a Populist, I am much more amazed to observe members upon the other side of this House dramatize indignation because a black man is occasionally deprived of life without due process of law, and in the same breath laud the Administration for shooting salvation and submission into the brown man because he wants to be free. . . .

Nations should have the same right among nations that men have among men. The right to life, liberty, and the pursuit of happiness is as dear to the black and brown man as to the white; as precious to the poor as to the rich; as just to the ignorant as to the educated; as sacred to the weak as to the strong, and as applicable to nations as to individuals, and the nation which subverts such right by force is not better governed than the man who takes the law in his own hands.[1]

Could human rights have been at issue? Indeed! Populism was greatly energized by that ideal. As much as anything, that humane preference had been responsible for the creation of William Neville's party ten years earlier.[2] It was therefore only fitting that when a war for liberty, a war to free Cuba from the "tyranny" of Spanish colonial rule, rapidly degenerated into a war of conquest on behalf of empire in the distant Philippines, the alarm would once again be sounded in resounding tones.

Such issues had existed from the nation's beginning. Lincoln could speak, as he did in Gettysburg with unrivaled historic eloquence, about a new nation having been created in 1776, "conceived in liberty and dedicated to the proposition that all men are created equal"; the frame of government, the national and state constitutions, the laws, and the system of rewards failed to measure up to the ideal. Only when practices were egregiously out of line, as in the case of slavery, did reality put the ideal to the test. The great economic revolution, which began well before the Civil War but which came to an explosive, discombobulating stage during the quarter-century after Appomattox, produced circumstances that suggested to some segments of the population, agrarians especially, that another great crisis was impending. From their perspective the situation was a significant threat to the America of the Declaration and was steadily progressing toward a new form of slavery, one possibly even worse than the old bondage that had produced the nation's bloodiest war.

Years ago, in a classic study that helped to shape the nation's understanding of its history, Vernon Parrington (1871–1929) came to this conclusion: "Since the rise of the slavery controversy the major parties, allied with masterful economic groups, have persistently ignored the Declaration of Independence, and repudiated in practice the spirit of democracy." Prevention of "so grave a treason to our traditional ideals, to assert the rights of the common man against the encroachments of a class, has been . . . the . . . mission of . . . third-party movements."

Populism was the culmination of all of these. It was, as Parrington knew firsthand, a movement of "homespun realists," who were losers yet at the same time winners. Their failure to establish a viable party—in name, at least—should not obscure their contribution to what Parrington also correctly identified as their major objective: the creation of a political system that would make it possible for "democracy to withstand the shock of the Industrial Revolution."[3]

If that objective was not secured nearly as well as it might have been—and it certainly was not—the fault was by no means theirs alone. Populists, despite a gale of criticism and outrageous misrepresentation, fought the good fight; they mounted what was, at least until the civil rights movement five decades later, the most significant mass democratic movement in American history, an extraordinary effort that continues, nearly a century later, to inspire and fascinate. Since the 1920s the Supreme Court and a very reluctant nation, with considerable backing and filling, have gradually struggled to reassert the Populist commitment to the humane preference.

Although conventional wisdom would suggest that Populism was eventually implemented, the original national program championed by the People's party, as will be seen, certainly was not fulfilled. The Populists nevertheless helped pave the way, not altogether intentionally or approvingly, for a more economically accommodative version of reform within both major parties called Progressivism.

Since Parrington's interpretation has been featured here, perhaps some additional comments regarding his scholarship are in order. With the benefit of more than six decades of hindsight, one can see that Parrington's brand of democracy was rooted in preindustrial, agrarian America. He was truly and proudly a Jeffersonian. Although long identified as a Progressive historian, he was surely as much a Populist as William Neville. Indeed, while he was still in his twenties, he himself had been a local Populist leader in that heartland of Populist fervor, southeastern Kansas. Unfortunate it is for the historical record that the essays Parrington had planned to write on Populism and Progressivism were unfinished when he died suddenly in 1929 while visiting England.[4]

Professor Parrington had launched this bold assertion from his academic base at the University of Washington as well: "It is, perhaps, not extreme to interpret the political history of America since 1790 as largely a struggle between the spirit of the Declaration of Independence and the spirit of the Constitution, the one primarily concerned with the rights of

man, the other more practically concerned with the rights of property."
For years, the scholarly community has been offended by the dualism
represented in that statement—to mention it is to raise the hackles in-
stantly.[5] An astute younger scholar, nevertheless, recently came to this
conclusion: "The literature on American Populism seems to be moving
toward a recognition of the republican roots of the Populist critique of
American capitalism. If, in fact, there were two late-nineteenth-century
American minds, one liberal and the other republican, Progressive historians may not have been too far off base in seeing a dualistic society.
One of the earliest major disseminators of this point of view, Vernon
Louis Parrington, probably knew of what he wrote."[6]

This is fair enough as regards the taproot of Populism. Questions about
its accuracy aside, the dualistic historical analysis certainly figured in the
thought of many people, especially in the South and West, where Populism flourished. As a frame of reference for judging and analyzing American society, it may very well have emerged in the aftermath of the
struggle for independence, concomitant with the economic revolution,
maturing with it, only to falter by the end of the nineteenth century. In
any case, by the time William Neville delivered his speech, which was
the product of that old radical or "republican" mind-set, there were more
American minds in contention than two. That such complexity existed
should surprise no one, as it has long been recognized that the 1890s
were truly a watershed in the rise of modern America.

In the 1890s this simple dualistic alignment was breaking down with
the emergence of "corporate liberalism" and "liberal corporatism." At the
same time the political alignment described by Robert Fisher for the
twentieth century, shaped primarily by the new industrial society, appears to have been forming, with reactionary, conservative, liberal, and
radical variants. These persuasions were still greatly complicated by the
old fissure along agrarian-versus-urban, country-versus-town, agricul-
tural-versus-urban-industrial lines. Yet the following definitions of the
terms—modified slightly for the frame of reference used here—seem apt
and will be employed throughout this study, unless otherwise indicated.
Reactionary represents "efforts to stop change and decrease the power
of lower-class and minority groups"; *conservative* represents "attempts
to maintain [and empower] the political and class status quo [closely associated with the dominant economic system]"; *liberal* represents "efforts to promote social changes which do not challenge [in a fundamental
way] the existing class and economic system"; and *radical* represents

"efforts to advance political, economic, and social democracy which often, though not always, see the capitalist system as the cause of problems."[7]

Too frequently the Populist movement has been treated as though it sprang from an historical vacuum. No doubt this has been caused by urban-industrial America's inability or disinclination to comprehend an agrarian world that all but vanished years ago. By the mid-twentieth century, to complicate matters, that world had been all but obscured by a mythical fog that has not yet found its Arnold Toynbee—or even its Richard Hofstadter—to name and interpret it. One might call this the Urban-Industrial-Capitalist Myth, which fused at least two powerful ideas—the notion of progress and the notion of an advancing, allegedly superior civilization—with the cause of unimpeded entrepreneurial growth. This potent construct emerged in the late nineteenth century to overwhelm and then later to replace another powerful mythology called the Agrarian Myth. Myths no doubt "relieve us of guilt," as Joseph Campbell has said. Unfortunately, they also serve to close the door on the past, denying humanity the opportunity to learn all that needs to be learned. More disastrous, they allow society to shun history or to use it primarily to confirm a specious present. In the process, those essential ties that connect humanity with generations past and future are all too frequently severed.

Not coincidentally, while practically every American history textbook offers at least a superficial—more often than not condescending—treatment of Populism, the segment is invariably positioned in advance of a discussion of the era's dominant beliefs, its revolutionary changes, its politics of drift, and above all its devastating assault on the democratic tradition. This subtly assures that the movement will come across as irrational or at best as idiosyncratic.

Populism in many ways represented the fulfillment, the last significant expression of an old radical tradition that derived from Enlightenment sources that had been filtered through a political tradition that bore the distinct imprint of Jeffersonian, Jacksonian, and Lincolnian democracy. Following the Civil War, Henry George (1839–97), an intrepid Philadelphia-born reformer, more than any other person endeavored to keep that tradition alive by updating and extending it in an attempt to assure its viability within the context of an urban-industrial nation.[8] Most Populists were not especially enamored of George's unique solution (the Single Tax) nor he with Populism. But his social analysis, as well as his reaffirmation of the old egalitarian theory of human rights, and especially his insistence that those rights were meaningless without an economic component, were central to the meaning of the movement. I have attempted to illustrate those connections throughout this study; they in fact constitute what has been called here the humane preference. In the process, I have highlighted the Kansas phase rather extensively; my justification for having done so, beyond familiarity, is the fact that Populism was nowhere more developed or more successful than in the Sunflower State. One would hope that insights derived therefrom would have some general validity.

Perhaps some comments regarding my historiographical background are in order. I suppose we all would like to think that we march to our own cadence, but the truth is that we all have our intellectual progenitors. The notes and the bibliographical essay at the end of this book spell mine out more completely. My agreement with V. L. Parrington has already been noted. Two other individuals deserve special mention. In 1931 John D. Hicks published his classic study, *The Populist Revolt: A History of the Farmers' Alliance and the People's Party*, and it quickly became the standard treatment of the movement. Although the book is seriously burdened by the ideological constraints imposed by Hicks's allegiance to the geographical determinism of historian Frederick Jackson Turner and his unconscious envelopment in the Progressive synthesis, it yet retains much to recommend it. Already under attack when Hicks published his book, the Turnerian school came under even heavier criticism thereafter and within a generation was much diminished as a way of making sense out of later-nineteenth-century American history. The resulting vacuum helped set the scene for an unfortunate historiographical detour down a dead-end road during the 1950s, portraying Populism as an unsavory, illiberal, retrogressive political interlude. The products of that detour, however, have since been essentially refuted by a long and still-growing list of carefully researched state and regional studies.

Nearly overlooked in this disputatious voyage through the historical composition room was another earlier historian, Chester McArthur Destler, who at the same time as Hicks attempted to direct the study of American radicalism and reform down a more productive road, one that historicans have ultimately resumed traveling, with some zigzags, since the 1950s.

Breaking free from the Turner straitjacket quite early (if indeed he had ever been in it), Destler discovered "urban [that is, eastern] origins" for "a number of supposedly rural stereotypes and remedial proposals that Turnerians . . . regarded as peculiarly western." The thrust of it all con-

vinced Destler that "a new radical synthesis," fashioned from "the ideological intercourse of country and city," may have "developed in the late
nineteenth century West."[9] It would indeed appear that the line cutting
across America's past was not nearly as geographical as it was industrial-
capitalist. On the one side of that line was a preindustrial capitalist and
anticapitalist (or at least mercantilist and antimercantilist) America with
urban and agrarian components; on the other was an emergent industrial
America with similar ingredients.[10] The two coexisted and interacted
with explosive and creative force over the last half of the nineteenth
century and were repeatedly invigorated, reshaped, and complicated by
an ever-changing landscape that included a moving frontier and a maturing urban-industrial environment. Populism emerged from that unique
caldron blessed with characteristics that pointed to the past and to the
future in ways that will undoubtedly furnish grist for historical debating
mills in perpetuity.

Chapter One

Tillers and Toilers

The Origins of Populism, 1872–1890

> *All political power is inherent with the people; . . . no government is*
> *worth preservation, or should be upheld, which does not derive its powers*
> *from the consent of the governed; . . . by equal and just laws, the rights*
> *of life, liberty and the pursuit of happiness shall be assured to all men,*
> *without distinction of race, color, or nationality; . . . the maintenance*
> *of these principles is essential to the perpetuity of our republican institu-*
> *tions, and . . . to this end the Federal Constitution, with all its amend-*
> *ments, the rights of the States, and the Union of the States, must be*
> *preserved.*
>
> —*Platform, Independent Reform party, Kansas, 1874*

> *The earth is the common heritage of the people; every person born into*
> *the world, is entitled equally with all others to a place to live . . . and*
> [*to*] *earn a living, and any system of government that does not maintain*
> *and protect this inalienable right is wrong and should be changed or*
> *abolished.*
>
> —*Platform, People's party, Kansas, 1890*

American historians now seem to agree that the era of the Civil War and
Reconstruction was an unfinished, halfway revolution. Because it was
that kind of epoch, it cast an exceptionally long shadow over the nation's
history. This was especially true of its politics. Those tragic years first
solidified and then virtually institutionalized a fundamental rearrangement
of the party faithful. Association with one or the other of the two major
parties came to be like belonging to the most evangelical of churches—

1

the Republicans' Grand Old Party or the Democrats' Lost Cause, Party of Our Daddies. In style at least, ethno-cultural-religious politics emerged supreme. As one historian has aptly written, "Sectional, religious, and racial loyalties and prejudices were used to organize the nation's two major parties into vast coalitions that ignored the economic interests of millions."[1]

It was not only the agrarian majority that was split asunder. The Civil War divided occupational constituencies generally along sectional lines—farmers, urban workers, and the commercial classes. A substantial majority of individuals within all these categories remained committed to their wartime loyalties into the 1890s. An exception was northern urban labor, which was loyal to the Republican-led Union cause but constantly supported the Democratic party. For these urban workers, economic, ethnic, and religious commitments (mainly Catholic) remained stronger than their sectional loyalties in determining their political allegiance. Spurned by the power structure, these people often supported political "machines," thereby rationally creating their own version of what another historian has aptly called a "ramshackle welfare state" in an age that loudly insisted it was "every man for himself and the devil take the hindermost!"[2]

From 1872 on, however, a liberated minority set to work to overcome the nation's myopia and cynicism, championing a line of thought that found a succinct rhetorical climax in Populism's 1892 Omaha platform: "We declare that this republic can only endure as a free government while built upon the love of the whole people for each other and for the nation; . . . it cannot be pinned together by bayonets; . . . the Civil War is over, and . . . every passion and resentment which grew out of it must die with it; and . . . we must be in fact, as we are in name, one united brotherhood of freemen." Twenty years of bitter struggle and preparation had been required to produce the sentiment embodied in that statement. In America's Gilded Age (1865–90) ideas of that kind had earned their advocates nothing but abuse.

Tumbleweed Politics

It has been said that the dominant version of postbellum politics was a "nonideological" creation of a "mature relationship between sectionalism, issueless politics, and the business direction of both major parties."[3] That assessment reads well, but I am convinced the era's politics was not so much nonideological and issueless as deceptively economic and flagrantly diversionary. On the northern side of the equation, that which Abraham Lincoln had described as a "new birth of freedom" was slowly but surely being translated into a new birth of economic license for new industrialists and the proponents of the inhumane preference—money and system over human beings.

As strange as it surely must seem, the American scholarly establishment would not discover the economic side of history until the twentieth century, but by the postbellum era, that factor was operating in extraordinarily unprecedented ways. Undeniably the North-South conflict played an especially important role in fashioning a political climate of inaction and drift in coping with the problems of the new industrial society—"tumbleweed politics," in the lexicon used here. But there was much more involved in the creation of the lag than the emotions, loyalties, and divisions created by the Civil War. The friends of democratic reform, particularly those who were convinced that without a measure of economic equality "all talk of liberty and fraternity, all equality before the law, [was an] . . . empty and sinister mockery," faced a number of other quite formidable obstacles.[4]

In the two decades before the creation of the People's party and beyond, the definition of reform itself contributed to the stalemate. To a degree, this accounts for why the reform chorus was manifestly discordant, frequently shrill, and generally ostracized. Considering all that was going on, it probably could not have been otherwise. The friends of democracy—those partisans of the humane preference—had to contend with a dominant intellectual climate that antagonized the very concept of reform itself. The age was especially bewildered by these questions: What is reform? Who are its legitimate champions?

Reform, in its more general sense, is (and was) the expression of a determination to make the real world conform to an ideal that in the mind of the reformer is blessed with positive moral qualities. Reform to the reformer is consequently perceived as a righteous upward movement, an effort to realize the "good society." To the extent that an individual has some rational conception of an ideal society and becomes involved in an effort to reshape the existing order according to that ideal, that person is a reformer.

The good-society ideal of reformers, in both the mainstream and dissentient traditions, drew heavily upon those more humane values explicit and implicit in the American Revolution, symbolized by the Declaration of Independence and to a lesser extent by the Constitution. There were, however, at least two major competing interpretations of the meaning of the democratic creed. The more influential and much less radical of the two stressed greater opportunity and, in its most compassionate rendition, it extended to the goal of equal opportunity (the Lincoln ideal, as many came to interpret it). The other interpretation was inspired by a more egalitarian vision and infused the democratic ideal with economic substance (Henry George à la the radical Thomas Jefferson). The goal of greater opportunity is, of course, not the same as equal opportunity itself; equal opportunity is not the same as actual equality. Much of the debate within American society over the years, especially among various and competing reform elements, has been related to those unresolved—at times even unrecognized—differences.

A huge transvaluation that political scientist Clinton Rossiter termed the "Great Train Robbery of American intellectual history" has particular relevance here, too. The ideal of the reform tradition was rooted in preindustrial, agrarian America; it was also solidly linked to laissez-faire individualism and was distinctly configured by the agrarian mold whence it came. As the industrial society matured after the Civil War with the ongoing technological revolution, it became increasingly obvious to some that individuals acting alone—or even in their associated occupational capacities—could not bring the process under control. The idea that technology was out of control and would likely destroy its creator was, after all, at least as old as Mary Shelley's 1818 English fictional character, Frankenstein's monster; only a cooperative and willful community would be capable of performing that task. But the prevailing political economy and conventional wisdom made a virtue of not controlling the process in a regulative or fundamentally reconstructive fashion. At the same time, aided and abetted by a voguish antisocial rendition of Darwinism, the champions of the new industrial capitalism were appropriating the older liberal tradition in order to turn back the reform effort, reinterpreting it in such a way that Adam Smith (1723–90), the patron saint of classic market liberalism, would not have recognized the doctrines linked to his name.[5]

Consequently, it was imperative that reformers sever their ties to the traditions of laissez-faire individualism and negative government, just as it was also necessary that they adjust their perceptions to accord with the new reality of a fast emerging urban-industrial nation. The great power and organizational dimensions of modern corporate enterprise required—if it were indeed to be brought under control—the use of state and national governmental power. Given the inherited tradition, these were conclusions not easily arrived at; once perceived, they were difficult to accept. The question of granting power for that purpose to the national government was especially divisive, particularly among most southern whites. In their minds the South's defeat—as well as challenges to white supremacy and an unprecedented and seemingly perpetual impoverishment—were closely identified with the North's victory and the resultant augmentation of national power. Furthermore, not only were the friends of democracy divided about granting that kind of power to the national government, the institutional devices necessary to control corporate enterprise were nonexistent. In fact, the structure of government, especially its legal and judicial systems, had already been reshaped to prevent the control of corporate enterprise and to stifle the attempt aimed at devising alternative institutions. At the same time, as the challenge to the neomercantilist order intensified in the decades after the Civil War, first at the state and then at the national level, new safeguards were being fashioned by corporation lawyers and a pliant judiciary to counter the drive for anticorporate, democratic reform.[6]

The quest for economic democracy was made even more difficult by the fact that the Civil War and Reconstruction combined to form that incomplete and unfulfilled revolution, which went quite far enough to rally the partisans of the inhumane preference but not nearly far enough to secure its opposite. The ultimate failure of Reconstruction, especially, severely compounded the element of disillusionment and cynicism within American society, endowing antidemocratic sentiments with new legitimacy and establishing an outrageous mythology and a twisted historical legend whose respectability would linger—even among leading scholars—for several generations.

Ultimately, the most dynamic and seemingly irrepressible force was the ongoing economic revolution. Economic change and material growth ruled the day. As a result, progress was increasingly measured solely by the materialistic yardstick. To that sizable group who thought merely in terms of greater opportunities, and even more to those who made no pretense of subscribing to the democratic creed, the business leaders fashioning the new industrial-capitalist world were the era's true reformers. Utopian capitalism was on the rise. Above all, the prevailing intellectual climate assured the nation that an unrestrained market economy was the only safe road to prosperity and future happiness. As its partisans would never weary of arguing, it was the only way of assuring fulfillment of the people's inherent property rights in accord with their ability and initiative. There was no denying that the ideal world of industrial capitalists was rapidly being converted into reality. Industry was indeed the coming thing. A lapse of time was probably to be expected before a significant number of Americans became sufficiently alarmed by that reality to challenge the new order and to begin viewing the leaders of the industrial advance merely as change-makers, most of whom likely had little or no regard for the democratic creed.[7]

Prelude to Populism: Kansas

The Populist movement grew out of a reform campaign that was actually two decades in the making. Many, if not most, of the movement's future leaders, those from outside the South especially, had been active in third-party politics at one point or another prior to the creation of the People's party. From that experience—more even than from farmer organizations—flowed much of the analysis, ideology, and program that informed and shaped the Populist agenda as set forth in the party's Omaha platform of 1892. Partly for that reason—and partly because the most influential recent study of Populism has implied otherwise—a closer look at this political prelude is in order.[8]

The case of Kansas is especially revealing. The first People's party materialized there, and the word *Populism* itself was coined in Kansas, probably because of that state's strong old radical or "neorepublican" tradition. After all, the state had a "bleeding," leading-edge tradition dating back to pre–Civil War days, and the problems confronting Kansas agrarians, although not nearly as desperate as those confronting the southern masses, were real and becoming more difficult with each passing year. By the 1870s—much more than Illinois, in fact—Kansas was the "land of Lincoln."[9]

Third-party activity in the Sunflower State got off to a premature and inglorious start. As early as February 1870, some dissidents got together at the state capital and organized what was called a "workingmen's movement." That effort soon collapsed, however, with barely a whimper, and its organizers were charged with "trying to rouse the rabble, destroy property, and to overthrow the government." But political dissent would not be so easily silenced thereafter.[10]

Nationwide, discontent with the country's course began to congeal midway through President Ulysses S. Grant's first term (1869–73). By 1872, an effort was under way to defeat the general's bid for reelection. That endeavor culminated in the formation of the Liberal Republican party, which won the support of many Democrats. Horace Greeley, editor of the New York *Tribune,* became the party's presidential nominee.

During the campaign, Liberal Republicans and Democrats denounced President Grant in scathing terms—even though the fraud and corruption for which the Grant administration was soon to be notorious had only just begun to take root; not until Grant's second term would it reach "full bloom, spreading from department to department."[11]

In Kansas, the extent to which President Grant personally was the issue was illustrated by the Democrats' state platform, which singled out the Hero of Appomattox for particular scorn. The man was said to be "utterly unfitted" for the presidency. He stood at the top of an administration, it was said, that had no rival in the nation's history "for shameless ignorance, nepotism, and gift-taking; for reckless disregard of law and forgetfulness of the honor of the Republic; for utter want of . . . dignity and statesmanship." His reelection, the Democrats said, would "degrade the nation" and threaten "the liberties of the people."[12]

In an extraordinary move, Kansas Liberal Republicans and the reform wing of the Democratic party met in convention to endorse the Greeley ticket. The platform they wrote was not especially noteworthy. Beyond determined opposition to the Grant administration, the coalition's stand against additional "grants of land to railroad or other corporations" and corrupt election practices, especially in the selection of U.S. senators, were its most significant planks. It was clear that the reform coalition in Kansas was plagued by inconsistencies and major unresolved philosophical differences. This was most evident in the state party's singling out for special emphasis that portion of the national Liberal Republican–Democratic platform that stressed states' rights as opposed to centralized power.[13]

Horace Greeley was soundly defeated; mere froth, he was, on an immature wave. The savage attacks to which he was subjected prompted from him one memorable line that had enduring meaning to later proponents of radical democratic reform: at times, he said, it was hard to tell whether he was "running for the penitentiary or for the presidency." Greeley, in fact, died only three weeks after his defeat, and the Liberal Republican party went out of existence. But beginning in 1873 the reform agitation mounted, much stimulated by the onset of the worst depression the country had ever experienced.[14]

Between 1872 and 1890 Kansas, like other states, saw the emergence of a multitude of reform parties. The rise and fall of these organizations was testimony to the volatility of the political climate, as well as to the extraordinary obstacles against which reformers were battling. The Independent Reform party followed the Liberal Republican–Democratic effort and waged two campaigns before it went out of existence, challenging the Republicans in 1874 and both major parties in 1876. The 1878 contest saw the Greenback party in the field against the Democrats and Republicans. In the three contests from 1880 to 1884, the Greenback–Labor party carried the banner of reform. In 1886 the Prohibition party (at the time thoroughly radical) continued the fight, and in 1888 the newly organized Union Labor party, the successor to the Greenback–Laborites, entered the contest. In addition, a number of lesser, splinter-group parties were active in several campaigns.

Analysis of the party platforms of the period reveal several general tendencies. From 1872 to 1886, the state conventions of the dominant Republican party formulated short, generally evasive, and noncontroversial platforms in presidential election years; in off-year elections they presented broad platforms, on rare occasions incorporating measures previously championed by one third party or another. Republicans also identified more with the use of national power to promote—but not to regulate—business enterprise; Democrats, while inclined to be critical of the use of government to aid business, were also reluctant to employ that power to regulate business, especially at the national level. The Democrats were also partial to states' rights and decentralization. The third parties of the period, on the other hand, called for a wide variety of reforms, embracing economic, political, and social activities. In fact, most of the proposals advanced in the later Populist decade were brought forward by these earlier third parties.[15]

Greeley's 1872 campaign had helped ignite the fire of reform. That year also was notable in Kansas for the establishment of a branch of the National Grange of the Patrons of Husbandry. Five years earlier, Oliver H. Kelley, a Minnesota farmer and Washington clerk, had originated the Grange to promote knowledge and sociability among farmers. Supposedly designed as a nonpolitical association of rural men and women, Grangers quickly became aware of their organization's political potential. In Kansas the Grange became a mass movement, growing with truly astonishing speed, as it did elsewhere in the West and to a lesser extent in the South. It reached its peak in 1874, the infamous "grasshopper year" in Kansas and the second year of a great nationwide depression. By then, Granger lodges were being chartered nationally at the rate of nearly two to three thousand or so each month.[16]

Segments of the nation's farm community were experiencing extraordinary ferment, and Kansas farmers too were on the march. Their rallying cry was "organize and cooperate." That sentiment produced a

Organizing farmers

significant first in the state—a farmers' convention in Topeka in March 1873. The convention, in turn, created the Farmers' Co-operative Association of Kansas, aimed primarily at helping farmers improve their economic leverage in the emerging corporate society.

Analysts have concluded that this convention was truly representative of the state's farm population. The delegates (167 total) were not all of one mind regarding either the causes of the farmers' plight or the solutions to it, but there was one vital area of agreement. John Davis, later a Populist leader and two-term congressman (1891–95), expressed this consensus when he wrote the convention's official summary statement. He insisted that the agrarian sector was now facing a stage in historical development when it was clear that farming in a go-it-alone, isolated manner was no longer adequate to insure justice to the many farmer producers. The new realities required reformation of the laws and institutions to insure equal justice. Cooperation among the nation's producers was absolutely essential. It would make "even the thieves tremble," wrote Davis. By association, he said, they would "rub off that cold prejudice, too likely to exist among men who live in isolation and seldom meet for social intercourse." And as was the case with "Great Peter of Russia, we are learning from our conquerors the art of victory. Very soon we expect to meet them, not as loose bands, or detached parties of Cossacks, but as organized veterans."[17]

The convention also issued a comprehensive statement of "desires and purposes" that went beyond anything that had been formulated in Kansas to that point. Not until the Texas Cleburne Demands, thirteen years later, would farmers again commit to as broad based a program. Condensed, the main points were: recognition that disorganization was the great handicap of the "producing classes"; a demand for reduction of "oppressive and unjust" taxes by government at all levels; support for state and national laws mandating just freight and passenger fares on railroads, and if necessary the construction of "national highways at the expense of the government"; condemnation of an act by the legislature "exempting bonds, notes, mortgages, and judgments" from taxation; opposition to the practice of voting municipal bonds as "pernicious in its effect," destined to "bring bankruptcy and ruin on the people"; and criticism of the national banking system as "but little less than legalized robbery of the agricultural classes."[18]

In 1874 the situation that produced these moves led to the creation of a Kansas branch of the Independent Reform party, which had the support of the Grange (in Kansas and elsewhere) and the state's Democrats. The old radicalism or neorepublicanism of the Independents came through distinctly in its less eloquent but modern paraphrase of the Declaration of Independence (prefixed to the introduction of this chapter), and they also made a point of stressing the need to preserve the "Constitution, with all its amendments."[19]

The party's most significant platform statement demanded that "railroad corporations . . . be made subservient to the public good" and called for laws to "secure the industrial and producing interests of the country against all forms of corporate monopoly and extortion." The Independents also called for restoration of the income tax and demanded the recovery of half a million acres of public land, to be set aside for schools in Kansas; an earlier Republican legislature had given the land away to four railroads. Special censure was also directed at the Grant administration, which was said to be "without parallel" in "its incapacity to meet the vital question of the day" by providing "for the general welfare." Curiously, no specific mention was made of the monetary system, nor was the national banking system ridiculed, as it had been by the farmers' convention. Apparently those issues had not yet become consensual among reformers.[20]

Kansas Republicans met after the Independents, eager to prove that they too were responsive to the state's farmers. After the usual reference to their Civil War record as savior of the Union, Republicans acknowledged that "parties cannot live upon glory. New issues are constantly arising and the party that deserves to live must be ready to provide for their solution." Yet the platform then declared that "the powers of the general government having been stretched to an unhealthy extent to meet the crisis of the Civil War and Reconstruction, [they] should now be restored to . . . normal." Republicans reaffirmed their confidence in the private national banking system, which was anathema to radical reformers, and they endorsed the need for "reasonable, just and uniform taxation." They acknowledged that the state's railroad corporations were "creatures of its legislature" and that it was "the duty of that body to subject them to such wise and impartial enactments" as would "protect the people of the state from extortion" and to provide "transportation of products, merchandise and passengers at reasonable rates." The party also went on record against additional "grants of the public domain to railroad or other corporations"—an action that the Liberal Republican–Democratic coalition had taken two years earlier.

Though the Independent Reform party was soundly defeated by the Republicans, Kansas reformers came closer to victory in that 1874 election than they would in any subsequent contest until the Populist earth-quake of 1890. Their 41.3 percent of the ballots left the Republicans with a plurality of just over 13,000.[21] Thereafter, this first reform wave began to recede. The state experienced a truly phenomenal period of settle-ment and economic growth. Rising prices for land and farm products coincided with a decline in zeal and membership in farm organizations that would not be reversed until the boom collapsed in the late 1880s.

Despite the decline of support at the grassroots, reform efforts con-tinued as determined as ever from 1876 to 1890. During that period, all reform proposals in Kansas politics were introduced by the third parties, apparently with only three exceptions. Some of their proposals would not be implemented until far into the twentieth century; with a few, the na-tion would still be struggling one hundred years later; many have never been implemented.

In 1876, for example, the Independents declared their opposition "to all banks of issue" and insisted that "banking on the part of corporations or private individuals . . . be confined by law exclusively to exchange, discount, and deposit." They called for an end to the national banking system and its replacement with a national paper currency backed by the credit of the national government. The Independents also condemned the 1873 act demonetizing silver, and they called the Specie Resumption Act of 1875 (due to take effect in 1879) "a fraud and an outrage," demanding its immediate and "unconditional repeal." They advocated a tax on all incomes over $1,500 (lowered to $1,000 in the 1878 platform) and called for the "immediate restoration" of silver as a "standard of value and . . . legal tender."

The 1877 Independent–Greenback platform was similar, but additional demands were included advocating criminal penalties for "watering" cor-porate stock, endorsing the creation of a postal money-deposit system, and requesting a congressional law for arbitration in disputes between corporations and their workers. The Greenbackers of 1878 added "equal pay for equal work" for both sexes and recommended that usury be made illegal. One of their platform principles made this revealing statement: "the claims of humanity should be considered first, and the claims of mere property second; . . . labor is the active and productive capital of the country, and should be protected and fostered rather than idle money." The Greenback–Labor party of 1880 first advocated women's suffrage, sponsored a law against convict labor, and called for an "equitable" ap-praisal of "all lands sold under mortgage or legal process, and an equitable stay or redemption law on forced sales of real estate."

Four years later, the Greenback–Laborites opposed all monopolies, singling out the railroad and telegraph systems for special attention. They advocated recognition and legalization of the right of laborers to organize and to bargain collectively in order "to enforce all their constitutional rights." Their platform demanded that the state mandate measures insuring "the health and safety" of those working in mines, manufacturing, and construction. They called for a reduction of interest rates and the creation of a bureau of labor statistics and went on record favoring a national constitutional amendment prohibiting the alien-absentee ownership of land. In their last platform of 1884 Greenback–Laborites combined the demand for women's suffrage with the earlier call for equal pay for equal work for both sexes. Since women could not vote except in municipal elections, one could hardly describe this as opportunistic.

In 1887 the newly organized Union Labor party first proposed public ownership for all facilities engaged in "transporting intelligence, passengers and freight." The next year the same party called for an extension of time on all foreclosures of real estate such as would allow the former owner to redeem the property at auction price. The Union Laborites also proposed revamping the laws so as ultimately to abolish "all interest."

The three proposed innovations of the major parties were exceptions. In 1874 and again in 1878 Republicans demanded that the state legislature establish "such passenger and freight tariffs as shall advance the interests and promote the industries of the people." In 1882 the Democrats first called for the direct election of the president, vice president, and U.S. senators; they also proposed in that same year that elections for federal offices be supervised by the national government.

If any of these reforms were to have a chance, it greatly depended on the attitude of the dominant Kansas Republicans. Between 1874 and 1890 the Republican party did occasionally voice support for one reform or another. In 1878 they denounced a monetary system based on the credit of the government, but in the same platform endorsed the withdrawal of national bank notes, replacing them with "greenback currency issued directly by the government." The 1878 promise list also endorsed a bimetallic standard. Neither of these proposals appeared again from 1880 to 1888. In 1882 Republicans called for a law to "prevent unjust discrimination by railroad companies." The next year the legislature created a railroad commission, supposedly to fulfill that pledge. It soon became clear, however, that the commission was impotent. (A prominent Republican leader later admitted that that had been the intention.) The

1884 Republican platform then demanded that the railroad commission be given the authority necessary to carry out its previously mandated legal function of regulation. In 1888 Republicans denounced "all great trusts as oppressive to the people" and called for "stringent laws to protect . . . workingmen against contract, pauper or Chinese [immigrant laborers]." The platform that year also advocated a reduction in the legal rate of interest to six percent on cash loans and a reduction in the maximum contract rate of ten percent.[22]

In the words of the Scarecrow, who is said to represent the farmers in *The Wizard of Oz,* "It is such an uncomfortable feeling to know one is a fool." One would have to be a fool to believe that platform statements guaranteed the passage of appropriate legislation, even when endorsed by a party as dominant as the Kansas Republican party.[23] All the parties contending in 1878 advocated legislation regulating railroad rates, but the issue remained to be thrashed out once again in the Populist decade. The 1884 Republican call for strengthening the powers of the railroad commission was likewise not attended to, and the issue carried over into the 1890s. The 1889 Republican legislature did make the change in interest rates that the party had supported in 1888, but much of the reform program—that which was most vital—required action by the national government. On that level the matter was even further beyond the reach of Kansans.

During most of the years from 1876 to 1888, there was not much either major party could have done to advance the reform program nationally, even had they been so inclined. But neither party was. The federal government was deadlocked as a result of the bitter sectional divisions induced by the Civil War and Reconstruction. Only in the years 1881–83 were both the presidency and the Congress in the control of Republicans. Perhaps, therefore, it was significant that just as the major outcry for reform began to materialize in 1888 the national government was once again in the hands of Republicans—the self-proclaimed most adept politicos at utilizing national power. Reform-minded voters were consequently inclined to measure the party's performance with a very critical eye indeed.

Farmers' Alliances, in Texas and Elsewhere

While these third parties were gaining modest successes in Kansas and the Midwest, a second and more powerful wave of discontent was growing in Texas. From there it would move back across the cotton belt of the Old South and then out upon the great wheat-growing regions of the West.

The Texas frontier was the salient point of convergence of the American South and West and so was appropriately the catalyst for what would be the last serious effort aimed at uniting the nation's traditional producing classes. The vehicle for that wave—the "vanguard" of southern Populism—was an organization that came to be called the Farmers' Alliance and Industrial Union.[24]

The movement began obscurely enough, sometime between 1874 and 1877 in Lampasas County, Texas, with the creation of a local farmers' association called the Knights of Reliance. The name was later changed to Farmers' Alliance, and the organization was duplicated in other counties; by 1878 Texas had what was called a Grand State Farmers' Alliance. The original organization disintegrated, however, after its unsuccessful and divisive involvement in the Greenback campaign. Organizational offshoots survived in Texas. In 1884, after having reconstituted itself as a state organization, the Texas Alliance began to experience phenomenal growth, becoming the dynamic organizational force among farmers.

Organizational activity was not confined to the Lone Star State. From the early seventies on, slowly but surely, a movement was forming in various parts of the country. It was not obliged to wait on the creation of Texas-style cooperative programs; when farmers and their allies began to come together in hundreds of local organizations to talk about the situation they confronted, then to formulate demands and strategy, a united community was created, and ferment escalated into what has been aptly called a movement culture.

At first the Granger movement held center stage, especially in Illinois, Iowa, Minnesota, and Wisconsin. In its old northwestern stronghold the Grange concentrated primarily on railroad malpractices. But after a few productive years its momentum ebbed, and the movement fell short of its major goals—too close, it would seem, to the "bloody chasm" (a contemporary reference to the Civil War) and not far enough into the industrial revolution for success. The internal dynamics of the Grange were also self-limiting. The order did manage to establish, with limitations, the right of the states to regulate railroads and grain elevators. The U.S. Supreme Court handed down seven decisions in 1876–77 (the so-called Granger Cases) that upheld—nominally, at least—the right of states to regulate and to determine "reasonable maximum charges" by railroads and other businesses vested with a "public interest." The primary doctrines of those cases have never been specifically overturned, although for a period of years after 1890 they were virtually nullified by the Court's application of the Fourteenth Amendment's due process clause as applied to corporations.[25]

During the late seventies and eighties a variety of new farm orders began to appear. In the nation's midsection, by 1880, the National Farmers' Alliance was founded; in Texas, by 1886, a Colored Farmers' Alliance had also been organized and was chartered nationally by 1888, as it expanded back across the South, apparently trailing the whites-only southern Alliance, which had been chartered nationally a year earlier. In Illinois and surrounding states the Farmers' Mutual Benefit Association established an effective presence; the Grange maintained a tenuous foothold also in various areas, and the Northeast produced something called the Farmers' League. Louisiana had the Farmers' Union; North Carolina, Farmers' Clubs; South Carolina, a Farmers' Association; Arkansas, the Agricultural Wheel and the Brothers of Freedom. By 1887, the Arkansas Wheel, established statewide in 1883, had in fact extended into six other states and the Indian Territory. Altogether, membership in farm orders was running over a million and increasing rapidly as the decade closed. Given the long history of disorganization among farmers, it was truly an astonishing development, and its participants understandably began to think in terms of impending revolutionary change. As a Kansas Republican foe of Alliance radicalism put it in 1889: "The air is full of lightning."[26]

Outside the South, the primary beneficiary of this growing militancy and class consciousness among farmers was the National Farmers' Alliance, an Illinois-based order. Its origins are as murky as those of the Texas Alliance. Founding credit has been given to a group in New York, which established an association early in 1877, and to an earlier organization founded in Kansas about 1873 or 1874, called the Settlers' Protective Association.[27]

The substantial beginning of this northern Alliance resulted from the efforts of Milton George, publisher of the *Western Rural* in Chicago. Early in 1880 he created a Farmers' Alliance in Cook County, Illinois, apparently modeling it on the New York order. George used his newspaper to promote the organization, then used the organization to promote his newspaper (probably his primary goal). Requests for local charters followed, and in October 1880 a convention was held in Chicago to organize nationally, resulting in the chartering of the National Farmers' Alliance. After an initial burst of enthusiasm and modest growth, the organization languished until about 1886, at which point it began to expand again. As the economic situation became even more desperate for many farmers by the late eighties, membership increased, in large part as a result of riding the coattails of the Texas Alliance. In fact until late 1889 George included the southern Alliance in his membership totals. By mid-1889, in any case, the northern Alliance had established a scattering of suballiances—from Kansas and Colorado north to the Canadian border—that had begun to show signs of life.[28]

Two years before Milton George renewed his enthusiasm for the Alliance, the Texas-based organization took on new life. The dire poverty that gripped the South simply had become too much to bear as the situation worsened year by year. As one historian has said, "In ways people outside the South had difficulty perceiving, the crop-lien system became for millions of Southerners, white and black, little more than a modified form of slavery."[29] The whole region, as another has said, was transformed into a "giant pawn shop."[30] Many thousands of southerners who had moved to the Texas frontier hoping to escape it all found themselves confronted with the same miserable grind or worse, consigned to the mercy of the furnishing merchant and various middlemen; they were eager recruits for those leaders determined to break the chains of peonage. Such a person was S. O. Daws, a thirty-six-year-old radical activist who had moved to Texas from Mississippi. Early in 1884 Daws was designated traveling lecturer of the Texas Alliance. It was a crucial choice; he would later play a key role in energizing the order, especially in recruiting dynamic new leaders for the local units. He also had much to do with a decision by the Alliance to emphasize cooperative purchasing and marketing arrangements. Success was obvious and contagious. Membership jumped from around 10,000 midway through 1884 to about 50,000 by the close of 1885.[31]

One of Daws's more significant recruits for the state leadership was William Lamb. Born in Tennessee, Lamb had migrated at age sixteen to the Texas frontier. He was named state lecturer when he was in his early thirties and already well established as a local leader. More genuinely radical than his sponsor, he soon had no peer in Texas as a movement organizer and energizer. Lamb became the primary advocate of cooperative buying and selling and was ahead of others in urging political action by the Alliance. Early on, he became an advocate of concerted action by the Alliance and the Knights of Labor. To quote an authority on Texas Populism, Lamb envisaged "a vast coalition of the rural and urban laboring classes to restructure American politics."[32] That vision was the radical side of the Alliance movement; it would soon be the very essence of Populism, until the movement was compelled to broaden its base.

The Texas Alliance continued to gain momentum, creating a movement that was at once self-energizing and marvelously transforming. Its development was expedited by a number of events. Internal debates over the issue of whether to join in support of Knights of Labor boycotts and the Great Southwest Strike of 1886 against the Jay Gould line touched off a battle within the Texas order between activists and more conservative elements that ultimately helped push the Alliance toward radical political action. But first the road led through Cleburne, a farming community outside Dallas, where a convention was held in early August 1886.

The report that came out of this meeting has been called "the first major document of the agrarian revolt."[33] But the Cleburne Demands, significant as they were, contained little if anything that had not already been brought forward by third parties and farm conventions since 1872. It would appear that Texas and the South had some catching up to do, and the Cleburne Demands represented that more than anything else. But it was not done without great turmoil. A sizable minority of delegates dissented and in fact seceded from the main body of the Texas Alliance. This was indeed a critical event. Dissension was created by what some, in retrospect, would see as the core of Populism-to-be—the Greenback–Labor critique of American capitalism.

The Cleburne Demands totaled sixteen (the seventeenth was an action directive addressed to the order's president). Five were concerned with labor, three with railroad abuses, two with the monetary system, and six with agricultural matters. Many—but not all—of the reforms previously surveyed in the case of Kansas third parties were included. The donnybrook was precipitated by the eleventh demand, which was the financial plank fashioned by Independents and Greenbackers the previous ten years.

One Texas historian said this about the dissidents and the affair generally: "While Alliance conservatives shared with the radicals an abiding concern over the plight of the farmer, they felt, or at least hoped, . . . they would not have to break with their received heritage to express that concern. . . . But the eleventh demand of the Cleburne document, the greenback plank, was unacceptable to the Democratic party." These dissidents, it was said, "expressed traditional attitudes . . . Alliance activists and Populists would have to cope with throughout the years of the agrarian revolt. For . . . the political ideology of both the parent Alliance and its . . . offspring, the People's Party, was grounded in the greenback monetary interpretation of . . . American finance capitalism."[34] Not all historians of Populism would agree that greenback ideology was quite that fundamental, but it figured prominently in the thought of a significant segment of the leadership, in Texas and elsewhere. Without it, Populism probably would have generated not much more than an agrarian version of Progressivism or a politics like that of the twentieth-century Farm Bureau, in which case it would have been appropriately consigned to the dustbin of historical topics long ago.

The radical input made for more colorful history. The revolt created by the Cleburne showdown brought to the forefront one of the more remarkable leaders produced by the Alliance. His name was C. W. (Charles W.) Macune. He was thirty-five years old, a lawyer and physician, largely self-taught, and blessed with extraordinary talent for organization, writing, and public speaking. Kenosha, Wisconsin, was Macune's birthplace in 1851, but his parents had moved from there when he was only an infant. As the family was moving to California, his father— a Scotch-Irish Canadian Methodist minister—died of cholera, and his mother returned to the Midwest, settling in Fremont, Illinois, where her son spent his boyhood. While still in his early teens, Charles Macune left Illinois on his own, spending some time in California and Kansas, then arriving on the Texas frontier at age nineteen.

In 1885 or 1886, Macune joined the Alliance in Milam County and soon emerged as a leader. At Cleburne he was elected chairman of the state executive committee. From that position he became the principal mediator between feuding Texas Alliance factions, emerging as president of the organization in the process. Thereafter, Macune was largely responsible for bringing the two factions together again at a January 1887 meeting held in Waco. By that time, the Texas order had grown to about 200,000 members, and Macune was soon to implement plans that would carry it to even greater heights.

An early Alliance historian said of Macune, after fully crediting his achievements, "Time proved him to be a man of erratic judgment, poor business ability, and uncertain ethical standards."[35] Macune in fact became an obstacle to the immediate creation of the People's party in the South. It was said he "revealed that his opposition to independent political action might emanate from a marked partiality toward the Democratic party, and that his loyalty might be based on an allegiance to white supremacy."[36] Mights aside, Macune was one of those legendary transplanted northerners who became—perhaps out of a desire not to be seen as a carpetbagger—more southern than native whites on the question of race. For the time being, however, Macune's style of leadership was quite effective.

Somehow, Macune managed to hold the Alliance together. By avoiding the question of independent political action, and insisting that the Alliance was merely a "business organization," while at the same time orchestrating an ambitious territorial expansion and a stepped-up cooperative marketing and buying program, he reconciled—temporarily—the order's conservatives and latent reactionaries to the radical Cleburne Demands. This was no small accomplishment. But there was an internal dynamic at work in this situation that superseded all else, and it was clearly working its way east and north from its Texas base. That dynamic might best be described by simply saying that hundreds of thousands of farmers and their allies were "mad as hell and just weren't going to take it anymore."[37]

As he formulated plans for expansion, Macune first considered joining forces with Milton George's National Farmers' Alliance, but he ultimately rejected the idea because of certain of its bylaws pertaining to organizational structure, financing, and membership. Especially objectionable was the eligibility of African-Americans for membership in the northern order, which was "unthinkable in the South." Macune wanted, according to one historian, "a strongly centralized order composed of [white—that is, European-American] farmers only, bound together by ties of secrecy and unified in purpose and procedure." Consequently, the decision was made to build—at the outset, at least—an organization with its primary base in the South. The first step toward that goal had already been consummated at the January 1887 Waco meeting, when the smaller Louisiana Farmers' Union merged with the Texas Alliance under a new name—the National Farmers' Alliance and Co-operative Union of America.

After the Waco conference the order began a massive organizational drive across the South's cotton belt. Organizers were dispatched to states throughout the region. Eight months later, the order was said to have established footholds in ten states, and enthusiasts had begun to look north to Kansas and beyond to the Great Plains for future growth.

In the meantime, southern consolidationists turned their attention to the Arkansas-based Agricultural Wheel, which was nearly as old as the Texas Alliance and as large or larger by 1887; the Wheel had also previously absorbed a smaller order called the Brothers of Freedom. In December 1888, after careful negotiations that avoided offending the considerable pretensions of both orders, consolidation was approved at a joint convention held in Meridian, Mississippi. Details were worked out thereafter, and in September 1889 the southern Alliance and the Wheel combined officially to create what was renamed the Farmers' and Laborers' Union of America.

The next logical step—a giant one, indeed—was to unite all organizations representing rural and urban labor, North and South. Consultation toward that end had been under way sporadically since early 1888. This consultation led to the scheduling of a national joint conference of all sympathetic farm and labor organizations to be held in St. Louis in December 1889; as one Georgia Alliance leader said, they desired "affiliation, possibly amalgamation, between the organized tillers and the organized toilers of the country." This St. Louis conference would be the first of a series of significant national meetings on the road to Omaha, Nebraska, where the People's Party of America would launch its first national campaign in 1892.

In early December 1889 delegates from all over the country and from five organizations assembled in St. Louis. The idea of merging all organizations representing rural and urban labor, however, was frustrated from the beginning. The American Federation of Labor refused to participate, and although the Colored Farmers' Alliance was meeting in St. Louis, it was apparently understood that the merger would not include the black southern order, considered "little more than an appendage" to the whites-only southern Alliance. The Knights of Labor and the Farmers' Mutual Benefit Association sent representatives, but by far the largest number of delegates—two hundred or so—were those that represented the Farmers' and Laborers' Union. The National Farmers' Alliance had about seventy-five in attendance. Representation probably approximated the relative size of the farm orders represented.

Combining even the two regional Alliances would have been a considerable achievement, but it was not to be. The majority of delegates from the northern Alliance balked at consolidation, citing three main reasons. First, they could not accept the southern order's new name, Farmers' and Laborers' Union; they suggested instead the order be called the National Farmers' Alliance and Industrial Union. The second had to do with the southern "whites-only" membership policy. The third pertained to the southern Alliance's secrecy requirements, which the northerners preferred as a state option.

The South met the North more than halfway. The first issue, the name, may appear trivial, but apparently it was not. Some northerners were evidently less eager to join with urban labor, and their reaction to the name revealed as much; in addition, the southern alternative incorporated the name of the northern order. But the southerners agreed to the change nonetheless. The southerners even agreed to eliminate the word *white* from membership requirements, leaving the matter to be determined on a state-by-state basis. More significant, southern whites were apparently also agreeable to having blacks serve on the organization's national executive council. The issue of secrecy was supposedly the insurmountable obstacle, although it need not have been. Despite their proclaimed opposition to it, secrecy had been practiced by certain of the northern orders, and within a year the main office would endorse the practice. Southerners regarded secrecy as indispensable to the success of the organization, especially in maintaining discipline and in its cooperative buying and selling programs. Yet the southern delegates tried to surmount even that obstacle by agreeing to a one-year delay in which to "prepare for secret work." All this was to no avail. The majority of northern delegates were a considerable distance short of having arrived at the level of organizational zeal permeating the southern Alliance and were looking for an excuse to avoid consolidation.

After this impasse was reached, northerners proposed the creation of an umbrella organization, a "temporary confederation." But southerners rejected the idea and stood firm on their generous previous concessions. Ironically, not much more than a year later, after the western and northern elements had begun pushing hard for a third party, southern Alliance leaders, led by Macune, would agree to a confederation of this kind but only to forestall the move toward a new party. The Knights of Labor and the Farmers' Mutual Benefit Association also declined the merger invitation but pledged cooperation. The Kansas Alliance delegation, a state that had already converted several months earlier, naturally accepted the invitation, and the North and South Dakota delegations left the northern Alliance at this meeting to become part of the newly reorganized National Farmers' Alliance and Industrial Union (NFA & IU).

Sectionalism, partisan fears, and concern regarding the effect of unification on third-party politics were primarily responsible for the failure of the two Alliances to come together. Ironically, the role of a third-body umbrella organization would eventually be fulfilled by the creation of the People's party, but the unresolved differences would by no means be eliminated. As a matter of fact, the two major parties would eventually exploit and exacerbate them for all they were worth.

Although the differences between the two Alliances were historically based, they were less than fundamental economically and socially. The extent to which that was so was demonstrated by the similarity of the set of demands that each agreed to separately. An early Alliance historian concluded that the "Southern Alliance . . . was interested more in financial problems than in anything else, whereas the Northern Alliance was terribly in earnest about the railroads and the disappearance of the public lands. But both organizations called for financial reforms of . . . [a counterdeflationary] nature, both protested against any landholding by [absentee] aliens, and both asked that the government take over and operate all means of transportation and communication." Except for the northern Alliance's omission of the silver issue, there was, he said, "on the three fundamental issues of land, transportation, and finance virtually no North and no South."[38] The fact that northerners but not southerners left out free silver was noteworthy, in light of the North's alleged greater attachment to that issue. Both farm orders embraced the Greenback monetary program, calling for the abolition of the note-circulating private national banking system and the substitution of a public system featuring "legal tender" currency (greenbacks) issued directly to the people and in sufficient volume to meet the growing business needs of the country. So the southern cooperative experience was not essential to produce a commitment to greenback ideology—on paper, at any rate.

Near the close of the conference, after the regular demands were approved, C. W. Macune introduced to the southern order the ultimate in greenback reform—the subtreasury plan. This crop-loan program (land was added later) was the most original measure to come out of the agrarian revolt. It was also to be by far the most controversial. The plan clearly had suggestive forerunners dating back to an 1816 tract by a Virginian by the name of Thomas Mendenhall calling for the creation of a national public banking system and a National Loan Office; much of it, however, was probably the product of Macune's fertile imagination and experiences.[39] Macune embraced the plan in the wake of the failure of the order's attempt to solve the credit problems that farmers faced by means of self-help cooperatives; his much-admired Texas Exchange had gone bankrupt several months prior to the St. Louis conference. Before that, Macune had left Texas to become editor of the *National Economist,* the Alliance's official national newspaper published in Washington, D.C.

Quite likely the plan recommended itself to Macune because it represented a way of resolving the problems of farmers without greatly enhancing the power of the national government and left undisturbed the social order built on the doctrine of white supremacy. He and many others in the Alliance movement, and to a lesser extent Populism later, were economically radical but socially, politically, and culturally conservative. Some were even latently reactionary. This helps to explain why some deconverted so readily once their economic plans were rendered impossible. I shall call this, albeit an awkward label, the humane preference–limited, the kind of thing that led to the contradictions Nebraska Populist William Neville identified in 1900 (see Introduction). It was a phenomenon destined to trouble the agrarian crusade to no end, and the two major parties even more. Macune's nearest counterpart on the northern and Republican side of the spectrum, for example, would be Mary E. Lease, whose behavior, rooted in psychological hangups spun off from the Civil War, would later contribute mightily to wrecking the Populist party in Kansas.[40]

Macune proposed that in every county in the Unites States where $500,000 worth of farm products were produced, there be built warehouses to which farmers could bring their crops for storage. Wheat, corn, oats, barley, rye, rice, tobacco, cotton, wool, and sugar were on the original list of commodities that could be stored. Farmers would then be eligible to borrow up to eighty percent of the current market price on the stored crops in legal-tender paper money at one (later two) percent per annum, plus a minimal charge for handling, storage, and insurance.[41]

The plan would have solved the farmers' credit problems, and it would have had revolutionary consequences for the economic system generally. Had it been implemented, the whole course of American economic development would certainly have been fundamentally altered. Its proponents never tired of saying it would "emancipate productive labor from the power of money to oppress."[42] They were probably right. Small wonder it became such a bone of contention and that it would rally the proponents of the inhumane preference as nothing else could.[43]

After St. Louis, the southern Alliance was truly the national Farmers' Alliance. It was, however, still in search of a comprehensive industrial union of producers. Early in 1890 its leaders moved with great vigor to carry the order as far west as Washington, Oregon, and California and north and east to Ohio, Pennsylvania, and New York. The question now was, could the NFA&IU achieve its goals without entering the political arena en masse? Or was some kind of third political entity necessary and inevitable to overcome the gulf that divided Republicans and Democrats? The answer would emerge from the politics set in motion along the Middle Border as the nation entered the 1890s.

Chapter Two

Amen, Dummy!

The Purification of Politics and the Campaign of 1890

The purification of politics is an iridescent dream. Government is force. Politics is a battle for supremacy. Parties are the armies. The decalogue and the golden rule have no place in a political campaign. The object is success. To defeat the antagonist and expel the party in power is the purpose. The Republicans and Democrats are as irreconcilably opposed to each other as were Grant and Lee in the Wilderness. They use ballots instead of guns, but the struggle is as unrelenting and desperate, and the result sought for the same. In war it is lawful to deceive the adversary, to hire hessians, to purchase mercenaries, to mutilate, to destroy. The commander who lost a battle through the activity of his moral nature would be the derision and jest of history. This modern cant about the corruption of politics is fatiguing in the extreme.
—*Senator John J. Ingalls, "Mr. Republican," Kansas, April 1890*

Who Was Leading Whom?

"If Texans led the farmers to the Alliance," said a Texas historian, "Kansans led the Alliance to the People's Party."[1] Indeed, and in the beginning, leadership came from a rather select group of radical activists belonging to a secret and thus enigmatic organization operating from within the Union Labor party. They called themselves the National Order of Videttes, and they played a key role in the development of the Populist movement.

24

Apparently the Videttes constituted a supra–steering committee. Its idée fixe was to free the nation from the grip of sectionalism and oppression by uniting massive numbers of farmers and laborers in support of a new party dedicated to the defeat of the regionally dominant, hidebound old parties, which they believed had become mere tools of the privileged few. The order was much influenced—possibly even conceived—by three brothers, surnamed Vincent, who published a weekly newspaper in a small country town in southeastern Kansas. The Vincent brothers— Henry, Leopold, and Cuthbert—were assisted by one of Benjamin Franklin's many direct descendants, William Franklin Rightmire. (The four actually signed off as Henry, Leo, C., and W. F.) With consummate precision, their weekly was called the *American Nonconformist and Kansas Industrial Liberator*; it began publication in Winfield, Cowley County, Kansas, in October 1886. The *Nonconformist* editors were, body and soul, committed to wresting "republican" America from the jaws of what they considered an industrial-capitalist monster.[2]

In an address W. F. Rightmire delivered before the Kansas State Historical Society in 1904 (unchallenged by any of the major players but much agonized over by historians since the early 1920s), the inside story of what really transpired back in 1888–89 was supposedly revealed. As he told it, in December 1888 in the wake of the Union Labor party's defeat the previous November, the Videttes got together in Wichita and created an organization called the State Reform Association to replace the executive committee of the Kansas Union Labor party and the Videttes. They then devised a plan aimed at organizing and politicizing farmers. This included a key decision to introduce the Texas-based Alliance into Kansas. That organization was selected, said Rightmire, because it "embodied every tenet of the platform on which the Union Labor party had waged its campaign." Thereafter, it was claimed, "three editors, members of the executive committee of the State Reform Association[,] went to Texas, and were initiated into the order." After returning, "they planted the Farmers' Alliance in Kansas by organizing a suballiance in Cowley County by changing a Northern suballiance at Cloverdale into a secret Alliance."[3] Rightmire identified the three editors as C. Vincent and W. F. Rightmire of the Winfield *Nonconformist* and John R. Rogers of the Newton *Kansas Commoner*. (Beginning in 1890, Rogers became an Alliance organizer in the state of Washington—or at the very least its advocate—and from 1897 to 1901 was the Populist governor.) The three then served as "recruiting officers to enlist organizers to spread the organization over the state." Subsequently, so the story went, from deep behind the scene they helped set in motion a monumental organizational snowball in Kansas and points north and west.[4]

Rightmire's account, as he presented it, clearly does not square with the story of the entry of the southern Alliance into Kansas that is on record. Seven months before this Wichita meeting occurred, one W. P. Brush—concerning whom little is known and who came from Clay County, Kansas, an area far to the north of Cowley County—had been commissioned to organize for the southern Alliance. Two months later, according to an Alliance historian who totally dismissed Rightmire's claim, Brush had organized "several suballiances" in Cowley County on the extreme southern border of the state.[5] The question is, did Rightmire fabricate the story of a plant to embellish his role in the creation of the People's party, or did he simply supply the wrong date—either as a result of error or by design? Another possibility suggests that plans were going forward on two disconnected fronts, but that would seem quite improbable, with the Vincent brothers, Rightmire, and other Videttes so much involved in what was going on in Cowley County.

Did Rightmire tailor the story to honor his supersecret Vidette oath? If that was the case, the plan he linked to the Wichita meeting of December 1888 could have been formulated by the Videttes and implemented before Brush received his commission. On 22 and 23 March, as a matter of fact, the council of the Videttes met in Yates Center, Kansas, with C. Vincent in a leadership role. The trip to Dallas most likely occurred— if it occurred at all—in April 1888, nearly a year earlier than Rightmire stated. Well before December 1888, the Kansas Videttes were fully apprised of the radical Cleburne Demands (August 1886) and were appreciative of the Texas order's cooperative programs, as well as its spectacular growth. Even more significant, C. Vincent was aware of a failed *direct* attempt on the part of the Texas Alliance—utilizing a Texas organizer—to establish a foothold in southern Kansas during the summer of 1887.

Indeed, it would appear that several of the Texas Alliance leaders were also Videttes.[6] In February 1887 Kansans—perhaps with the help of Texans and Arkansans—had promoted and achieved a national Vidette order at the Union Labor party convention held in Cincinnati. Select delegates from each state participating in that convention—mainly former Greenbackers, Antimonopolists, and Knights of Labor leaders—were said to have been initiated into the secret order and commissioned as organizers.

Sixteen years later, Rightmire, by attributing the scheme to the new and open State Reform Association, would have been able to claim credit for an activist cadre without fully exposing the earlier machinations of the Videttes. That secret order had since become infamous (probably undeservedly so) and was much hated and feared among that parade of respectables that ruled Kansas politics. Memories of it remained vivid enough in 1904, when Rightmire, by then an established Topeka lawyer with a reputation to safeguard, addressed the historical society. Back in the 1888 campaign, Kansas Republicans had in fact sensationalized the accusation that the Videttes were a wild and murderous band of anarchistic dynamiters plotting to destroy the government.

On the other hand, Rightmire may very well have been claiming too much. The role played by the Videttes and the State Reform Association may have been confined—and this after December 1888—to the important task of organizing new suballiances, to converting northern ones to the southern affiliation, and to consolidating the two Alliances. Perhaps one day some really tenacious historical detective will clarify the situation definitively.

The strategy for building the Alliance, according to Rightmire, was to seek out "some Republican farmer in each county" who had served in the legislature but who had been subsequently spurned and thus felt alienated. That person was to be encouraged to take on the task of organizing his county's farmers with the assurance that when or if the Alliance went into politics, the "founder" would be rewarded, receiving "any place he desired" in a restructured political regime. The plight of many Kansas farmers took an even more drastic turn for the worse after 1887, and the plan—if it was indeed implemented—evidently worked better than anyone could have anticipated.[7]

Initially, the northern Alliance seemed on the verge of capturing the support of Kansas farmers. Its first suballiance had been organized early in 1881, but the order sputtered along with little success until 1888, at which point it began to grow. On 2 August 1888 the association was finally able to hold its first state meeting. At Lyons, Rice County, 150 delegates representing organizations from seven counties constituted the core of the *first* state Alliance in Kansas. On 6 February 1889 the same order met again in Topeka and reelected I. M. Morris president. A short six months later, however, the northern Alliance had been largely supplanted and ultimately absorbed by the southern Alliance, which apparently had been established as a state organization *only* after 22 December 1888, with Benjamin H. Clover of Cambridge, Cowley County, Kansas, as president.[8]

The ascendancy of the southern Alliance was apparently even more rapid than this overview would suggest. On 19 April 1889 John Rogers published in the Newton *Kansas Commoner* the southern order's statement—a product of the meeting in Meridian, Mississippi—that "a consolidation with all, or nearly all, other farmers' and laborers' organizations has been affected and the consolidated association will soon be known by the name of the Farmers' and Laborers' Union of America." Kansas meetings followed, in Wichita in May and in Peabody in June, that prepared the way for a 14 August convention in Newton (a few miles north of Wichita). There the remnant of the northern affiliate was officially absorbed under the name Farmers' and Laborers' Union of America. All the while, membership totals were skyrocketing. According to one careful estimate, there were 21,000 members by April 1889; they were on the way to surpassing 100,000 by May 1890 and had gone from 700 suballiances to around 2,000.[9]

Kansans Create a People's Party

As early as 1888 unusual signs of an impending political storm were visible in Kansas. Although in the election that year Republicans soundly defeated their divided opposition, more than a few formerly devout followers had begun to question the Grand Old Party's course. Thousands of old-party members had by then been enlisted in the Alliance and had been repeatedly hit with the argument that they had been bamboozled for a generation.

One such individual was Percy Daniels of Girard, Crawford County, in the state's southeastern corner. Forty-eight years old, a Republican since Lincoln's first election, a Rhode Island native, a distinguished Civil War veteran, a resident of Kansas since 1867, a civil engineer, a farmer, a Granger, and a brigadier general in the Kansas militia, Daniels would soon help organize the People's party and serve one term as lieutenant governor. It was during the summer of 1888 that he began to reevaluate his Republicanism with a very critical eye indeed. Local Republican chieftains were about to nominate him for the state senate. In response, Daniels announced through the press that he was honored to be considered but would not accept unless the party approved of the following proposition, to which he was firmly wedded: "THE TIME HAS COME WHEN EVERY INSTINCT OF CHARITY, JUSTICE AND PATRIOTISM DEMANDS THAT THE POWER OF CAPITAL FOR WRONG AND OPPRESSION BE CURTAILED."[10] Having shot himself in the foot, so to speak, the general was not nominated.

Shortly after launching his insurgency, Daniels initiated a lively and revealing exchange of letters with John J. Ingalls, Kansas's senior U.S. senator. "The public," wrote Daniels, "is rapidly coming up to the point of asserting that positive legislation must interfere." Daniels then emphasized, "Assertions of these wrongs in resolution, nor idle and perfunctory discussion in legislative bodies will long suffice to satisfy this growing conviction." Senator Ingalls responded:

I belong to the school of politicians who think . . . government should interfere as little as possible in the affairs of its citizens. I have no sympathy with the paternal idea, but believe . . . the best results are attained when the people are left to settle the great questions of society by individual effort. All that legislation can do is to give men an equal chance in the race of life. We cannot make poor men rich, or rich men poor, except by making the natural capacities of all men exactly alike. The difficulties in society arise from the fact that Providence has established unequal conditions, making some men wise and others foolish; some men provident and others thriftless; some men industrious and energetic and others idle and self indulgent.

Perturbed by what he considered an especially glib and historically inaccurate response, Daniels fired back: "I cannot see that the distribution of wealth is very closely allied to our individual capacities. There are men in Kansas . . . barely making a living raising grain, who are as able and *unscrupulous* as any of the Wall Street financiers, or the men who divided a quarter of a billion in the various Pacific Railroad deals. Opportunity is the larger factor in most of these transactions—lack of integrity taking second place, and capacity third." Daniels suggested Ingalls rank his fellow senators according to their wealth and then judge whether there was a correlation between the size of their fortune and their abilities. If that were the case, Daniels said, Kansas would likely take offense at being represented by one so near the bottom of the list as Ingalls.

By this point, like many formerly complacent Kansas Republicans, Percy Daniels was firmly committed to altering the nation's course. He began speaking and writing to promote a number of measures he believed would be beneficial, but his favorite reform—then and for more than a

decade thereafter—called for a graduated tax on wealth. In an 1889
speech he said, "As a nation we are rapidly growing in wealth and power,
but . . . our growth is not a healthy one." According to his calculations,
more than ninety percent of the "annual increase in wealth" was being
appropriated by fewer than five percent of the nation's citizens. It was
to reverse this trend that Daniels became an outspoken advocate of a
graduated tax. He would have the revenue used first to provide for veterans and then for the employment of "all idle American labor on extensive internal improvements in every state, in building and improving
country roads and waterways, and in constructing and maintaining storage reservoirs and forest parks."

The Daniels plan obviously necessitated expansion of the role of government, which would mean a decided break with the idea of the negative
state or, as Ingalls put it, with letting individuals do for themselves. That
was surely the larger import, ultimately, of the whole reform agitation
and undoubtedly its most enduring influence. But for what purpose would
the state's positive interventions be made? That was the rub. Would it
be intervention to restore an older, largely mythical competitive order,
or would it be intervention to bring about some kind of cooperative society? To complicate the matter even more, were there not positions
somewhere between these two extremes? Beginning in 1889, these issues began to surface quite distinctly, revealing a degree of dissension,
indecision, and conflict that would plague the American polity thereafter.

These issues were discussed in dozens of pro-Alliance newspapers
across the state. In the fall of 1889 much attention was also devoted to
implementing the plan for a State Alliance Exchange that had been approved at the Kansas Alliance's Newton consolidation meeting. The Exchange was described as a "corporation" whose purposes were: "To
conduct a general mercantile business. To act as agent for the purchase
and sale of all kinds of farm and orchard products and general forwarding
agent for all kinds of commodities. To erect, manage and operate warehouses, stockyards, grain elevators, packing-establishments as may be
found necessary." The enterprise was to have $500,000 of capital stock,
split into shares of five dollars each, with no one individual or suballiance
eligible to own more than fifty shares. It was a corporation designed—
certainly on paper—to be and to remain democratic in ownership and
control. The Exchange was to begin operation once $10,000 in shares
had been subscribed.[11]

During the summer and fall of 1889 the question of what political
course to pursue commanded ever-greater attention. Throughout the

summer of 1889, William A. Peffer, editor of the influential Topeka *Kansas Farmer,* continued to advise against making any hasty political moves. Peffer believed there was little chance that a successful new party could be formed. As he saw it, "it is better for farmers and workers in general to form associations for the purpose of discussing principles, leaving details alone for the present." But he conceded, "The masses want reform in directions other than those in which the great parties are going . . . , but certain leading questions have controlled . . . elections, as they will . . . until the people in non-partisan associations . . . demand their consideration by legislative bodies."

Farther south, Murdock's Rebellion was the topic of conversation. In May 1889 Marshall Murdock, editor of the influential *Wichita Daily Eagle* and a leading Republican, blasted the 1889 Kansas Republican legislature. Murdock hastened to assure his readers that he was not an "anarchist," but he believed the state had "grown too much one-sided" and that "revolution" was required to clean up the mess. Murdock kept up this attack through the summer. In August the Republican editor of the *Fort Scott Monitor* responded by arguing that reform had to come from the Kansas legislature. Murdock saluted that flag with this: "Bah! It would be more sensible to go to the devil for pointers necessary to a circumspect life. That legislature is in and of itself one of the most prominent causes for the Rebellion. For years it has not only proved a disgrace but rottenness itself. . . . The only power to which to look, the only power from which there can come any relief, is from the people, and not from a Kansas legislature or from any of its creatures."

Murdock would stay with the Republican party during the rebellion, but growing numbers of Alliance enthusiasts were willing to follow his kind of reasoning to a logical conclusion. One of these was Stephen McLallin, editor of the Meriden *Advocate* in Jefferson County, in northeastern Kansas. A native of Pennsylvania, where he had been born in 1837, McLallin had moved to Kansas about 1869. Civil War service, graduation from New York's Albany Medical School, and some seventeen years as a practicing physician preceded his entry into journalism in the mid-1880s. A "compound of a Greek philosopher, . . . the austere, undemonstrative Scotchman, and the modern socialist"—or so his associate editor and fellow Populist Annie Diggs later aptly described him—Dr. Stephen McLallin was above all a genuine humanist and avant-garde political and economic commentator.

Editor McLallin, whose paper had been designated the state Alliance's official organ at the Newton consolidation meeting, led the way in the move for a new party. On 21 September 1889 he wrote: "It is urged . . . we should go into the primaries and by energetic and persistent efforts work out a reformation in the existing parties. We have tried this for the last twenty years without success. We have the same class of party leaders that have stood at the head during all these years and they are still as hungry as though they had never fed at the public crib." As he saw it, "Nothing short of civil revolution seems capable of effecting a change in the interest of the people." The old parties could not be used successfully, he reasoned, because bitter memories of past political struggles would not allow their former opponents to join. What was needed was a chance for the adherents of reform "to cut loose from their old moorings without a formal surrender of the colors under which they have so gallantly struggled heretofore." This, he felt, would enable people of all parties "to unite upon the issues that are now supreme, and insure their . . . triumph by overwhelming majorities."

McLallin believed that a conventional nonpartisan approach to reform, such as was then being advised by William Peffer, would be self-defeating. In his mind it meant that Alliance members would continue to be divided along the "old lines, precisely as they have been divided before they became members of the Order." A truly nonpartisan effort, to McLallin's way of thinking, would mean cooperation with neither old party.

As 1889 closed, the sentiment for third-party action in Kansas intensified. The new disposition of the Farmers' Alliance pointed logically and thus inexorably in that direction. In November 1889 one of Ben Clover's first official acts as president of the reorganized Alliance was to send out a circular letter directing all suballiances to submit, by resolution, the platform of the state Alliance to their congressmen—all Republicans— asking for their endorsement. When this was done, every single Kansas representative and Senator John J. Ingalls either avoided giving an answer or responded evasively; only Senator Preston B. Plumb gave it his unqualified support.

Soon thereafter, state Alliance leaders directed the suballiances to submit their demands to Peffer's *Kansas Farmer.* Perhaps that move was not without influence. Beginning in December, Peffer began publishing in the *Farmer* his analysis of contemporary problems, entitled "The Way Out"; he also took to the lecture circuit in behalf of the Alliance platform.

It was in this context that a Franklin County Republican leader named William Kibbe sounded an alarm that the atmosphere was "full of lightning." Kibbe took heed; he soon became a Populist. Storm warnings were even more obvious as the new year and the new decade approached. On the surface, the state's official Republican newspaper, the *Topeka Daily Capital,* appeared oblivious to the existence of any unusual ferment. The *Capital* told its readers that prohibition enforcement was the primary issue of Kansas politics and that the Republican party alone stood between them and the menacing reign of John Barleycorn, inspired by a concerted "Copperhead" and "Rebel" conspiracy. Farmers who perused the pages of the *Capital* discovered that "hard work" was their "salvation." These were cold words, indeed. Farmers could find little solace and even less support in the state's leading Republican newspaper.

The Alliance cause was not without a journalistic voice in the state capital. There was Peffer's *Farmer,* of course, and on 9 January 1890 McLallin published the first edition of the *Advocate*—soon to be the leading Populist paper in the state—from its new location in Topeka. He introduced it as "devoted to the Interests of the Farmers' Alliance and Industrial Union and other Kindred Organizations." Although McLallin favored third-party action, he was careful to appear as though he were being led rather than leading; Peffer had not yet abandoned the hope that Alliance demands could be met within the two old parties—which in his case meant the Republican party.

On 10 February 1890 Peffer wrote a personal letter to Senator Ingalls, which was published in the *Farmer* on 26 February. He asked Senator Ingalls to state his views for publication on the following issues: farm relief, expansion of the volume of circulating money, the national banking system, and the free and unlimited coinage of silver. The senator told Peffer that his views on the issues would appear "in a few weeks" but through some other channel than the *Farmer.*

Whatever else may be said of this response, it was a dumb move by an obviously bright politician. The senator was "Mr. Republican" in Kansas politics. Over the years, his condescending approach to farmers, combined with his abrasive rhetoric and his strident probusiness/antilabor positions, had earned him implacable foes. Union Laborites had even singled him out for special scorn in their 1887 and 1888 state platforms. In the latter year he had been called "a traitor unfit to represent the State of Kansas." By ignoring the demands of the Alliance and by ignoring Peffer's request, Ingalls helped the cause of his opponents immensely, even by helping to make himself a major issue. By this point, his strongest adversaries were firmly in control of the Alliance and were capable of turning the wrath of that by-now potent movement squarely upon him.

On 3 March 1890 Ben Clover took a crucial step in that direction.

Apparently following the advice of the State Reform Association, commanded by W. F. Rightmire, the president of the state Alliance issued a call for a meeting of the county presidents in Topeka on 25 March. The stated purpose was for "consulting about matters of vital importance to our order and farmers and laborers in general." Actually, as State Reform Association insider Stephen McLallin later revealed, the object "was to take preliminary steps for the organization of a new party." The county presidents, according to McLallin, knew that was the purpose of the meeting, although a number of them opposed it and believed Clover had exceeded his authority in calling the meeting.

Whether he had or not, on 25 March 1890 sixty-eight county presidents assembled in Topeka. At the meeting they approved several significant resolutions. Among them, one denied support to Senator Ingalls; another declared that "the speedy control of the legislative and executive departments of our state and national government by the industrial classes uniting their strength at the ballot box is an imperative necessity; and to secure this result, we most earnestly invite the Knights of Labor, trades unions, and trades assemblies of all incorporated cities of the state to unite with us." Another declared that "we will no longer divide on party lines, and will only cast our votes for candidates of the people, for the people, and by the people." The meeting also directed the president to appoint a member of the Alliance from each congressional district to be known as "the People's state central committee." This was the culmination of a trend that had started with the 1889 local elections, when "People's tickets" had been presented in at least the Kansas counties of Cowley, Jefferson, and Harvey.

The Rubicon had been crossed. This 25 March meeting of the Alliance county presidents was the decisive turning point in the move to create a new party. On 5 April President Clover asked the members of the Alliance, through the *Advocate,* to select members from their districts whom they wanted to represent them on the central committee. The following month, on 14 May, Clover published the official call for a meeting of this committee in Topeka on the second Tuesday in June. Included in this call was a recommendation by Clover that the Alliance send three members from each district; he also suggested that "the Grange, Farmers' Mutual Benefit Association, Knights of Labor, and all labor organizations having for their object the betterment of the laboring classes, send at least one or two delegates in order that all interests and orders may confer together for the best good of all."

In the meantime, in an interview with a reporter from the *New York World,* Senator Ingalls gave his famous answer to the question about whether political ends justify the means. It was published on 13 April and was reprinted soon thereafter throughout Kansas by all papers sympathetic to the Alliance. The comment appears at the opening of this chapter. From squarely within the antidemocratic tradition that had previously been invoked in defense of slavery (see especially George Fitzhugh's *Sociology for the South,* published in 1854), Ingalls basically answered, "Amen, dummy!" People were *not* entitled to equal rights. Dirty tricks were in order; anything necessary to advance party fortunes was fair game. In politics ethics was for fools and yokels, and "the purification of politics" was "an iridescent dream." When his response drew fire, Ingalls attempted to explain it away by saying he had been describing how politics was, not how it ought to be. But he convinced none of those who were already disgusted by what they viewed as a severe case of degenerate Republicanism, and he likely caused even more of the party faithful to reconsider their allegiance. His remarks rhymed all too well with countless earlier statements, and they fitted perfectly the picture that his many foes were painting of him. As far as proponents of reform were concerned, the interview was a precise summary of Republican philosophy. In the campaign that fall, Populists took each sentence—separated and numbered—and presented it as a plank of the Republican platform.

Significantly, on 30 April, Peffer announced he and the *Kansas Farmer* "put the Alliance before party, and we advise friends . . . [,] in all cases wherein this new party question arises, . . . consider what is best for the Alliance." On 14 May Peffer made this announcement: "Senator Ingalls having declined to answer our questions, the KANSAS FARMER will not support his claims for re-election, but, on the contrary, will support the claims of any other competent man upon whom the opposition shall unite."

Would Kansas abandon the grand old parties and Senator Ingalls? At the time Ben Clover certainly captured the attitude of many people: "Kansas farmers," he said, "have learned by sad experience that kinks twisted off the British lion's tail will not pay mortgages, even though the mortgage may be held in England." True, Senator Ingalls was the greatest Rebel "Democrat skinner" of them all, but Kansas farmers had also learned that "brigadier skins are the thinnest clothing a shivering family was ever wrapped up in." So much for two major-party ploys; it was Clover's most brilliant statement, either as Alliance leader or later as a one-term Populist congressman.

The Cowley County farmer had spoken from experience. Clover was then fifty-three and was loaded down with debts. Apparently he had done fairly well for a while in Kansas after moving west from Ohio in 1870. By

the late 1880s, however, his farm was said to be encumbered with an
$18,000 mortgage, on top of which was stacked another $1,800 in ac-
crued interest on notes and renewals. Given the monstrous deflation
afflicting the economy in those years, it was a heavy burden indeed.

Most farmers were not as deeply in debt as Clover, but indebtedness
was widespread and deadening. These debts came due in a period of
severe economic contraction, which was intensified by the collapse of an
expansionist boom, aggravated by a severe winter, followed by drought,
and a constant decline in farm income. The situation seems to have been
favorable for some kind of political revolt. One should also note—and I
want to emphasize this very strongly—that for many, especially for those
who had been committed to the reform cause for years, it was not just a
matter of debts; more important, it was a question of the survival of the
republic as they wished it to be.

Beginning in April and May 1890, county Alliances in various other
parts of the state followed the examples of Jefferson, Cowley, and
Harvey counties and began to organize for political action. On 12 June,
in response to Clover's call of the preceding month, forty-one Alliancemen, twenty-eight Knights of Labor, ten members of the Farmers'
Mutual Benefit Association, seven Patrons of Husbandry, and four representatives from Single Tax Clubs gathered in Representative Hall in
Topeka to further those political aspirations. Clover was elected to pre-
side over the meeting, which by resolution voted *unanimously* to present
a full slate of candidates in the upcoming election under the name "People's party"—not "the Alliance ticket," as one historian has maintained.[12]
A committee was then created with John F. Willits, president of the Jefferson County Alliance, as chairman, charged with the responsibility for
summoning a state nominating convention. This group, in turn, issued a
call for a delegate-state convention in Topeka for 13 August.

In this rush of events, the convention was no doubt facilitated by the
Alliance organizational structure in most areas. Where party apparatus
existed, it was usually inseparable from the Alliance. After Ben Clover
declined consideration, the convention not surprisingly nominated John
Willits, chairman of the state People's party central committee, as its
candidate for governor. The nomination for chief justice went to W. F.
Rightmire, who shortly before the convention had been elected secretary
of a new state organization called the State Citizens' Alliance. Mainly
because of Rightmire's efforts, this body was to play an important role
in the reform movement until the national People's party was fully
formed. The first local organization of its kind had been created in Olathe,

Kansas, a few months earlier by D. C. Zercher, a former Greenbacker and Union Laborite, who was elected president of the state organization. It would appear that the Citizens' Alliance, as a state order, was promoted by the State Reform Association in an effort to enlist residents of cities and towns who were ineligible for membership in the Farmers' Alliance, such as Rightmire himself. The State Reform Association disbanded after the Citizens' Alliance was created. The fact that Ben Clover, John Willits, and other Alliance leaders were also members of the Citizens' Alliance adds considerable weight to Rightmire's claim that the State Reform Association was closely linked to—if not calling the shots for—the Kansas Alliance. In January 1891 a National Citizens' Industrial Alliance would also be created by these Kansas activists.

Others on the ticket were not especially well known either before or after their nomination. A farmer and a rancher headed the slate, and two lawyers, two ministers, four former Republicans, one former Democrat, one former Union Laborite, one black man, and one white woman were represented; the coalition-building strategy was obvious. Even so, the new party's choices bore the look of spontaneity. About principles, there was more continuity and less originality. The platform was simply constructed, but it began with a statement that created some controversy. The party, the platform said, "recognize[d] Almighty God as the rightful sovereign of nations . . . from whom all just powers of government are derived, and to whose will all human enactments ought to conform." This has been taken out of context by at least one prominent historian to illustrate an abnormal theocratic bent.[13] Actually, it was there primarily because of Senator Ingalls's contention that the "decalogue and the golden rule" and morality generally had no place in politics. The party was, however, deeply and without apology influenced by the idea that human rights derived from some force superior to mere mortals—a divine spark, so to speak. The platform then reiterated the 1889 St. Louis demands, with five additional resolutions, having to do with railroads and labor-management relations, that were appended at the request of the Knights of Labor. In this unspectacular manner the stage was set for what was the most remarkable political campaign the state had ever witnessed.

Good-bye to One Old Party

As Kansans were creating their People's party, the campaign to elect candidates pledged to the St. Louis platform was gaining momentum across the South and throughout the West. The Alliance leaders in the southern states, apparently viewing the world through the lost-cause and racist prism, or at least making their plans in accord with that peculiar cultural baggage, convinced themselves that they could gain control of the Democratic party. Along the Middle Border—particularly from the Dakotas down through Nebraska, Kansas, and Oklahoma Territory—out upon the Mountain West and beyond to the West Coast, action closely paralleled the Kansas course.

Large portions of the area west of the Mississippi River were afire with activity. Throughout that vast region the same ferment was at work and remarkably similar moves were made toward independent, third-party action. An authority on the Rocky Mountain West found that antimonopolism was the common denominator actuating the political uprising.[14] The monopolistic targets differed somewhat from state to state, but throughout the region the perceived threat of monopoly posed a challenge to a deeply entrenched way of life and to an ideal vision of how American society was presumably supposed to function—the promise of American life. This threat constituted the core, energizing force that drove the revolt. The most comprehensive and scholarly study of southern Populism has arrived at a similar conclusion for that region.[15]

The situation in Nebraska proceeded much as it had in Kansas, except for one critical difference—third-party activists were not as much in command. This was reflected in the greater reluctance on the part of Nebraska's more conservative Alliance leaders to pursue the third-party option. The call for action, in fact, came from the rank and file—by petition—forcing a call for an independent nominating convention that was held in Lincoln on 29 July 1890. The Alliance, supported by the Knights of Labor, Grangers, and Union Laborites, named an Independent ticket with Alliance president John Powers as its gubernatorial candidate. The Nebraska platform, like the one in Kansas, closely resembled the St. Louis demands. The Nebraska movement, while not yet as radical as the Kansas movement, was headed in that direction. To say, as one historian has, that Nebraska had nothing but a "shadow movement" or that "Populism" did not exist "there at all," would establish an historically incredible orthodoxy test regarding what did or did not constitute Populism.[16]

Reflecting, no doubt, their ties to the southern-affiliated Alliance, farmers and their allies in the two Dakotas moved almost as quickly as Kansans toward third-party action. Calling themselves Independents, South Dakotans held a meeting in Huron on 7 June and decided to call a nominating convention. Since this was nearly a week before the meeting of the Kansas People's party central committee that made the decision to summon a convention in that state, the claim has been made that South Dakota was the "birthplace" of the People's party. H. L. Loucks, president of the South Dakota Alliance, was later named to head the Independent ticket nominated by that convention. North Dakota followed a similar course, ultimately nominating Walter Muir, who was also president of the Alliance.

Minnesota's third party emerged entirely from the northern Alliance structure and appropriately called its alternative to the old parties the Alliance ticket. Colorado's effort was a product of concerted action by a combination of former third-party and Alliance activists, calling themselves the Independent or Farmers' Alliance party; in Michigan the Grange and the Alliance worked together to present a slate called the Industrial party; in Indiana former third-party leaders and several farm groups came together to create what was also called a People's party. In the meantime, the ferment had begun to take hold in Wyoming, Montana, Idaho, Washington, Oregon, California, and the Southwest. In a few states, such as Iowa, where significant action might have been expected, no elections were scheduled; in others, like Illinois, only insignificant offices were at stake.[17]

An ominous sign in all this was the singular unwillingness of white southern Alliance leaders to cut their ties to the Democratic party and join their northern and western brethren in forming a new party—Populists called this the middle-of-the-road approach. Indeed, the deepest shadow hanging over the movement was symbolized less by the relatively weak "greenback critique of American capitalism" north of Kansas than by old-fashioned colorphobia and loyalties to the party of the lost cause to the south and east of Kansas. It would be difficult to imagine a more tragic and pathetic situation. All that was required of these white southern farmers to take the first step toward freeing themselves was to reach out and clasp hands with their black neighbors (who were, of course, just about as determined to hold on to the Republican party) and create thereby a formidable—maybe even irresistible—political force.

A recent study written from what amounts to a refreshing Texas neo-populist perspective has speculated that the movement would have been much more successful had the northern Alliance's base been converted, as it was in Kansas and the Dakotas, to the southern Alliance, with its greater commitment to fundamental economic reforms and cooperative programs.[18] No doubt that would have made a difference. But more appropriate speculation could be made about the much greater difference that surely would have resulted had white southern Alliancemen been able to put aside their race phobia and the lost cause in order to join forthrightly in creating a genuine People's party—multiracial and multi-sectional in nature; if not that, at least one along the lines pursued, for a brief, lonely, and courageous moment, beginning late in 1891, by Georgia's Tom Watson. [19]

Leonidas L. Polk was directing the Alliance's southern strategy. This North Carolinian had been elected president of the NFA&IU at the December 1889 St. Louis meeting and was staunchly backed by the *National Economist,* which was founded and edited by C. W. Macune and published in Washington, D.C., since early in 1889. Understandably, neither Polk nor Macune cared what happened to the Republican party, but both deeply preferred remaining with the Democrats. For Polk, but not for Macune, the Alliance gradually assumed greater importance than the "party of the fathers"; Polk was willing to pursue the third-party option if it became obvious that the Alliance would not be able to reshape the Democratic party to its liking.

Powerful southern Democrats were as determined to use the Alliance for their own purposes as the Alliance was to use that party. Their way was made easier by the fact the region's New South and Old South leaders both placed white supremacy high, if not at the top, of their agendas. The Old South leaders had a strong base in the agrarian camp, a bastion that would constitute a southern "shadow movement" and that would continually trouble the reform quest. This "shadow movement" (the phrase was coined by Lawrence Goodwyn) came to the fore early in one of its more grotesque forms, soon known throughout the country by the eponym Tillmanism. In the South, certainly, as it has been said, "Alliance radicalism was Populism," but the Alliance combined both conservative and radical agrarianisms, creating tremendous tension within the order. This conservative-to-reactionary agrarianism—agrarianism laced with colorphobia, actually—found its most talented and forceful leader in Benjamin R. Tillman, the fiery, "One-Eyed Plowboy" of South Carolina.

Ben Tillman—like many thousands of white southerners—was part of that bitter harvest that had been sown during the nation's "halfway" revolution. The Edgefield County farmer had emerged as the leader of white South Carolina "upland" farmers before the Alliance began its organizational drive in the state. Working through what was called a Farmers' Association and later the Farmers' Alliance, Tillman put together a rural-white political machine that gave him control of the state's Democratic party in the 1890 election and that put him into the governor's chair for four years, then into the U.S. Senate, where he remained until his death more than twenty-three years later. This "Alliance Democrat"—a racist demagogue par excellence and no one's fool—never became a Populist. In fact, he used his influence to work against the effort to bring the nation's farmers and workers together in a new party. The troglodyte image Tillman widely conveyed (he was the likely inspiration, incidentally, for the Wicked Witch of the West in Frank Baum's 1900 children's classic, *The Wonderful Wizard of Oz*) was gleefully exploited outside the South by the enemies of Populism in order to collapse the two agrarianisms into one, thereby tarring both with the same brush.[20]

This racist shadow movement was present in all the southern states but nowhere quite as crudely as in South Carolina (although Mississippi, by the turn of the century, probably surpassed South Carolina as the home of race-baiting politicians). Throughout the region, on into 1891, there was considerable and not altogether unrealistic hope that the Alliance could capture the Democratic party. Without hindsight, who could be sure it was an illusion, a tar baby in disguise?

"Bloodless Revolution"

By late summer 1890 a remarkable political ferment had developed along the Middle Border—and nowhere more than in Kansas. One observer wrote, "The upheaval that took place . . . can hardly be diagnosed as a political campaign. It was a religious revival, a crusade, a pentecost of politics in which a tongue of flame set upon every man, and each spake as the spirit gave him utterance." The ground had been well prepared by the Alliance and its allies. Hundreds of speakers traveled about the state addressing themselves to issues and mobilizing the masses. But it was not only recognized leaders who sounded the call for action; in the words of this same observer, "The farmers, the country merchants, the cattle-herders, they of the long chin-whiskers, and they of the broad-brimmed hats and heavy boots, had also heard the word and could preach the gospel of Populism." Never before, perhaps, had ordinary people been so involved in politics. From August to November 1890, political fervor consumed the state like a prairie fire, as tens of thousands of Kansans flocked to the banner of the People's party intent on demonstrating that the purification of politics was not an iridescent dream.

The discontented did not have to look far for champions. Numerous third-party campaigners eagerly joined the crusade, rejuvenated by the prospect of the masses at long last awakening. Their political and analyt-

ical skills, in many cases developed over a twenty-year period, immediately and logically catapulted these reformers to positions of leadership.
The Alliance movement, moreover, provided the forum whereby many
new personalities moved to the front.

Mary Elizabeth Lease was the most spectacular of the newcomers.
She was thirty-seven and always introduced herself—at least, formally—
as Mrs. Mary E. Lease. Her detractors soon took liberties with the "E,"
rendering it as "Ellen," since it rhymed with "Yellin."[21] Born to Irish-
Catholic parents named Clyens in Pennsylvania and educated in New
York through high school, Mary Clyens moved west in 1870 to teach in
the parochial school at Osage Mission in southeastern Kansas. There she
met and married a druggist named Charles Lease, and the couple moved
to a farm in Kingman County. Not too long thereafter, they moved to
Denison, Texas, then back to Wichita, Kansas. In the meantime ten
years had intervened. During this period Mary Lease brought four children into the world, managed the household, and in her "spare time"
studied law. In 1885 she was admitted to the Kansas bar, becoming one
of a very small number of woman lawyers.

Between 1885 and 1887, Mary Lease began to build a reputation as a
lecturer. The Irish National League, women's suffrage, and temperance
commanded her attention. She was a Republican until 1888, when she
left the party to work for Union Labor, and she made a political debut of
sorts that year by speaking before that party's state convention. She
gained considerable experience from her activities in the 1888 election
and a certain amount of notoriety in the middle counties of Kansas. From
there she moved wholeheartedly into the reform agitation that led to the
creation of the People's party. Her natural talents, which were considerable, soon brought her to prominence among the party's many
orators.[22]

A powerful, melodious voice was of course a great advantage in an age
that was yet without electronic amplifiers. Mary Lease certainly had that.
Annie Diggs, who rivaled and ultimately surpassed Lease as the most
admired among many Populist women, considered it her greatest "distinguishing gift." Journalist William Allen White said he had "never heard a
lovelier voice." He said she had "a golden voice—a deep, rich contralto,
a singing voice that had hypnotic qualities." Concerning her persuasive
powers, White felt Lease conveyed in her speeches a quality that was
lost in cold print. "They were dull enough often," said White, "but she
could recite the multiplication table and set a crowd hooting or hurrahing
at her will." The Republican loyalist, rather short and plump himself,

described her appearance in a less complimentary fashion. "She stood nearly six feet tall," he said, "with no figure, a thick torso, and long legs. To me, she often looked like a kangaroo pyramided up from the hips to a comparatively small head. . . . She wore her hair in a Psyche knot, always neatly combed and topped by the most ungodly hats I ever saw a woman wear. She had no sex appeal—none!"

One's impression of Mary Lease was greatly influenced by one's political persuasion, as White's account illustrates. A more sympathetic observer described her this way: "Mrs. Lease is a tall woman—fully five feet ten inches, and rather slender. Her face is strong, good, not pretty, and very feminine. There is no mark of masculinity about her. She is woman all over. Her hair is a dark brown and evenly parted in the center and smoothed down at the sides with neat care. Her nose, chin and cheek bones announce themselves strongly. However, they give no sense of harshness to her face."

Mary Lease had that special something that momentarily made her one of the nation's most magnetic orators. Early in 1891 one interviewer said she seemed "one of those radical, strong, warm natures which feels and has impulses rather than thoughts. She can see a wrong and feel an injury quickly, but would be slow and far from sure in her remedies. Her mind is untrained, and while displaying plenty of a certain sort of power, is illogical, lacks sequence and scatters like a 10-gauge [shot] gun." Much of her effectiveness does seem to have derived from her ability to feel and articulate, as few could, the concerns of the masses, a demagogic trait invaluable to movers and shakers and not disastrous if tempered by other qualities. Apparently in her case, those tempering qualities were in short supply. She was indeed more a barometer of discontent than a leader or originator of reform thought. Reform so pursued could be quite effective as long as the impulses were reasonably convergent; otherwise it was capable of turning on itself. This may help explain why Mary Lease and a number of other Populist leaders, in Kansas and elsewhere, later followed an erratic course.

For the moment, however, the Lease style was made to order. Unquestionably, she played a huge role in that first whirlwind of a campaign. She moved about the state, her reputation growing steadily, roasting opposition male politicians in a manner that quite a few men would likely have toned down a bit out of fear of physical reprisal. A classic example of her effectiveness is the reaction of a Republican editor in Wellington, Kansas, after a Lease visit: "At the opera house last Monday night," he snorted, "a miserable caricature upon womanhood, hideously ugly in feature and foul of tongue, made on ostensible political speech, but which consisted mainly of the rankest kind of personal abuse of people in this city, among which [sic] the editor of this paper understands that he came in for the principal share." He went on to write that he did not know exactly what were the "old hag's reasons" for the attack. "All we know about her is that she is hired to travel around the country by this great reform People's party, which seems to find a female blackguard a necessity in its business, spouting foulmouthed vulgarity at $10 a night." He was certain that "the petticoated smut-mill earns her money, but few women want to make their living that way." He capped off this bit of vitriol by noting sardonically, "We thought at first we would write her up in something after her own style of expression, but upon reflection concluded . . . the space could better be devoted to something else. Her venomous tongue is the only thing marketable about the old harpy, and we suppose she is justified in selling it where it commands the highest price." Besides, "In about a month the lantern-jawed, goggleeyed nightmare will be put out of a job, and nobody will be the worse for the mud with which she has tried to bespatter them."

Since she spoke extemporaneously, few of Mary Lease's speeches from the 1890 campaign or later made it into the written record. Late in March 1891, however, she delivered an oration in Kansas City that was reported more fully by the *Kansas City Star*. The reporter said it was "a crazy-patch of perhaps a dozen different speeches." So it would seem. "Wall street owns the country," she said. "It is no longer a government of the people, for the people, by the people, but a government of Wall street, for Wall street, and by Wall street. The great common people . . . are slaves, and monopoly is master. The West and South are bound and prostrate before the manufacturing East." And so it went. On 7 August 1891 the *Salina Republican,* edited by Joseph Bristow, quoting the *Kansas City Star* but citing no date, made this announcement: "Mrs. Lease's parting injunction to a meeting of Harvey county farmers: 'And now I say to you as my final admonition, not knowing that I shall meet you again, raise less wheat and corn, and more hell.'" That famous bit of advice that she was alleged to have given Kansas farmers has apparently never before been documented to the period of its origin. Interviewed in 1896 and again in 1914 on the matter, Lease insisted it had been invented by reporters, but she said she had let it stand because she thought "it was a right good bit of advice." If she said it, she apparently did not say it in the 1890 campaign but in Harvey County sometime before this quote appeared. It could well be that someone working for the *Kansas City*

Star simply manufactured the line, such as William Allen White—who along with Joseph Bristow and others was one of the founders of a young Republican, anti-Populist organization called the Kansas Day Club. Whether she said it or not, it became famous; it was the kind of advice many farmers could surely appreciate.[23]

Although not nearly as flamboyant as Mary Lease, another remarkable woman, Annie Diggs, proved to be an effective campaigner and Lease's superior, by far, in intellectual ability and political sagacity. Populists knew and loved her dearly as Little Annie. Nearly a decade after the 1890 campaign, a journalist drew this verbal picture: "Imagine a little woman, slender . . . , barely five feet tall and weighing only ninety-three pounds. Picture . . . a face on which shines the light of zealous endeavor and enthusiastic championship of a beloved cause; rather thin lips, an intellectual forehead from which the hair . . . is brushed back pompadour like; twinkling eyes which alternately squint almost shut, then open wide as she expounds her favorite doctrines of socialism; a trifle nervous, a soft voice and an occasional musical little laugh as she talks, and you have a fair photograph of [Annie Diggs]."

Annie La Porte was born in 1853 in Canada to a French-Canadian father and an American mother. When she was only two, her parents moved to New Jersey. Although she was not a college graduate (a fact she said on several occasions that she truly "regretted"), she had a better than average education, via private tutor, the public schools, and for a short time, a convent school. An adventurous soul, she first pursued a journalism career in Washington, D.C., while still in her teens. At age nineteen (in 1873), she decided to become part of the great westward movement as a single woman. She moved to Lawrence, Kansas, where she found a job in a music store. Shortly thereafter she met and married A. S. Diggs, an employee in the Lawrence post office, and the Diggs family soon included three children.

After a few years, Annie Diggs became active in the Woman's Christian Temperance Union and in behalf of women's right to vote, which she and most western Populists regarded as a natural right denied. She also involved herself in the activities of the Unitarian Church, the Social Science Club of Kansas and Western Missouri, and the Kansas Liberal League. In the early 1880s she returned to the East on several occasions to lecture before Unitarian conferences. Then she resumed her career in journalism, in Boston, as correspondent for several Kansas papers. She retained her interest in reform; in fact, her thinking was greatly influenced by what she observed in the nation's industrial heartland.

About this experience she later said: "While I studied conditions in the East I became all the more convinced . . . the reforms which we sought were after all economical rather than moral questions." She convinced herself that "there was little hope in the East because the wage earners were afraid to say their souls were their own. But if the farmers could become interested there was, I thought, some promise of success. You cannot evict a farmer whose farm is his own. He is a sovereign." No better description was ever given of how the process of urban-rural, East-West cross-fertilization occurred and nourished the reform quest.

Annie Diggs returned to Lawrence just as the Alliance was beginning to receive notice. She persuaded the editor of Lawrence's Republican newspaper to add an Alliance column that she would write. The day after her first effort, the editor disavowed any responsibility for the views expressed in her column, but she was allowed to continue and her work received notice outside Lawrence. Stephen McLallin subsequently asked her to become associate editor of the Topeka *Advocate,* a position she assumed in March 1890, and with her help the paper was on its way to becoming the state's leading reform weekly, with a circulation of around 80,000.

In spite of her considerable public exposure before 1890, Annie professed to be apprehensive about campaigning actively. But once she was enlisted in the cause, she adjusted with ease and became quite effective. In her speeches she drew upon her acquaintance with conditions in the East and in the West, employed a conversational style, added a large dose of factual argument, and in a tightly reasoned, soft-spoken, and pleading oratorical manner, she became a favorite.

Mary Lease, Annie Diggs, and many other less heralded women added considerable luster to the campaign. But not all the excitement was generated by women. Some enthusiasm was also created by the party's congressional nominees, all males. Ben Clover led the fight in the third congressional district, which encompassed nine counties in southeastern Kansas. Big, insipid, malleable, and superficial, the Alliance leader nonetheless used a bulldog determination to hammer home arguments he had perfected since leaving the Republican party in 1888.

In the north-central portion of the state, John Davis was nominated to represent the fifth congressional district. His selection capped a personal career as a member of the Knights of Labor, farmer organizer, and reform editor over the previous twenty years. His primary theme was one that had emerged over and over again throughout the dislocations and the explosive changes that characterized American society in the after-

"new slavery"

math of the Civil War—"the new slavery." He liked to ask: "Have we
abolished slavery? Ask the factory girls, the sewing women, the coal
miners, the iron workers, the farmers and all the men and women of toil
who form the great public which the Vanderbilts would damn to perpetual
servitude!" The antebellum slave system, he said, "rested on three millions of blacks, whom it pauperized, but [at least] fed and clothed." The
old slave "masters never became millionaires. They were brutal and
overbearing, but they had not the means to purchase great lines of railroads and telegraphs, and through them to levy tribute on whole states."
The "new slavery" was much worse, said Davis. It "rests on sixty millions of people. It makes paupers which society must feed; and it has
created thousands of millionaire slave masters."

The same theme could be heard in the campaign speeches of John
Grant Otis, a Granger state lecturer and the party's nominee in the fourth
congressional district. Born on a Vermont farm in 1838, Otis was a
twenty-year reform veteran. He had been a dairy farmer for quite some
time, but his background was exceptional. Before moving out to Kansas
Territory in 1859, he had attended Burr Seminary in Vermont, Williams
College in Massachusetts, and Harvard Law School. He practiced law in
Topeka briefly before going into dairy farming. In politics he had been a
Republican, of "abolitionist vintage," and during the Civil War he had organized and briefly commanded a contingent of black troops. In the mid-
seventies, however, he left his former party to fight for reform,
sequentially, as a Granger, Greenbacker, and Prohibitionist. Apparently,
at the time of his nomination Otis was still a Grange leader and not a
member of the Alliance.

Otis was deadly serious about the magnitude of the threat he believed
citizens of the republic faced. Early in 1890 he informed Alliance president Clover by public letter of his belief that fundamental reform was
necessary. His formula: "When the American people shall introduce cooperation into the field of PRODUCTION as well as into the field of DIS-
TRIBUTION, and shall organize for 'work' as we organize for 'war'! then
will we behold PROSPERITY such as the world has never witnessed."

Otis's major campaign theme may well have reflected the influence of
Henry George à la Edward Bellamy. "This great industrial movement,"
he said, ". . . is but another advancing step in the forward march of human society. We are emerging from an age of intense individualism, supreme selfishness, and ungodly greed to a period of co-operative effort.
Competition is giving way to unite[d] action." It would appear, said Otis,
as though we were awakening from a "mesmeric sleep of a selfish age,

to find ourselves closely related to the whole human family." Consequently, old issues were being relegated to the dustbin of history, while people lined up on one side or the other of a "portentious contest." On the one side of the line were the minions of capital; on the other were the producer masses. Events indicated, he assured his listeners, that the struggle was about to be won by the strength of the combined forces of labor, which would lead to a new society built on the principle of "mutual co-operative effort."

William Baker, an Alliance district lecturer, was the party's nominee in the sixth congressional district of Kansas, an area encompassing twenty-two counties in the northwestern corner, Baker was fifty-nine, a rancher, and a former Republican from Lincoln County. Although he had been engaged exclusively in ranching since his 1878 arrival in the state, his background was diverse. After his graduation in 1856 from Waynesburg College in his native Pennsylvania, he taught school, served as principal, studied law and was admitted to the bar, and engaged in the mercantile business for sixteen years. His style of oratory was far from spectacular—during his six years in Congress he would speak for the record very infrequently—but his remarks were apparently convincing. Speaking primarily from experience, he emphasized the particular difficulties confronting farmers, ranchers, and small businessmen. It was an approach many hard-pressed homesteaders in the northwestern Kansas counties clearly appreciated, for Baker survived the Republican comeback of 1894 and as a result became the only Kansas Populist to be elected to three consecutive congressional terms.

Thirty-six counties in the southwestern quarter of Kansas constituted what was generally referred to as the Big Seventh. Like the sixth district, the seventh had become a hotbed of Alliance activities after 1888; political revolt was a certainty. In late July there emanated a cry of horror and anguish from a Republican editor in Holton (a town not in the district but in which the nominee had first resided) that the seventh was about to nominate "a rabid fiat greenbacker with communistic tendencies." That political monstrosity was Jeremiah Simpson, the "Sockless Jerry" of political legend.

Simpson, who would become one of the most popular and renowned of all Populist leaders, was born on Prince Edward Island in 1842. From as far back as he could remember, however, he had been a New Yorker, because his Scotch-Irish parents had moved to that state when he was only six. There he received a limited common-school education, then left home at fourteen to follow a seafaring life. For more than twenty years (excluding a short period during the Civil War when he served with an Illinois regiment until he was incapacitated by illness), he sailed the Great Lakes as cook, sailor, mate, and captain. Marriage in 1870 and family responsibilities then greatly altered the pattern of Simpson's life, and a few years later he traded in his ship, so to speak, for a prairie schooner. In 1878, after a brief period on a farm in Indiana, where he was introduced to an agricultural depression and the Grange, he moved his family to Kansas and purchased a small farm and a sawmill near Holton in Jackson County, in the northeastern corner.

Years later, when asked by a journalist what had prompted his move to the state, Simpson answered: "The magic of a kernal, the witchcraft in a seed; the desire to put something into the ground and see it grow and reproduce its kind. That's why I came to Kansas." Undoubtedly, he also had hopes of a better life, but it was not exactly smooth sailing. Not long after their infant daughter died in a tragic logging accident, the Simpsons moved to a ranch in the southwestern part of the state near Medicine Lodge. Having invested all their savings in land and cattle, Jerry and Jane Simpson were soon introduced to the hard times facing those who were trying to sustain themselves as family farmers and ranchers. In the mid-to-late 1870s, Jerry Simpson left the Republican party to become a Greenbacker, and in 1886 he ran unsuccessfully on the Independent ticket for the legislature. Then came the severe winter of 1886–87, followed by drought, and the savings of a lifetime were swept away. Already a reformer by temperament and affiliation, Simpson was all the more committed to third-party politics. But he was much disheartened by the Union Labor party's defeat in 1888, on whose ticket he had again run for the legislature.

The few manuscripts Jerry Simpson left behind reveal that he was a horrible speller. Apparently his education had simply been deficient in that respect or—more likely—he had some kind of impairment, such as dyslexia, that affected his ability to put words to paper. He was certainly very intelligent and (his six years in Congress abundantly documents this) few—if any—politicians could match his ability to speak and think on his feet.[24] He was, at the same time, an omnivorous reader, and his many years aboard ship had given him ample opportunities to read. William Allen White later recalled: "He was smart. He had read more widely than I, and often quoted Carlyle in our conversations, and the poets and essayists of the 17th century. His talk . . . was full of Dickensian allusions, and he persuaded me to try Thackeray, whom I had rejected until then." One of his favorite books was Henry George's *Progress and Pov-*

erty, and he took from it not so much George's Single Tax solution as George's perceptive critique of society's ills and insistence that something needed to be done to secure and to protect human rights. More than anything else—except perhaps common sense and the postgraduate school of hard knocks—that was the source of Simpson's personal philosophy.

Above all, Jerry Simpson was a reformer with an extraordinary sense of humor—a rare quality that was seldom present in the era's politicians. It was, in fact, central to his personality, adding that one simple but magic touch that elevated him above his fellows. The acclaimed novelist Hamlin Garland observed him in action on Capitol Hill late in 1891 and fashioned a word portrait not likely to be surpassed:

He is about fifty years of age, of slender but powerful figure, whose apparent youthfulness is heightened by the double-breasted short sack coat he wears. His hair is very black and abundant, but his close-clipped moustache is touched with gray, and he wears old-fashioned glasses, through which his eyes gleam with ever-present humor. The wrinkles about his mouth show that he faces the world smilingly. His voice is crisp and deep and pleasant to the ear. He speaks with the Western accent mainly; and when he is making a humorous point or telling a story, he drops into dialect, and speaks in a peculiar slow fashion that makes every word tell. He is full of odd turns of thought, and quaint expressions that make me think of Whitcomb Riley. He is a clear thinker, a remarkable speaker, and has a naturally philosophical mind which carries his reasoning down to the most fundamental facts of organic law and human rights.

By the end of the 1880s Simpson had been forced by economic circumstances to supplement his income as best he could. As happened with so many other third-party leaders, the Alliance movement claimed him and he claimed it. But in his case the stakes were much higher; the city marshal of Medicine Lodge—for that was the position he held at the time of his nomination—was a candidate for Congress.

In that 1890 contest, Jerry Simpson was subjected to extremely bitter abuse by the Republican press. Among other things, his indictment included lack of patriotism, dishonesty, larceny, atheism, anarchism, communism, and worst of all, having "simian" characteristics. But Jerry stood up well under attack; in fact, with his confidence, self-esteem, sense of humor, and extraordinary wit, he usually managed to turn abuse to his advantage. An example of this was seen in his speech at Harper, Kansas, in late August. He began by stating: "You may be surprised to see me in the form of a man, after the descriptions of a partisan press, but I'm no zoological specimen—not even a monkey or an orangutan." There followed a great roar of laughter from a crowd made up primarily of farm men and women who were only too aware they too were generally regarded by the powers that be as "hayseeds" and "hicks," who were not quite with it. Simpson had thereby attuned his audience for the remainder of his talk.

Just as in this Harper speech, Jerry Simpson liked to stress that in spite of "improvements in wealth producing machinery," the farmer was worse off than twenty years earlier. What was the problem? The "People are without a medium—less than $10 per capita in circulation." Railroads also shared in the blame for hard times. "We have all the machinery for the finest government on the face of the earth, but we are fast becoming entangled in the web of the giant spider which controls our commerce and transportation. We must own the railroads or enough of them to do the necessary carrying. 'Tis idle talk to say we have not the authority. The government is the *people* and *we* are the people." Land was another subject dear to his heart. The existing land system, he said, was just plain "robbery." Then in good Georgian rhetoric he insisted: "Man must have access to the earth or he becomes a slave." And so he spoke, here and there interjecting a pertinent and usually humorous story to emphasize a point and to retain the interest of his audience.

For their congressional candidate, Republicans of the seventh district nominated "Colonel" James Hallowell, apparently a rather sedate Kansan, who was actually referred to as Prince Hal. Much was made of the contrast between Hallowell and Simpson. "The opposing candidates are opposites in every way," asserted the state's major Republican newspaper. "Colonel Hallowell is a brilliant, experienced and competent man who would add strength to the Kansas delegation; Jerry Simpson is an ignorant, inexperienced lunkhead." In the editor's opinion, "Jerry would disgrace the state in congress; scarcely able to read and write, unacquainted with public affairs, without experience as a legislator, raw, boorish, fanatical with the fanaticism of sheer ignorance, he would render Kansas a laughing stock."

Given such prospects, Republican leaders ignored a cardinal rule of political warfare—to not underestimate one's enemies—and suggested that the two candidates be brought together for a debate. The obscure city marshal of Medicine Lodge, they thought, would be wiped out by the Republicans' polished and dignified Prince Hal. The debate was arranged to take place toward the end of the campaign, and Hallowell, as agreed, was assigned the opening and closing speeches. Jerry Simpson in a much later interview recalled the event as follows:

> He was a handsome fellow, a good dresser, and his followers had dubbed him "Prince Hal." He was a splendid talker, and long before he had finished his speech I knew he had the crowd with him and that I would have to do something drastic to jar them loose. He poked considerable fun at me. The idea of sending a man to Washington who had no public experience, other than being city marshal of Medicine Lodge, was really funny. He, Hallowell, on the other hand had . . . legislative experience. He knew how laws were made, etc.
>
> When my turn came I tried to get hold of the crowd. I referred to the fact that my opponent was known as a "Prince." Princes, I said, wear silk socks. I don't wear any. The crowd laughed at this but it was not enough and I had to try again. Now, I said, Hal tells you that he has made laws. I am going to show you the kind of laws that Hal makes. Reaching over on the table and picking up a book I opened it and, tapping on the page with my finger, I said, here is one of Hal's laws. I find that it is a law to tax dogs, but I see that Hal proposes to charge two dollars for a bitch and only one dollar for a son of a bitch. Now the party I belong to believes in equal and exact justice to all.[25]

The crowd of course loved it, and Jerry once again had his audience right where he wanted them. Having blundered in bringing the two together in the first place, the Republican press compounded its error by inadvertently providing Simpson with an invaluable sobriquet. From that day forth it was "Sockless Jerry" Simpson. No Populist parade thereafter was said to be complete without a float featuring several young ladies knitting socks for Jerry.

As the story of Jerry Simpson demonstrated, Kansas Republicans were inordinately out of touch with ordinary people. One Republican editor frankly admitted that "abuse and vituperation" of People's party candidates was the main strategy. The *Topeka Daily Capital* waged a somewhat more comprehensive campaign, which amounted to one part each of personal abuse, bloody shirt, and prohibition. The editor of the state's leading Republican paper, lost in the past, repeatedly informed his readers the only thing at stake was prohibition—whiskey was the issue. Speaking of the leaders of the new party, he wrote: "They are unworthy of citizenship and belong in the penitentiary." The 12 October edition offered this commentary: "Members of the people's party: Your man Polk appears to be an unscrupulous trickster; your man Clover an unprincipled demagogue; your man Willits a low-lived perjurer; your man Rightmire an indicted swindler, and your man Ives a creature of the rum-soaked democracy." The same issue ran an article entitled "The People's Party is the Scheme of Ex-Rebels."

The editor of the *Capital* and Republicans throughout the state and nation were shocked by the effrontery of Kansas voters, who went to the polls early that November and delivered a stunning blow to the Grand Old Party. As one Republican editor saw it, "The people's party managers trusted for victory to the ignorance of the people, and to the shame of Kansas their confidence was not misplaced." Republican governor Lyman Humphrey was reelected by a small plurality, as was the rest of the executive ticket, with one exception: one Republican was defeated by a former Democrat on the People's ticket running for attorney general. But the People's party elected Clover, Davis, Otis, Baker, and Simpson to Congress, and 96 of 125 members of the lower house of the state legislature. All this happened in a state where Republicans had grown accustomed to having a comfortable majority approximating that of 1888, when the party elected 120 of 125 members of the lower house and 39 of 40 members to the state senate.

Comparing the returns for 1888 (a vote for presidential electors) and 1890 (a vote for secretary of state), the vote had shifted as follows:

Party	1888	1890	Loss	Gain
Republican	182,800	120,969	61,831	—
Democratic	102,600	55,873	46,727	—
Union Labor	37,600	—	37,600	—
Prohibition	6,700	1,316	5,384	—
People's	—	115,933	—	115,933
Total	329,700	294,091		

The total vote of 1890 had declined by about eleven percent from 1888, mainly because of the exodus of people from the state and because of the normal decline for an off-year election. By reducing the vote of each party by that amount (subtracting 11 percent of the 1888 total from the loss column), its real loss can be approximated. On that basis one can reasonably conclude that the rank and file of the new party included about 41,000 former Republicans, 35,000 former Democrats, 33,000 former

Union Laborites, and 4,500 former Prohibitionists. The Kansas People's party was, be it noted, from the beginning a coalition of nearly equal components drawn from the two old parties and the minor parties. If they were nearly equal, they were by no means altogether compatible, for it would prove to be a very difficult coalition to hold together.

For the moment, Populists were jubilant; Republicans were simply dumbfounded. The latter could console themselves, as did the editor of the Topeka *Capital,* by noting: "While the people's party controls the house by a very large majority, the senate is still republican by 38 to 1, and a governor's veto also stands in the way of radical legislation of which businessmen and capitalists might have stood in dread. There is no danger of the passage of any measures which would render capital unsafe." There was, on the other hand, a strong possibility that Senator John J. Ingalls, the hero of those Republican "businessmen and capitalists," would be retired from his post.

The Kansas legislature that convened the following January presented an interesting contrast in membership. The typical People's party representative was forty-six, a farmer or stock raiser, and more often than not a native of Ohio, Indiana, New York, Illinois, Virginia, or Kentucky who had moved to Kansas in 1878. About one in nine was foreign born; one in three had been active in third-party politics for years; one in five was a college graduate. Only eleven of the total had previous legislative experience, while one in three had held local office only. The typical Republican representative, on the other hand, was forty-five, a native of Pennsylvania, Ohio, Indiana, or New York, and a business or professional man who had moved to Kansas in 1877. One out of four had previous legislative experience; one in five was a college graduate; and only one of the group was foreign born.

The holdover Republican senate contrasted even more sharply with the Populist house. The Republican senator was, compositely, forty-five (forty-three at the time of his election), a lawyer, a proprietor of a business or a banker, and a native of Ohio, Pennsylvania, or New York who had lived in Kansas since 1868. Only four of the thirty-eight Republican senators were farmers. One of two had previous legislative experience. Six were college educated.

In short, the major difference between Republican and Populist legislators was a matter less of age or education than of occupation. To use the terminology of historian Lee Benson, it was a case of the agrarian-minded versus the commercial-minded—a showdown with wild cards and jokers between a party of "businessmen and capitalists" (the proponents of a metropolitan-entrepreneurial ethos) and the proponents of a democratic radicalism deeply rooted in the agrarian tradition. My examination of the major leadership of Kansas Populism has pointed up a less distinct occupational contrast as between Populists and their old-party opponents but, if anything, an even more intense commitment—certainly in the beginning—to this same radical democratic tradition.

The most important immediate task facing these legislators was to elect a U.S. senator. John Willits and William Peffer were the main contenders. Between the two, Peffer was regarded as the more conservative prospect. Nearly all the former third-party legislators and the activist cadre of leaders on the outside opposed the editor of the *Farmer.* One of them later revealed that "they lacked faith in his loyalty to the principles on which the campaign had been fought, and believed . . . he would really act with the Republicans after going to Washington." But the majority of the party caucus supported Peffer, and his election was assured as long as there was no break in ranks. To avoid that, Peffer's caucus opponents and that activist cadre met separately and agreed to go along with the majority rather than run the risk of reelecting John J. Ingalls by pushing for their preference.

The ranks held, and the new Kansas party had a U.S. senator to go with its five representatives. The defeat of Mr. Republican signified the close of the 1890 Kansas campaign. Never one to be caught without a sarcastic retort, Ingalls described himself as "the innocent victim of a bloodless revolution—a sort of turnip crusade, as it were." It remained to be seen how revolutionary the outcome would be.

Alliance Victories Outside Kansas

To many observers the 1890 election in the southern states seemed to confirm the arrival of the Alliance and a "coming revolution" in southern politics. Alliance gubernatorial candidates were elected in South Carolina, Georgia, and Tennessee. In Texas, the man the Alliance had endorsed won. Many Alliancemen were elected at various levels in states throughout the region. Alabama, Florida, Georgia, Missouri, Mississippi, North Carolina, South Carolina, and Tennessee were said to have elected legislatures "safely" under the control of the order. One account estimated, "Perhaps as many as forty-four of its candidates—men who had definitely committed themselves to the support of Alliance principles—had won seats in Congress." Two, perhaps three, U.S. senators from the South were also said to be pro-Alliance. Late in 1891, however, when Congress convened, only Thomas E. Watson from Georgia's tenth congressional district, which included Augusta, would forthrightly join the People's party caucus in Congress and fight for the radical Alliance program. As Texas radical William Lamb recognized a bit sooner than most southerners, the Democrats had done a better job of taking over the Alliance than the Alliance had of taking over the "party of the fathers."[26]

Where independent action occurred outside the South, the results were more immediately gratifying—particularly in Nebraska. Independents won control of both of that state's legislative houses. Two Populist congressmen-to-be, Omer Madison Kem and William Arthur Mc-Keighan, would join the five already elected from Kansas. In South Dakota and Minnesota Alliance forces came out of the election holding the balance of power in their legislatures. In South Dakota this made possible the election of another U.S. senator, James H. Kyle, a thirty-nine-year-old Congregational minister, who began his ten-year senatorial career. Kyle would come in as an independent, join the Populist caucus, and then drift back toward independency and the Republican camp toward the end of his tenure. Minnesota also elected Kittel Halvorson to Congress. Along with Watson, this meant that in the Fifty-second Congress, (due to convene in December 1891) the Populists would count nine representatives and two senators in their delegation.[27]

In North Dakota, Michigan, Illinois, Indiana, and Colorado the Independent–Alliance effort achieved no significant breakthroughs, but it did cut into the Republican vote enough to contribute to the election of an unusual number of Democrats. This had happened in Nebraska, too, where a young Democrat named William Jennings Bryan was elected to Congress.[28]

All in all, it was an impressive first effort. After the election, the Kansas party chairman sized up the situation well when he announced that supporters could be "justly proud" of their victory but that they should "not forget . . . the war is not yet at an end. We have still a great work to accomplish. We must maintain and strengthen our organization for the great conflict of 1892." Their agenda included the work of the various state legislatures in 1891, the perfection of a national party organization, and the education of the public to build support for their principles.

Chapter Three

Common People, Uncommon Politics

The Road to Omaha, 1890–1892

We meet in the midst of a nation brought to the verge of moral, political, and material ruin. Corruption dominates the ballot-box, the legislatures, the Congress, and touches even the ermine of the bench. . . . The newspapers are largely subsidized or muzzled; public opinion silenced; business prostrated; our homes covered with mortgages; labor impoverished; the land concentrating in the hands of the capitalists. The urban workmen are denied the right of organization for self-protection; imported pauperized labor beats down their wages; a hireling standing army, unrecognized by our laws, is established to shoot them down, and they are rapidly degenerating into European conditions. The fruits of the toil of millions are boldly stolen to build up colossal fortunes for a few . . . ; and the possessors of these, in turn, despise the republic and endanger liberty.

—Preamble to the Omaha Platform, People's Party of America,
July 1892

On 4 July 1890 picnic rallies were a common occurrence wherever the Alliance had established a foothold. They occurred throughout the state of Kansas. An estimated six thousand people turned out for festivities in little Winfield, the home base of the Vincent brothers and the *American Nonconformist*. The special attraction was a speech by Leonidas Polk, national president of the Alliance and a favorite from among "the boys in gray." The popular North Carolinian disappointed no one, boldly challenging the politics of divide and conquer: "I tell you this afternoon that from New York to the Golden Gate the farmers have risen up and have inaugurated a movement such as the world has never seen. It is a revolution which I pray God may be peaceful and bloodless; a revolution which shall roll on . . . till some of the great wrongs of the world shall be righted."

The crowd, of course, included a great many former "boys in blue," who retained vivid memories and in some cases visible reminders of the North-South conflict. The ex-Confederate colonel assured Kansans that southern farmers were their "brothers." Naming no names, he said, "Some people have stirred up sectional feeling and have kept us apart for twenty-five years." Those who have "waved the bloody shirt" and "taught" their "children the poisonous doctrines of hate" have "chained us hand and foot. They have placed upon us manacles that are worse than those that have fallen from the African slaves. They know that if we get together and shake hands . . . their doom is sealed." Therefore, "I stand here today, commissioned by hundreds of thousands of southern farmers, to beg the farmers of Kansas to stand by them."

The Alliance president revealed that he had already been up to the nation's capital to promote their program. Congressional leaders had told him that "overproduction" was the cause of the farmers' woes; and the New York City commercial center defined their reforms as nothing more than the wild, mistaken notions of "hayseed socialists and demagogues." Polk was not about to accept that interpretation: "There is something besides overproduction that has caused it." With the subtreasury plan foremost on his mind, he added: "Congress could give us a bill in forty-eight hours that would relieve us, but Wall Street says 'nay.'" It was clear to Polk that the major "parties are afraid of Wall Street. They are not afraid of the people."[1]

If old-party politicos were fearful of the financial elite but not of ordinary folks, could it be because "the people" had a gun that was designed to "do everything but shoot"? An inveterate Minnesota reformer, Ignatius Donnelly, had arrived at that conclusion years before regarding the nonpartisan approach of the Grange. Despite some encouraging rhetoric and a quasi-endorsement for third-party action outside Dixie, such nonpartisanism was still the official position of Polk and the southern wing of the Alliance. Fortified by the results of the 1890 election, nonetheless, an activist cadre composed primarily of Kansans set out to create a gun for the people that would shoot—and that preferably would not explode in their faces. President Polk had, after all, assured Kansans in his Winfield speech that there would be "no Mason and Dixon's line on the Alliance maps of the future."[2]

Cincinnati, via Ocala and Omaha

In early December 1890 the Supreme Council of the NFA&IU assembled in Ocala,[3] Florida. The organization's phenomenal growth in the year since the St. Louis meeting was plainly evident. Delegates were present from an area extending from border to border and coast to coast, representing thirty states and perhaps as many as one and a half million farmers. Organizational enthusiasm was clearly on the rise, and this meeting was considered a crucial step in furthering the cause of America's farmers.

Having previously graduated to the political arena, Kansans traveled to Florida determined that the tail would wag the dog. The key was to persuade southern delegates to help create a new party. Not only did third-party activists and radical Alliance leaders support the idea; so did more conservative Alliance members who greatly feared that if most white southerners did not join the revolt, the movement in Kansas and elsewhere in the North and West would merely become a feeder for the Democrats.[4] While some moderates feared that farmers would defect to the Republican party, radical leaders were convinced the movement was already "larger than the Alliance" and needed to be immediately nurtured to insure success. There was only one way, they believed, to bring about a multisectional political alignment to wage the fight of the "masses against the classes," and that was through a new party.

Alliance historians have left some things unexplained regarding this Florida conference. Few members, if any, from the southern white (that is, Euro-American) Alliance, at this stage, seem to have been willing to come out openly in support of a new party.[5] Leaders representing the Colored Farmer's Alliance warmly embraced the call, although they were present only in an observer ("fraternal") role, thus symbolically albeit futilely extending a hand to their white neighbors. One can only wonder how the inclusion of an African-American on the Kansas People's party state ticket was received in the South.

There probably was more disagreement than met the eye since Alliance rules discouraged public disagreement or open attacks of one member on another. Kansans and a few other northern delegates, in any case, appear to have been left standing with "egg on their faces."[6] Wishful thinking to the contrary, there was still a Mason-Dixon line on the Alliance map, and a racial one as well. Until it became clear that reform through the Democrats was not going to happen, white-southern logic dictated that they wait and see how the many candidates who had been elected throughout the South with Alliance support measured up in 1891. A move to form a new party would require a reason compelling enough to overcome deeply ingrained sectional, religious, and racial loyalties and prejudices on the part of race and historically conscious white southerners—a barrier too great for many to surmount.

Before the Ocala meeting, Rightmire, the Vincent brothers, and Stephen McLallin had been working closely with others operating through the Kansas State Reform Press Association (which would be organized nationally at Ocala) and the Kansas State Citizens' Alliance. They had taken preliminary steps to schedule a conference for early in 1891 to organize a national party.[7] Backing for that call was secured outside the South, and C. A. Power, a third-party activist and Indiana Alliance delegate, was recruited by the Kansans to issue it at the Ocala meeting. This he did, and according to Rightmire, it "gave great offense to the delegates from the southern states." Kansans, according to Rightmire, then "suppressed and withdrew the call, and as a reward were given two of the national offices."[8]

As he had at the earlier Cleburne conference, C. W. Macune once again played the role of mediator, this time by helping to suppress the call for a new-party conference. The Texas editor of the *National Economist* was then—and would remain—adamantly opposed to the creation of a new party. To defuse the third-party bomb, he suggested a wait-and-see strategy. Southern Alliance supporters, in the meantime, could judge the outcome of reform through the South's one-party system. If the outcome was unsatisfactory, the new-party option would still be available, and arrangements for that move could be made by a delegate convention in time for the coming national election. As part of the compromise, Macune suggested such a meeting be held in February 1892. If at that time the delegates—drawn from all "organizations of producers upon a fair basis of representation"—agreed to the formation of a new party, so be it. The strategy was agreed to, and for a short time the political movement was put on hold.

Also included in Macune's compromise was an agreement to create a confederation of "industrial" organizations. This was nothing more than that umbrella entity that had been suggested by the northern Alliance but rejected by the southern at the December 1889 meeting, when the effort to consolidate the "tillers and toilers" and their allies had failed. Macune, Ben Terrell, and some others viewed the confederation as little more than a tactic designed to head off the creation of a new party.[9]

The vast majority of white Alliance members (at the leadership level, at least) were by no means ready to abandon the Democratic party, but if they were seriously committed to their program, they were going to be abandoned by that white supremacist and more economically conservative party of their "fathers."

The Ocala platform helped to assure that. The demands were much the same as those that had been adopted at St. Louis. The subtreasury plan was incorporated, by this time extended to include land as well as crops, "with proper limitations upon the quantity of land and amount of money." It was number two on the list of demands, right after the call for the abolition of the private national banking system. Probably reflecting the end of the courting ritual directed at the North, the order backed away from the St. Louis convention's unqualified advocacy of government ownership of the means of transportation and communication, calling instead for regulation, with government ownership relegated to a last resort.

For the first time, the Alliance specified that the amount of "circulating medium" (coin and legal tender notes) be "speedily increased to not less than $50 per capita." According to one study by an economist, this monetary objective called for a "currency volume to population" that would not be achieved until nearly midway through the twentieth century, long after the disappearance of most of the small-to-marginal farm operators for whose assistance it was designed. Other financial measures called for "the free and unlimited coinage of silver," a "graduated income tax," legislation to make it illegal "to deal in futures of all agricultural and mechanical productions," a prohibition against alien-absentee land ownership and implementation of a program to reclaim land already held by individuals and corporations of foreign nationality, and in a related category, the reclamation of "excess" land controlled by American "railroads and other corporations."[10]

It was not a program calculated to endear the Alliance—or the national People's party, soon to appear—to money impresarios and corporation stockholders and employees in any capacity. From among the lowly furnishing merchants, petty wholesalers and retailers, assorted middle dealers, small-town bankers, and lawyers (corporate and otherwise), on up the line to the great merchants and tycoons of Wall Street and dozens of other metropolitan financial centers nationwide, bitter opponents soon moved to the front, and they wore the labels Democrat and Republican. Distinct evidence that this had already begun was reflected in the national press coverage devoted to the Ocala conference, particularly by newspapers based in New York City. Events would soon assist mightily in focusing these attitudes even more intensely to produce a potent counterattack.

Two developments in January 1891 were important in drawing the emerging battle lines. The first occurred in Omaha, Nebraska, where the northern Alliance held its annual meeting. Independent sentiment, looking to the creation of a new party, clearly dominated the conference. Resolutions were adopted that began with the flat statement that "we most emphatically declare against the present system of government as manipulated by the Congress of the United States and the members of the legislatures of the several states." Delegates then endorsed the call for a February 1892 meeting "to nominate" an independent presidential ticket.

The Omaha demands differed only slightly from those of Ocala. The northern Alliance also began by advocating elimination of the private national banking system, suggesting that "surplus [government] funds be loaned to individuals upon land security at a low rate of interest." Included also was the demand for an expansion of "the volume of currency . . . to $50 per capita." A closely related measure demanded that landowners be allowed "to borrow money from the United States at the same rate of interest as do the banks." All of these could have been facilitated by the subtreasury system, but no specific mention was made of the southern plan. Other significant planks included "government ownership of all railroads and telegraphs"; "free and unlimited coinage of silver"; "prohibition of alien landownership and of gambling in stocks, options, and futures." In sum, the northern Alliance was following the course prescribed at Ocala even more closely than the Kansas component of the NFA&IU.

Making good on the Ocala compromise that targeted a meeting for February 1892, C. W. Macune moved in late January 1891 to create that umbrella organization promised as part of the deal. Representatives from the NFA&IU, the Knights of Labor, the Farmers' Mutual Benefit Association, the Colored Farmers' Alliance, and the Citizens' Alliance got together in Washington, D.C., and formed what was called the Confederation of Industrial Organizations.[11] Ben Terrell, Macune's fellow Texan and Good Man Friday, was named chairman. A representative from the northern Alliance was conspicuously missing from the Confederation. The date for a conference of various "industrial orders" to decide whether to pursue the new-party option was set at 22 February 1892; the conference was originally scheduled by third-party opponents to meet in Washington, D.C., but was later changed at the request of state leaders to a more convenient St. Louis site.[12]

At the same time events were going forward on yet another organizational front. At Ocala, C. W. Macune had also been named president of the newly formed National Reform Press Association (NRPA). Apparently, the idea was to convert a reluctant Macune and others to the third-party movement. All of the NRPA's other officers were confirmed third-party advocates. Scott Morgan of Arkansas was secretary-treasurer, and the executive committee included none other than C. Vincent, Ralph Beaumont (the "socialist national lecturer" of the Knights of Labor and editor of the *National Citizens' Alliance* in Washington, D.C.), and Texas activist William R. Lamb. Clearly the radical political ferment that had sprung to life within a triangular area intersecting Texas, Kansas, and Arkansas—roughly, from Washington-on-the-Brazos to Newton, Kansas, and from there to Pine Bluff, Arkansas—had begun to reach far beyond its base.[13]

In the meantime Kansans assumed nearly full control of the movement's vibrant political phase. Unsatisfied with the course prescribed by the two regional Alliances, an activist cadre—250 strong by this point—operated through the newly created National Citizens' Industrial Alliance (NCIA), which had been incorporated under Kansas laws in January 1891. This cadre took the initiative in reactivating the call that had been issued and then withdrawn or "postponed" after the Ocala meeting.[14] The NCIA "instructed" its secretary, W. F. Rightmire, to reissue the call when it was deemed "advisable." Soon thereafter, said Rightmire, he obtained "by correspondence the call issued at Ocala . . . with all the signatures attached." In early February, after obtaining a number of additional signatures of prominent Kansas party leaders and legislators, Rightmire released the supplemental call to the press. This move was reportedly "received with great enthusiasm by the reformers of the Northern states, and with coldness and opposition by the Alliance leaders and press of the Southern states."[15]

By April 1891, however, the solid southern front had begun to crack a bit. The struggle to hold Democrats to the Ocala platform—the subtreasury plan, above all—was pushing southern white Alliance brethren toward a parting of the ways. Texans again led the southern charge, and some energetic and talented outside encouragement was provided by Henry Vincent and M. L. Wilkins of Kansas and Ralph Beaumont of Washington, D. C., among others, representing the National Reform Press Association. The occasion was a conference of the Texas Alliance held in Waco in mid-April. The meeting culminated in a crucial decision on the part of the Texas Alliance to send a delegation to the Cincinnati convention. Out of this meeting also came the Texas Reform Press Association and the Texas Citizens' Alliance. These two Kansas creations had quickly become the third-party organizational vanguard, given the reticence of the southern-dominated NFA&IU. With their formation, the wave that had begun with the Texas Alliance and spread northward in 1888 to Kansas and beyond had now returned to its point of origin, making a bid to take Texas and the southern Alliance one large and painful step further.

The Waco conference featured a showdown between the forces advocating reform through the Democrats (led by C. W. Macune) and the radical new-party element (led by William Lamb, Harry Tracy, H. S. P. "Stump" Ashby, James H. "Cyclone" Davis, and others). More than a little irony was involved in the affair. As a Texas historian has aptly said: "Lamb's radicalism, splitting the Alliance founders in 1886, brought Macune to power; Macune's organizational creativity constructed a national constituency of farmers that made possible Lamb's dream of a third party of the laboring classes; and their shared objective, economic parity for farmers . . . was symbolized in the sub-treasury plan, which Macune conceived as an instrument of economic reform and Lamb converted into one of political revolt." As a result, standing up and being counted for the Ocala platform increasingly became the rallying cry throughout the South. In the end, "Macune's sub-treasury, in Lamb's hands, defeated Macune and [ultimately] created Southern Populism."[16] But the move would likely have gone nowhere without significant previous movement outside the South, and it remained to be seen whether the southern phase had begun to develop soon enough and with sufficient strength to assure the success of which its devout followers dreamed. Perhaps the Cincinnati conference would be the test. For sure, a good many dedicated reformers thought so as they packed their bags and headed in that direction in response to the call.

On 18 May 1891 the *Cincinnati Enquirer* headlined one of its columns: "THEY'RE HERE.\The Great Industrial Army.\Thousands More on the Way." Unfortunately for reformers, not quite all came, leaving two critical gaps in the ranks of this army: one was sectional, and the other involved urban labor (even though Terrence Powderly was present and seemingly—by the end of the conference, at least—promising the support of the Knights of Labor somewhere down the road). Officially, just over fourteen hundred delegates were seated, representing thirty-three states plus Oklahoma Territory and the District of Columbia. Few, if any, who asked to participate were turned away, and the zealous, or those within close proximity, were most numerous. Representation was consequently greatly skewed in favor of the new West and the old Northwest. Fully one-third were Kansans; Ohio's delegation was nearly as large and together with that of Kansas constituted more than half the delegates. Altogether, from the old Confederacy there were only forty-eight delegates (Nebraska alone had twice that many), and more than half of those were from Texas—the only southern state (Kentucky excluded) with anything more than token representation. Less surprisingly, a total of twenty-eight delegates appeared from only six northeastern states. Fully seventy percent of the participants were, in fact, drawn from eight states; ranked in order of delegation size they were Kansas, Ohio, Indiana, Nebraska, Illinois, Kentucky, Iowa, and Minnesota.

The original and supplemental calls had summoned eleven different associations and three minor parties to Cincinnati, and the delegates reflected that diverse and general mix.[17] Numerous third-party and single-issue proponents, some self-appointed, jumped at the opportunity. A few of these people could display reform credentials dating back to the anti-slavery crusade. A Washington, D.C. reporter asked a former Greenbacker, who had remained behind in the nation's capital, to provide an assessment of these old campaigners: "A large majority," he said, "are honest, well-intentioned men, a few are dead-beats, and too many are like the French people of whom a witty American lady said: 'They don't know what they want, and will never be satisfied until they get it.'"[18]

Most of the delegates, however, had ties to one or the other of the various Alliances (Farmers' and Citizens') or to the National Reform Press Association, and they knew exactly what they wished to accomplish at the conference: to organize a new party dedicated to advancing the "laboring classes." An influential minority shared that goal but counseled delay. The Kansas congressional delegation, for example, was split on the matter. Jerry Simpson had arrived from Washington, D.C., accompanied by C. W. Macune, who had undoubtedly persuaded Simpson, John Davis, and Ben Clover (also NFA&IU vice president) that it would be best to delay the decision regarding formation of a third party until February 1892. Presumably, Macune and L. L. Polk led the congressmen-elect to believe that delay was in the interest of bringing along more southerners. An ideal solution would somehow have to be found to satisfy both positions. When it was found, that solution, coincidentally or not, closely resembled the course Kansans had pursued ten months earlier.

W. F. Rightmire, one of the principal architects of the Kansas phenomenon, called the convention to order on the afternoon of 19 May. Having that honor was testimony to the leading organizational role he had played, and it was also the high point of his political activities; it was as though his one and only goal had been merely to assist in the creation of a national people's party.[19] After the original and supplemental calls were read, Rightmire said: "It's only right that the Conference come together at the call of Kansas, for on her plains was shed the first blood in the struggle that freed 6,000,000 slaves, and on her soil was fought the first battle which is to free 63,000,000 industrial slaves."[20] Despite his exaggerated figures, it would be hard to imagine a statement that conveyed more forcefully the gravity of the situation or the sense of mission that clearly dominated and defined the convention.

Somehow, the delegates managed to keep their attention concentrated on their economic agenda, despite the persistent clamor from the stronger single-issue advocates of their day—the prohibitionists. The battle against John Barleycorn was joined, at points, with the fight for women's suffrage, to the detriment of the latter. Women's rights advocates, however, were given a fair hearing, and a number of women delegates participated in the work of the convention. Eva McDonald, a Minnesota Alliance state lecturer, conceded at one point that the involvement of women in politics was "rather unique" but, she quickly pointed out, "you men have had the ballot for more than a hundred years, and look what a mess you've made of it." Sarah E. V. Emery of Michigan, known for a widely circulated economic treatise, *Seven Financial Conspiracies,* was the most influential woman present and was, along with Emma Curtis of Colorado, elected to the new party's national committee.[21]

Potentially the most troubling issue that bore on the movement's future—especially as it related to support from the South—was the treatment afforded American citizens of African ancestry. The problem of colorphobia cannot adequately be described as merely white racism or Anglo-Saxonism, complicated as it was by unusual historical baggage. M. H. Brian, a delegate from Louisiana (the same area, incidentally, that would later produce Huey P. Long), when quizzed on the matter, told a reporter that the people of his parish were "ready for a new party. We find that we can manage the colored men in the Alliance very well, and

we are not a bit frightened about negro supremacy." Such racist paternalism—the humane preference–limited—was clearly in evidence, although the leader of the Colored Farmers' Alliance, R. M. (Richard)
Humphrey of Houston, emphasized that "colored men in the Alliance all
want a third party."

The most dramatic scene relevant to the rights of African-Americans
occurred toward the close of the conference. Only one delegate was
present from North Carolina, the home base of the president of the Euro-
American Alliance. Ben Colvin of Michigan was recognized to announce
that "there was a colored delegate present from North Carolina. He had
paid his expenses here, but did not have enough [money] on which to
return home. We don't want him to walk!" A collection was called for,
and a "storm of quarters and half dollars poured into a hat." His name
was John A. Sawyer; he had, in fact, served on the convention's most
important committee—platform and resolutions. The reporter noted,
"the colored brother was appreciated." If it is true that R. M. Humphrey,
colored Farmers' Alliance and Co-operative Union (CFA&CU) "superintendent," had no African lineage, as a Texas historian has claimed, Sawyer may have been the only representative of his race serving as a
delegate. Being also the only delegate from an important southern Alliance state whose whites had shunned the convention, one can appreciate
why Sawyer was appreciated.

After the hat had been passed, the cry echoed through the hall demanding that the North Carolinian be given a chance to speak. It was
said he was "a fine-looking young colored man and a rattling talker." His
remarks, as filtered through the reporter's notes, included these
comments:

The interests of the white man and colored man were identical, and what hurt
one hurt the other. The people of his State were greatly interested in this movement. They were willing to follow the lead of the whites, but he asked them for
God's sake not to lead them astray.

He had been asked why there were not more people of his color here. He
would say that they were too poor to come and probably that the convention was
glad that more had not come if they had to be cared for the same as him.

He closed by saying that this movement would find a strong ally in the colored
people all over the country, but particularly in the South.

The shadow of the Civil War and Reconstruction was ever present. In
fact, the most dramatic moment of the conference involved a display of

unity between Confederate and Union veterans. A resolution expressing support for Union-veteran benefits sparked the scene. The resolution was reputedly endorsed unanimously by former Confederates—a "genuine rebel yell" greeted the announcement. At that point, a "long-tall Texan," James H. Davis, the "cyclonic" orator of later Populist fame, dressed in a white suit that accentuated his slender six-foot-plus frame, made a short speech saying, among other things, that "the day meant resurrection for principles and burial for rings and monopolies." Following that, a Union veteran from Indiana by the name of Wadsworth returned Davis's conciliatory remarks, emphasizing that "the noble braves who wore the gray had been just as honest as those who wore the blue." As he saw it, "Both had been duped since the war. They had been kept divided, while the trickster got away with the country. Now they would stand together to fight a common foe more formidable than the rebellion." When he finished, Davis approached Wadsworth carrying a U.S. flag, and they clasped hands and paraded about the stage with Davis waving Old Glory high over the head of "his former foe."[22] R. M. Humphrey, identified by the reporter as "the colored delegate from Texas," then joined them waving a flag of his own. Shortly thereafter, the whole convention got in on the act, touching off a demonstration that lasted "fully fifteen minutes." It was, reportedly, a sight to behold, "the most sensational scene of the conference."

The conference moved straight ahead toward its main goal, despite the spurned but determined foes of alcoholic beverages and a few of the more conservative delegates who were opposed to forming a new party, chief among whom were John H. Powers of Nebraska and L. L. ("Lon") Livingston of Georgia, both state Alliance presidents. One report indicated that those who opposed the immediate formation of a new party realized they had made a mistake in sending only their leaders to the conference, where they were vastly outnumbered. Had they urged their members to participate fully, it was said, "they could have controlled its action without trouble." Those who favored forming a new party simply overwhelmed their opposition. At one point, a letter was read from L. L. Polk urging delay. It was "received with painful silence," until a delegate from Arkansas shouted: Let us "sit down on that communication as hard as we can." That sentiment was greatly applauded, and the letter was referred to a committee for burial.

Not long after Polk's message was read, the report of the committee on resolutions was declared ready. Chairman Donnelly explained that the committee had arrived at a plan it hoped would avoid dividing "the friends of reform." Confronted with one demand that they "proceed without regard to any previous movement and build a party on an entirely new foundation," and another demand that they await action by the conference scheduled for February 1892, the committee struck a strategic balance. It recommended the creation of a national central committee for what it recommended be called the People's Party of the United States of America. This group would then be directed to attend the conference scheduled for February 1892. If a new party was endorsed by that meeting, the committee was to "unite" with it; if not, it was to be directed to "call a national convention not later than June 1, 1892," to nominate a presidential ticket.

The desire to bring everyone on board the good ship reform was even more clearly reflected in the platform recommended by the committee on resolutions. Donnelly announced that the committee had endorsed the St. Louis, Ocala, and Omaha documents. "If the South is not with us," said Donnelly, "we are with the South." Indeed they were because where the St. Louis and Omaha platforms had differed, the Cincinnati platform had given way to the purely southern Ocala document. After Robert Schilling of Wisconsin had read the report, the secretary announced that Confederate veterans had unanimously approved the attached resolution relating to compensation of Union veterans; this touched off the demonstration previously described. After it ended, a motion to adopt the report was made and seconded. "Loud cries for the question" were heard, but when William Lamb of Texas was recognized, he attempted to slow the political steamroller by asking that the report be read again. "Let's not get so enthusiastic," said Lamb, "we have until 1892 to decide the matter." Opposition was immediate, and Lamb backed off, uttering this somewhat muddled yet revealing comment: "the People's party would win in 1892 peaceably, and if not, in 1896 with bloodshed. One great fault of the people is that they cling to the party name and forget the principle. What they wanted was American principles. A debt has been created for the benefit of the bond-holder and the people will have something to say in the future." A bit later, another Texas delegate, Thomas Gaines, attempted to slow down the proceedings. "The idea of adopting a platform," said Gaines, "after only one reading was ridiculous." It was reported that the Texan "was roundly hissed and finally cried down." Then after yet another attempt by the prohibitionists to add their resolution from the floor, the platform was overwhelmingly adopted.

With a central committee in place and a national nominating convention assured, the Kansas solution of March 1890 was virtually duplicated at

"Populist" — term's debut

the national level. One prominent historian, with some uncertainty, credited Donnelly with the "formula."[23] It seems more likely, however, that others were also involved in ways that were not revealed to the press. The Texans seemed to have been shocked by what the report included. With James Davis sitting on the committee, this seemed a bit strange. Was Davis working at odds with others in his delegation, or had a key segment of the report been added at the last minute? Perhaps both of these factors were involved, in which case Davis's emotional performance after the platform was read may have been less than spontaneous. It would seem that at the last minute it was decided to recommend formation of a committee representing a party, rather than merely a conference liaison-contingency group. According to one inside account, something like that happened. W. F. Rightmire said he had worked confidentially with S. F. Norton of Illinois, M. L. Wheat of Iowa, and Robert Schilling of Wisconsin ("the secretary") to insert a clause pertaining to the election of an "executive committee" and to organize supporters to push it through to approval before the opposition could rally their forces.[24]

However it was done, the formula ultimately pleased nearly everyone. Shortly thereafter, even Macune's *National Economist* would describe the steps taken in Cincinnati as "wise and conservative," an arrangement well designed to serve as a "link that will unite the farmers with all other occupations in the great approaching conflict."[25] The People's party national committee was elected, and Henry E. Taubeneck of Illinois chosen as its chairman. John Otis of Kansas nominated Taubeneck and William Lamb of Texas seconded his selection. (Otis and Lamb would later distinguish themselves as extreme antifusionists—that is, opponents of cooperation with other parties.) They nominated Taubeneck because he had proved he was a "true blue" independent as an Illinois legislator, was the "Big One" holdout in the Illinois senatorial election of 1891, and would stick to the middle of the road, waging all-out war against both old parties. Ironically, the new chairman was later willing to cooperate with reform-minded Democrats.

Party Expansion

In the aftermath of the Cincinnati conference, perhaps as that huge Kansas delegation was returning home on its special section of railroad cars, the word *Populist* made its debut. Because it was an oral creation, later sources tell slightly different stories of its origin, but all point to a conversation involving William Rightmire and David Overmeyer, the latter a prominent Kansas lawyer and Democratic leader. Rightmire reportedly pointed out how awkward it was to refer to a member of the new party as a "People's-party woman or man." Said Rightmire, "We need a shorter name for conversational purposes." Then turning to Overmeyer, "Dave, you are long on words—give us a nickname." Overmeyer thought for a moment, then came up with the Latin word *populus,* meaning "people." Rightmire was said to be skeptical about that because he could see journalists shortening it to "Pops." Overmeyer replied, "So much the better. You want a short name. You can't find one much shorter than 'Pops.'" Several unnamed journalists, probably from the *Kansas City Star,* who were either eavesdropping or involved in the conversation subsequently used it in their columns, spelling it as they misheard it. Soon thereafter, the terms *Populist, Populism,* and *Pops* spread like wildfire; they almost as quickly found their way into the dictionary.[26]

As these newly christened Populists made firm plans for the great contest of 1892—their first and last legitimate battle, as it turned out— events in the South propelled growing numbers of Farmers' Alliance members toward political revolt. They increasingly saw reform through the Democrats as a sham. Southern Alliance leaders—especially in North Carolina, Georgia, and Texas—were particularly angered by the negative reception the subtreasury plan continued to receive from Democrats. Several weeks after the Cincinnati conference, President Polk attempted to utilize the threat of third-party action to bring the Democrats into line, as he had done at every opportunity for almost a year. "The new party," he said, "has adopted . . . Alliance demands. . . . Does anyone suppose intelligent Alliancemen will vote against a party that adopts those demands, and in favor of a party that not only fails to adopt, but resists [them]?"[27] A few months later, Polk finally despaired of enlisting the support of the Democratic party in behalf of the Ocala platform. The NFA&IU president was deliberate, if nothing else; he and many southerners were by this time facing up to a stark reality of which a growing minority of Americans had in fact been painfully aware since the 1870s: the structural reformation they desired was anathema to the regionally dominant old parties.

In June 1891 the new party's five-member executive committee met in St. Louis and took steps to organize an agency to distribute reform literature throughout the country. Plans were also made regarding campaign fundraising and a speakers' bureau. The committee focused primary attention on the South, dispatching a number of party leaders from

Kansas to the region to urge their Alliance brethren to join them. In late summer Polk made another trip to Kansas, where he spoke in three different locations urging continued effort and once again hinted that southern assistance would likely be forthcoming.

Jerry Simpson, Mary Lease, Annie Diggs, and William Peffer were among the more prominent Kansans who made the swing through the South. According to an Alliance historian, the "picturesque features of the campaign of 1890 were reproduced, and orgies of speech-making went hand in hand with picnics, barbecues, and similar festive occasions."[28] Mary Lease, it seems, had lost none of her powers—she again elicited personal attacks from the "gentlemen of the press"; they even rivaled those of Kansas's Republican establishment.

Interviewed in Washington, D.C., shortly after returning from this southern tour, Jerry Simpson provided this assessment of the movement: "We are in the midst of the greatest political revolution the world has known." An abusive establishment press to the contrary, its "leaders are not Jacobins, nor are they anarchists or socialists. They believe in equal rights, exact justice and free competition." The modern situation, however, required some fundamental adjustments. "All industrial enterprises which are essentially monopolistic, such as railways, telegraphs, etc., should be under government control, but everything else should be left in private hands." He went on to say that the movement was based on "sound political economy" and was "sustained by the scientists." To emphasize his point, he announced that the "doctrine of Prof. [Richard T.] Ely, as presented in his last work on political economy, is our doctrine." More clearly in the category of wishful thinking, Simpson also said, "The old Democratic scarecrow of Negro rule has lost its potency in the South as thoroughly as the bloody shirt has lost its influence in the North."[29] Although it was obscured somewhat by momentary enthusiasm and hope, the lost cause and colorphobia remained highly potent in the South, just as did the bloody shirt and prohibition in the North and West. Contrary to at least two prominent studies, one by Peter Argersinger and the other by Lawrence Goodwyn, I believe this combination of irrationality, moralism, and prejudice—more than the silver panacea or fusion politics—would prove to be Populism's supreme nemesis, externally and internally.[30]

In the meantime, organizing efforts went forward. Kansas Populists were especially active throughout the latter half of 1891 assisting in the creation of Alliances and party organizations in other states. In the month following the Cincinnati conference, efforts were under way in at least

Iowa, Wisconsin, Illinois, Indiana, Ohio, and Pennsylvania. State parties were organized in Iowa in June, in Ohio in August, and in other states of the North and West where variously named third parties had earlier been established. With the help of the Kansas party and the national executive committee, the Vincent brothers' *Nonconformist* was moved from Winfield to Indianapolis to support the Indiana People's party and to build support in that critical sector encompassing the Old Northwest, where the Alliances had not been very successful.

The ever-popular Jerry Simpson made a second trip to the South in the fall of 1891, promoting the new party in North Carolina and Louisiana. He returned to Washington convinced that events were headed in the right direction for the party. His contacts convinced him that southern Alliance members would hold their political leaders—congressmen, in particular—to the Ocala platform. Significant support for that belief came from Tom Watson. The newly elected Georgia congressman had been leaning toward the new party since its formation at Cincinnati. By the fall, he was firmly committed to holding southern Alliance congressmen to the test of their program. And on 1 October 1891 Watson launched his soon-to-be highly influential *People's Party Paper* to further that belief and to promote concerted action between the South and the West.

Prior to this, some Texans finally took the plunge. On 17 August 1891 the "founding meeting" of the Texas People's party—the first in the South—was held in Dallas. Most of the state's prominent white Alliance leaders were present. Several black leaders were also there. R. M. Humphrey, Colored Alliance superintendent, at one point told those who seemed to be intent on fashioning a segregated and paternalistic party apparatus: "This will not do. The colored people are part of the people and they must be recognized as such." A Texan of African ancestry, R. H. Hayes, saw even more clearly what was essential for the success of Populism all over the South and indirectly throughout the nation. "If you are going to win, you will have to take the Negro with you," said Hayes. The Texas convention agreed to include two blacks on the new state executive committee. It remained to be seen how far southern Euro-American Populists were willing to take Afro-Americans with them. It would not be nearly far enough, although it would be adequate to galvanize the many pathological colorphobes among whites. Despite this shortcoming, these southern Populists were headed in the right direction. They certainly deserved better treatment than they were going to receive at the hands of the South's self-proclaimed "conservative better elements."[31]

St. Louis via Indianapolis

In November 1891, Indianapolis, the new home of the *American Non-conformist,* was the site of the NFA&IU's annual meeting. The politics of third-party action was the major topic of the conference. Leonidas Polk had decided the time had come for him to make his break with the Democratic party, and the People's party executive committee was also there trying to win the official endorsement of the NFA&IU. That would not happen, but Polk advised the conference "to be deceived no longer." The unanimous reelection of Polk, together with the election of Henry Loucks (who had been on the new party's central committee since the Cincinnati conference) as vice president clearly signaled the direction in which the order was headed.

Tom Watson's representatives at Indianapolis, supported by Jerry Simpson, gained approval for a resolution instructing all congressmen who had been elected with Alliance assistance not to "enter . . . any party caucus" that did not make the Ocala platform the "test of admission." Watson—present but not a delegate—predicted that congressional friends of the Alliance would meet separately to nominate their own candidate for Speaker of the House. Said Watson, "Georgia is ready for a third party and will sweep the state with the movement."

The shift in sentiment that had occurred since the Ocala meeting, eleven months earlier, was sharp indeed at Indianapolis. Kansas activists were especially struck by the change; clearly they believed they were riding the crest of a huge wave that was about to alter the course of history. Several weeks after this meeting, on 1 December the central committee of the Kansas People's party issued an address to the people of Kansas that served as a kind of Populist manifesto (until it was superseded by Ignatius Donnelly's more famous and partly derivative preamble to the St. Louis and Omaha platforms).[32] The Kansas address included this indictment:

the wealth of the country [since the Civil War] has been concentrating in [ever fewer] hands. . . . Every branch of business is depressed. The merchant fails for want of trade and the banker from depreciation of values. Labor is unemployed or inadequately paid. Our cities are the abodes of poverty and want and consequent crime, while the country is overrun with tramps. Starvation stalks abroad amid an "overproduction" of food and illy-clad men and women and helpless children are freezing in the midst of an "overproduction" of clothing. . . .

We hold that these conditions are the . . . result of vicious legislation in the interest of favored classes . . . [and] appeal to the great body of the people, irrespective of occupation or calling, to rise above . . . partisan prejudices . . . and calmly and dispassionately examine the facts which we are prepared to submit in support of our claims. We appeal to reason and not to prejudice, and if the facts and arguments we present can be refuted we neither ask nor expect the support of the people. "Come and let us reason together."[33]

How would it be possible for the general public to "reason together" when not even the Alliance could manage such a feat? The elections of 1890 had raised expectations that there would be forty-four southern congressional representatives pledged to the Alliance program. By the time the new Congress was ready to convene more than a year later, however, that optimistic count was much reduced. The preliminary meeting of "Alliance representatives" that assembled in the office of the *National Economist* actually drew only twenty-five congressmen, and these few almost immediately split into two factions and wound up glaring at one another. Lon Livingston was the principal leader of sixteen southerners at this meeting who were adamantly opposed to a third party; the remaining nine were led by Tom Watson and Jerry Simpson.[34]

John Otis, Simpson, and Watson challenged Livingston and his fellow southerners to abide by the Indianapolis resolution. At one point Watson addressed himself directly to Livingston and, among other things, said that "farmers trusted you, and now you want to betray them for your own personal interest." The two Georgia leaders came close to blows, and the meeting ended with Watson conceding that an "irrepressible conflict" existed "between the two factions." The Livingston group departed to join the Democrats, and the nine insurgents adjourned to Senator Peffer's apartment, where they were joined by Senator Kyle. There the first People's party congressional caucus was called to order. Still hoping to gain the vital support needed from the South, they chose as their house leader and candidate for speaker the only southerner to honor the Alliance's Indianapolis resolution—Tom Watson. Since the resolution was Watson's creation—the product actually of the Georgia battle between Livingston and Watson that began the previous August—it would have been strange indeed if he had not supported it. The idea was to put to the test the issue of what came first: loyalty to the South's Democratic party or commitment to the Alliance platform. To Populists, the results of this early test were none too satisfying; one of an estimated forty-four southern Alliance congressmen, or even one of seventeen, was hardly a score to brag about, even though that one was a person of Watson's considerable talents.

Those who refused to leave the Democratic party denied that they had abandoned Alliance principles. Some pointed to their subsequent support of Charles Crisp of Georgia for speaker as an indication of the value of working from within the Democratic party. Since Crisp was thought to be more sympathetic to the cause of bimetallism than his closest party rival, his election was viewed as a small reform triumph. In fact, the *National Economist,* still the official national Alliance paper, commended these southern Alliance congressmen for ignoring the order's instruction and proclaimed that the "victory is not in securing Crisp but in whipping the bosses of both parties, and securing supremacy for the wishes of the people by making the money question the great issue in 1892."

If C. W. Macune's paper continued to reflect the will of the southern Alliance (definitely a questionable proposition by this point), the order had become an exponent of a brand of financial reform that fell far short of the greenback-antimonopolism characteristic of its platforms since 1886. Stephen McLallin of the Topeka *Advocate,* among others, was greatly disturbed by this whole affair. McLallin wrote an editorial reminding Macune (the "economic radical") that "free coinage of silver, while . . . one of our demands, is of minor importance. . . . The power to issue money and control of its volume must be taken from corporations and restored to the people, where it constitutionally and rightfully belongs, or all ostensible monetary reforms are a failure and a farce."[35] The Kansas editor felt strongly enough about this development that he made a special trip to Washington, D.C., so he could personally confront Macune and others on the issue.

It was a strange and ironic position for Macune to have taken. Something was sure enough "rotten in Denmark"—that is, the nation's capital—and it was spelled just like the name of the editor of the *National Economist.* Less than a year earlier, Macune had in fact confronted McLallin and Kansans generally with this truly profound piece of advice:

It is your duty as Alliance men to discuss and thoroughly understand the subtreasury plan, and if it is not correct we should know it at once and stop advocating it, because if we can eliminate that from our platform the Democratic party in the south and the Republican party in the north will swallow the platform whole and never make a face at it. Wall street does not care for free silver now, but they thought it was best to keep it as an issue in the next campaign. Wall street will not object to doubling the value of money when it can take plenty of time to prepare for the change so as to make it profitable to Wall street, but they will fight the sub-treasury to the bitter end. Why? Because the sub-treasury is based on an underlying principle of free government and seeks to establish a representative currency which shall expand or contract automatically as the necessities of business require, thereby destroying "the power of money to oppress by its scarcity," and rendering it impossible for any combination of capitalists to depress the price of the produce of the country by means of "corners" and trusts or pools. This will establish and maintain the principle for which Abraham Lincoln contended: . . . in the conflict for supremacy between labor and money labor should be supreme.[36]

No one ever utilized the old radical Lincoln ideal more effectively in defense of Populism's economic program.

Crisp, as Watson pointed out, had been an early opponent of the sub-treasury plan, and he clearly viewed Alliance radicalism and Populism as an even greater menace than the Republican party. Watson and other Populist leaders naturally had no reason whatsoever to celebrate the Georgia Democrat's election as speaker. Their goal was not a modestly reformed Democratic party, but a new party that would replace the regionally dominant old parties—the Democratic party in the South and the Republican party in the West.[37] It was an extremely difficult—if not impossible—mission that would confront both blind and calculated resistance, as well as cynical and sincere co-optation, intensifying as Populism grew as a legitimate threat.

In the end, the old-party insurgency called Progressivism that came over much of the nation at the turn of the century accomplished a semblance of the regional political transformation desired, without abolishing the old parties. By and large, however, Progressives supported neither the fundamental economic reforms nor the advancement of the cause of the laboring classes that were at the core of prefusionist Populism. (But this observation takes us too far ahead in the story.)

Attention was now focused on the St. Louis conference called by that Confederation of Industrial Organizations that C. W. Macune had arranged more than a year earlier. This meeting in late February 1892 was to determine whether to wage a third-party campaign. After some delay to sort out the delegate situation, the conference awarded seats to around eight hundred individuals representing twenty-two organizations. Just over seven hundred of these, however, were assigned to the eight main orders that were included in the call.

Colonel Polk was elected permanent chairman, beating Macune's man, Ben Terrell—a sure sign that third-party sentiment was strong. In his speech to the convention, Polk was wildly cheered, especially when he said: "The time has arrived for the great West, the great South, and the great Northwest, to link their hands and hearts together and march to the ballot box and take possession of the government, restore it to the principles of our fathers, and run it in the interest of the people."[38]

During the conference, third-party advocates won all the critical showdowns with their foes, a substantial minority led by Lon Livingston and made up primarily of southerners. The attitude of the "antis" was stated bluntly by Livingston: "We don't care what they do in Kansas and other western states. They can have a third party if they want one; in fact, a third party in Kansas is probably a good thing with which to overthrow the Republican party, and in that good work we wish them success; but in the South we want no third party."[39] With that attitude so strong, the convention's leaders delayed the decision for third-party action as long as possible and concentrated instead on the platform. The document they produced continued the large area of consensus among the various orders since the 1889 St. Louis convention regarding a program. Positions were more clearly defined, but in only one area was there anything significantly different in this second St. Louis platform. The NFA&IU Supreme Council at Ocala had dropped the first St. Louis platform's call for government ownership of the country's railroad, telegraph, and telephone systems, opting instead for regulation. The Cincinnati convention had continued this alteration, but the delegates at this St. Louis meeting restored the earlier demand.

Apparently, northern and southern leaders had to engage in some logrolling, unconscious or otherwise, to achieve that outcome. In the eyes of many white southerners, public ownership of the transportation and communication systems was the epitome of a detested "paternalism and centralization" (generally entangled with white supremacy), and northerners were much less enamored with the subtreasury plan. The return to the earlier St. Louis position reflected the stronger influence of the North and West, as well as an element of concession in the interest of retaining the subtreasury plan. For the first time the plan was presented in such a way as to make it clear that it was a means and not an end—and not even an indispensable means. The end was clearly public ownership of and control over the monetary system, to maintain an adequate supply of money and credit. McLallin had stated the end quite succinctly, and the first and most fundamental plank in the St. Louis platform did so now. It declared:

We demand a national currency, safe, sound, and flexible, issued by the general government only, a full legal tender for all debts, public and private, and that, without the use of banking corporations, a just, equitable, and efficient means of distribution direct to the people, at a tax not to exceed two per cent per annum, to be provided as set forth in the sub-treasury plan of the Farmers' Alliance, *or a better system; also, by payments in discharge of its obligations for public improvements* [my italics].[40]

The platform came from committee with something quite new and re-markable—a preamble written by Ignatius Donnelly, which was later de-scribed by one noted historian as "a masterpiece of political invective." A key segment of the preamble, somewhat revised for the later Omaha platform, heads this chapter.[41] Donnelly read the portion he had written with a great deal of feeling and oratorical skill. The demands and reso-lutions, which were shorter and not nearly as spirited, were presented by another member of the committee. Then, according to a reporter, the delegates and spectators, "as if by magic," sprang to their "feet in an instant and thundering cheers" and "shouts for Donnelly" echoed "from 10,000 throats" celebrating what they had heard "as the road to liberty." The demonstration went on "fully ten minutes." With considerable clarity and a dash of hyperbole, the reporter said "the din was indescribable" and compared it to "the lashing of the ocean against a rocky beach during a hurricane."[42]

When calm was restored, Livingston moved the adoption of the plat-form without specifically mentioning the preamble with its condemnation of both old parties and implicit third-party mandate. It was a transparent attempt to put one over on the convention and to further his strategy of weakening the Republican party beyond the South. A Georgia delegate from Watson's wing of the Alliance quickly moved to make it clear that the preamble was included. With that accomplished, the convention came to an end.

At this point C. W. Macune, briefly and for the last time, assumed center stage at the front of a movement he had played such a key role in building, before sabotaging it and then deserting the cause. It was a tragic story; Populism sorely needed his considerable organizing talents and diplomatic skills. On behalf of the now defunct Confederation of In-dustrial Organizations, the Texan single-handedly reassembled the con-vention as a committee of the whole to arrange for the selection of a group to meet with the People's party executive committee. This was done, and these delegates were quickly merged with the People's party central committee. Careful and comprehensive plans were then made for organizational structure and delegate selection from precinct through county, congressional district, and state levels. The date for the national convention was set at 4 July 1892, and Omaha, Nebraska, was chosen as the site, from a list that had included Kansas City, St. Louis, and Indianapolis. [43]

A "Second Declaration of Independence"

Shortly after the St. Louis delegates decided to join the People's party, Stephen McLallin noted in the *Advocate* that Kansas Republican newspapers had generally responded to the meeting somewhat like the editor of the Lawrence *Journal,* who claimed "the conference was composed of two classes—demagogues and lunatics. The demagogues framed the platform and the lunatics adopted it." The preamble especially drew fire. McLallin conceded that it contained "a terrible indictment against the old parties." The charges, he said, were "either true or false. If true, who will dare say that those parties are worthy of further confidence. If not true, all that the [old-party] press . . . has to do in order to destroy the new party is to demonstrate that single fact." It would not do, said McLallin, to engage merely in "ridicule and abuse."[44]

This was, perhaps, wishful thinking. Ridicule and abuse, not reasoned response, would continue to be the main line of attack throughout the country by both old parties. Lon Livingston, for example, hurried back to Georgia immediately after the conference ended to spread the word that the meeting had been "composed of a lot of cranks and men without character or influence." Worse yet, he reported that Ignatius Donnelly had said that "the New Order of things would wipe out the color line in the South." If these people were to succeed, white southerners would probably have "to eat and sleep with niggers." For colorphobes, proof enough of this could be had simply by noting that nearly one of every eight delegates in attendance at St. Louis had represented the Colored Farmers' Alliance—97 of about 800, which was actually a fair and representative proportion.[45]

After St. Louis, the relationship between the Alliance and southern Democrats rapidly deteriorated. The Democratic party in several southern states, including Texas and Tennessee, adopted a policy of requiring members to sever their ties to the Alliance before being allowed to participate in party activities. In the remainder of the South, except for South Carolina, Alliance candidates were simply "outmaneuvered or outvoted." Tillmanites endorsed the Alliance program in South Carolina but

Omaha platform

remained committed to the Democratic party on all levels. Most Alliance leaders were in fact still unwilling to break with "the party of their fathers."

The shaky hope that the South would finally come to the aid of the People's party received a heavy and unexpected blow on 11 June 1892 with the sudden death of Leonidas Polk, who undoubtedly would have become the Populist candidate for president less than a month later. Only Polk had earned the kind of confidence among both southerners and westerners that was essential for a serious South-West reform coalition. The man had worked slowly but effectively toward his goals. Only a few weeks before his death he had called a special conference, attended by Alliance leaders from eleven southern states, in Birmingham, Alabama. There he had tried, with amazing patience and diplomacy, to get his fellow white southerners to endorse the new party; his efforts had nearly been successful, for he apparently came within three votes of gaining a majority among those in attendance. After Colonel Polk's departure from the scene, prospects were bleak. As Colorado Populist Davis Waite recognized at the time, "in order for the People's Party to succeed, WE MUST BREAK THE SOLID SOUTH." The death of the popular North Carolinian may not have signified the complete demise of hope, since that state of mind seemingly springs eternal, but it was truly a critical setback.[46]

The magnitude of the loss was undoubtedly masked by the rush of events. Barely two weeks after Polk's funeral in Raleigh, Populists were preparing for the trip to Omaha to launch their national campaign. On 2 July nearly fourteen hundred delegates and three thousand or more spectators witnessed opening ceremonies and organizational activities in Omaha. The platform committee was instructed to report before nominations were made early on Monday, Independence Day. Although the platform differed only slightly from the St. Louis platform, this document would subsequently acquire a revered quality in the eyes of Populists as a "second Declaration of Independence," known simply as the Omaha platform. An ordinary political document it was not. To Populists it contained a sacred creed, a master plan to save the republic—and the hour was late.

In spite of its familiarity, the reading of Donnelly's preamble and the demands was followed by a reception even more exuberant than the one in St. Louis. It lasted more than thirty minutes and was reportedly accompanied by "sustained cheering, clapping, yelling and crying." An unsympathetic observer sensed the frightening specter of "socialism and communism," probably comparable to "the enthusiastic Bastille demonstration in France" during the French Revolution. The crowd was finally brought under control when the band played not "The Marseillaise" but "Yankee Doodle." As one very astute observer recognized, "this dramatic and historical scene must have told every quiet, thoughtful witness that there was something at the back of all this turmoil more than the failure of crops or the scarcity of ready cash."[47] Indeed there was.

This Omaha platform became the bible of the movement, and as scripture, it merits careful attention. First of all, it was clearly the culmination of a third-party campaign that had been under way since the mid-1870s, and it enshrined the Alliance demands as they had been perfected since 1886. Its program of economic reform was designed to rescue an older, predominantly agrarian America from the onslaught of urban-industrial America.

On a number of occasions these reformers had avoided making their cause over into a crusade to enforce a particular moral standard—the campaign to prohibit alcoholic beverages especially. Once again they did so. Apparently, this plea from the preamble was quite genuine:

While our sympathies as a party of reform are naturally upon the side of every proposition which will tend to make men intelligent, virtuous, and temperate, we nevertheless regard these questions—important as they are—as secondary to the great issues now pressing for solution, and upon which not only our individual prosperity but the very existence of free institutions depends; and we ask all men to first help us to determine whether we are to have a republic to administer before we differ as to conditions upon which it is to be administered.

The entire platform was embodied in three planks that challenged the nation's prevailing capitalist, so-called free-market system at its core. The first, encompassing five coequal subordinate proposals, involved financial or monetary arrangements, treated under the heading "Money." The second concerned the transportation and communication systems. These two were followed by a third, relating to "Land." It viewed land in the broadest sense, as the ultimate source of all "wealth" and "heritage" of all "the people." Populists reasoned that these three areas existed—or were meant to exist—to benefit the people. Having been usurped by corporate and individual interests, they had to be reclaimed and conducted by means of public agencies, owned and administered by the public.

This agenda, the sum of Populism's first national platform, was followed by ten resolutions. These were measures that the delegates supported but that were "*not . . . part of the platform of the People's party* [my italics]". This needs to be emphasized because more than a few historians have misunderstood or ignored the platform and this disclaimer and have focused instead on one or more of these nonplatform, generally noneconomic, protoprogressive reforms to illustrate the meaning of Populism. The ten resolutions included: (1) a secret ballot, (2) the application of revenue to be derived from a graduated tax to reduce the "burden of taxation" on "domestic industries," (3) pensions for Union veterans, (4) immigration restriction, (5) an eight-hour law for government work, (6) an end to the Pinkerton (private, corporation armies) system, (7) initiative and referendum, (8) one term for the president and vice president and direct election of senators, (9) an end to subsidies to "private corporations," and (10) sympathy for a Knights of Labor strike then under way.

Although it was an expanded list of party sentiments, the Cincinnati convention's advocacy of "universal suffrage" and the St. Louis convention's support for "female suffrage" were omitted. Apparently the result of a desire to make the document more palatable to those enamored of or enslaved by conventional sexist and racist mores—especially Democrats, North and South. It was a significant omission for a party professing to represent the people. It could hardly have been an oversight. During opening ceremonies Mary Lease's youngest daughter, Louisa, who was said to have inherited "her mother's wonderful voice," gave a recitation that "brought down the house." She closed her address by ad-libbing this comment: "The motto of the Alliance is: 'Equal rights to all and special privileges to none,' but you are not true to that motto if you do not give woman her rights. It has been said that the hand that rocks the cradle is the hand that rules the world, but we have made up our mind that there will be no cradle to rock nor babies to put in them if you don't give us our rights."[48]

The new party's platform was nonetheless a remarkable document that had gradually taken shape over a period of years. The decision regarding a presidential ticket, however, had to be made with virtually no preparation. The death of Polk had eliminated the party's best prospect. From the standpoint of raw talent and popularity, a Watson-Simpson ticket would probably have been strongest. But the Canadian-born Simpson was ineligible, and Watson was considered but passed over—ultimately even for the second spot, when former Confederate general James G. Field of Virginia was nominated for the vice presidency merely to balance a ticket headed by former Union general James B. Weaver of Iowa.

Weaver was fifty-nine and a veteran of the third-party struggle whose political roots extended back to the antebellum period. A native-born westerner, he had entered politics as a Free-Soil Democrat but became a Republican in 1857. Twenty years later he came to the conclusion that the party of Lincoln had been absolutely corrupted. He then became a Greenbacker and with the support of Democrats in his district had been elected to Congress in 1878, 1884, and 1886. In 1880 he had been the Greenback–Labor party's candidate for the presidency, waging perhaps the first modern presidential campaign, in a sense, by making an extensive personal speaking tour in behalf of his party and principles.

General Weaver was nominated on the first ballot. Despite his third-party background, the Iowa lawyer clearly was associated with the party's more conservative or pragmatic wing. His selection played a key role in determining the party's future course; by 1892 he was convinced that the cause of reform was likely to go nowhere without the support of many old-party voters—especially Democrats. It was said he "was always ready to cooperate with other parties provided they were willing to support the principles in which he believed."[49] His nearest competitor for the nomination was Senator James Kyle of South Dakota, who had only reluctantly consented to have his name placed in contention.

Shortly before the nominations were made the convention also adopted what was henceforth supposed to be a "fundamental" party "ordinance"—the self-denying ordinance, as it came to be known. It declared: "No person holding any position of official trust, or emolument under the federal or any state or municipal government, including senators, congressmen, members of the legislature, shall be eligible to sit or vote in any convention of this party, and a copy of this ordinance shall be annexed to every call for any future convention." Thus "the people," and not professional politicians, were to be assured "permanent control."

In a welcoming speech that could have served as a close, Omaha's Republican mayor assured the convention: "You have laid the foundation of a great party. You have broken down the barriers of sectionalism, buried the bitterness of the past, extinguished the glowing embers of the campfires of hate, [and] wiped out the imaginary line that separated the north and south." The optimism and hope generated at Omaha was contagious. A Kansas Populist paper headlined its coverage of the convention, a "Great Political Love Feast." It described the upcoming campaign as though it were a prize fight: in opposite corners one had "The Plain, Common People of the North and South vs. the Corporations, the Trusts and the Monopolies." Political cartoonists could do wonders with the metaphor, even though the lines were not nearly so clearly drawn. The stage was thereby set for the first great battle of 1892.[50]

Nebraska's delegates to the Independent party (later the People's party) state convention, 1890. *Courtesy Nebraska State Historical Society*

William V. Allen, Populist U.S. senator from Nebraska, 1893–1901. It was said that Allen stood head and shoulders above his colleagues, both intellectually and physically. Allen also presided over the turbulent St. Louis convention that nominated William Jennings Bryan for president on the Populist ticket in 1896. *Courtesy Nebraska State Historical Society*

William A. Peffer, U.S. senator from Kansas, 1891–97. Some were convinced that "Pefferism" was populism. *Courtesy Kansas State Historical Society*

James Baird Weaver, the 1892 Populist party presidential candidate. Weaver earnestly believed that populism had a "mission to restore" to the American government what he called "its original and only legitimate function"— the task of "assuring to all its citizens . . . their inalienable rights."

Ignatius Donnelly of Minnesota, author of the preamble to the Omaha platform of 1892. "We meet in the midst of a nation," he wrote, "brought to the verge of moral, political, and material ruin." *Courtesy Minnesota Historical Society*

Mary Elizabeth Lease, Populist orator without equal and according to some, a "demagogue in petticoats," ca. 1890. "The West and the South are bound and prostrate before the manufacturing East," she said. *Courtesy Kansas State Historical Society*

Marion Butler, Populist U.S. senator (1895–1901) and national party chairman from North Carolina. *Courtesy North Carolina State Archives, Raleigh*

Jeremiah Simpson, U.S. representative from Kansas, 1891–95 and 1897–99. The "Sockless Jerry" or "Sockless Socrates" of political legend. *Courtesy Kansas State Historical Society*

Jerry Simpson on the hustings during one of his later campaigns for Congress. *Courtesy Kansas State Historical Society*

Annie L. Diggs, "Little Annie" of Populist politics and later, according to her opponents, the "Lady Boss" of the Popocrats (Populist-Democratic fusion forces), ca. 1900. *Courtesy Kansas State Historical Society*

L. L. Polk of North Carolina, president of the National Farmers' Alliance and Industrial Union (1889–92), who was denied his rendezvous with destiny. *Courtesy North Carolina State Archives, Raleigh*

Populist faithful on their way to a rally, Dickinson County, Kansas, 1890s. *Courtesy Kansas State Historical Society*

Thomas E. Watson, U.S. representative from Georgia (1891–93) and the Populist party's candidate for vice president in 1896. Watson warned that merging with the Democrats would be to "play Jonah while they play the whale." *Courtesy Southern Historical Collection, University of North Carolina, Chapel Hill*

Republican assistant sergeants-at-arms, attempting to assure Republican control of the legislature, display their weapons in Topeka during the Kansas "legislative war" of 1893. *Courtesy Kansas State Historical Society*

"BLOWING" HIMSELF AROUND THE COUNTRY.

In this anti-Populist cartoon of 1896 William Jennings Bryan blows hot air at some Neanderthal types representing the farmers of America. *Courtesy Kansas State Historical Society*

COPYRIGHT'08
BY R.B.HINDMARSH

William Jennings Bryan, 1908, standing outside the Lincoln, Nebraska, office of the *Commoner,* the weekly newspaper he founded in 1901. *Courtesy Nebraska State Historical Society*

Chapter Four

When Push Came to Shove

The 1892 Election and Its Aftermath

> *All new parties in America have believed in the equality of men before the laws. . . . [That important principle has, nonetheless, been jeopardized because] there has grown up another person, little known to the fathers of the republic. It is a legal entity, endowed with more privileges and powers, and fewer responsibilities than belong to common men.*
>
> *This artificial person, created by law, is stronger than Samson and Hercules combined. It is more tyrannical than King George, and less merciful than chattel slavery—a monster, powerful, aggressive, and grasping, which to-day dominates society. . . .*
>
> *This new creation . . . [is] making justice between man and corporate power unusual, if not impossible. . . . This new tyrant does not even come into court, except by proxy. Without body, it cannot be imprisoned or hanged. Without conscience, it cannot suffer the pangs of remorse. Without soul, it is not concerned as to the rewards and punishments of the future.*
>
> *. . . The old parties of rapacious greed are friendly to their offspring, and will not afford relief. Is it any wonder that society is organizing against this new form of tyranny—this "communism" of capital? and that a new political party is rapidly forming for defensive purposes?*
> —*John Davis, "Communism of Capital: The Real Issue Before the People,"* The Arena, *September 1892*

Shortly after the Omaha convention Tom Watson was asked by the editors of the *Arena* magazine to contribute a short piece explaining why the next president should be a Populist. The Georgia congressman summed up his response by writing: "the People's Party . . . is pledged to *real, vital, imperative reforms,* whose purpose is to destroy *class rule* and to restore to the people the government."[1] That comment captures, as completely as any brief summary can, the meaning and mission of the Populist party as viewed by the faithful. The opposition would deny that the old parties were fronts for class rule—or even for an incorporating America; indeed, they would argue with equal certitude that Populism was itself a class movement, narrowly and sectionally derived. There was more than a little truth in the indictments of each.

At the time, no one analyzed the situation with greater clarity and insight than Eva McDonald, a young Minnesota prolabor activist with Farmers' Alliance and Populist ties.[2] She conceded that, with the significant exception of the Knights of Labor, the party had taken "but little cognizance . . . of any class of workers except those engaged in agriculture or kindred pursuits." It was essential, she wrote, that urban workers be effectively mobilized in support of the party. The "mass of city workers" had not been represented at the St. Louis conference of February 1892. If that was the product of "antagonism, or even indifference," she said, "it might prove fatal to the success of the new movement." Why? "For if the People's Party, in its ultimate development, only represents a class, no matter how large that class, its work must necessarily partake of a sectional character, and, from lack of breadth and depth, fail to accomplish those great reforms which mark epochs in civilization."[3] One might add that if the movement was perceived as representing only the agricultural community, in whole or in large part (apparently that was her unstated concern), failure would surely be its reward.

Although she wrote before the Omaha convention had named its presidential ticket, McDonald made another observation about Populism that remained valid—unfortunately for the new party—throughout its brief history: "It is a peculiarity of the People's movement," she wrote, "that it has not yet produced a leader. It has teachers—earnest, thoughtful, and progressive. It has statesmen of good parts. But a leader, in the true sense, is yet wanting." What the people's movement would get in due course was a triad of leaders reflecting the unreconciled (and unreconcilable, hindsight suggests) diversity of the movement. On a right-to-left continuum, they were William Jennings Bryan (technically not a Populist), Tom Watson, and Eugene Debs.

All three leaders clearly had ties to an old radical, neorepublican tradition with roots deep in the subsoil of a preindustrial, predominantly agrarian America. The question was, could the movement for which they would become heroes overcome implicit and inferential class and sectional barriers to generate the support needed to carry out "those great reforms which mark epochs in civilization"? Or was it already too late to avoid the restraints imposed by what John Davis had called a "new form of tyranny"? This campaign of 1892, more than the "Great Battle of the Standards" four years later, would be the movement's crucial moment.

"Welcome Honorable Allies"

Kansas ✓

While the Populists organized nationally, the reform effort had gone forward at the local and state levels in various parts of the country. The performance of the party in Kansas was especially watched and was probably indicative of what was going on elsewhere. Since it controlled only the lower house of the Kansas legislature as a result of the 1890 election, there was little chance that the party would be able to enact much of its program. The holdover Republican senate, however, faced a reelection contest the following year and was not unaffected by the political earthquake. Several important reform measures were passed despite the standoff. Among them: an act prohibiting alien-absentee land ownership; an eight-hour law for all workers employed by the state; a measure providing for the regulation of warehouses and for the inspection, grading, weighing, and handling of grain; a bill prohibiting combinations designed to prevent competition among persons engaged in buying or selling livestock; and another creating a banking regulatory agency headed by a bank commissioner.[4]

The defeated measures were even more significant. Populists drafted a bill to regulate and establish "reasonable maximum" rates for railroad freight within the state, which included provisions prohibiting discrimination in short-haul, long-haul charges and providing for the popular election of railroad commissioners with "full power and authority to control, fix, and regulate the charges and rates." The senate committee on railroads, contrary to the 1890 state Republican platform, rejected the bill, saying it was likely to invite "an almost limitless field of legal and business absurdities." The house also passed a bill that Populist sponsors claimed "would have driven unscrupulous Shylocks—robbing the people by a usurious interest of from 25 to 100 per cent. per annum—out of the state or forced them to become honest, law abiding citizens, by loaning their money at a legal rate of 10 per cent." The measure required the "forfeiture of both principal and interest in case of usury" and was said to be "nearly a copy" of a New York state law. The senate judiciary committee rejected this anti-usury bill as "a declaration of animus" that, they contended, would unduly discourage capital investment. A bill providing for an Australian (secret) ballot expired on the senate calendar and a number of important measures were defeated more directly by senate Republicans. Among the latter were those providing penalties for bribery, prohibiting the corrupt use of money in elections, outlawing child labor and the use of private-detective forces (that is, private armies) by railroad management in labor disputes, and yet another giving women the vote.

The enfranchisement of women was the most divisive issue the legislators faced. Early in the session a Populist introduced a bill granting women the vote and acknowledging their right to hold public office. Notably, this was to be accomplished by legislative fiat: its sponsors argued that a state constitutional amendment was not required to confer the rights at issue, only to prevent a future legislature from repealing the statute. Accordingly, the bill was voted on, and it was defeated, falling three votes short of the needed simple majority. By special order, the measure was again brought before the house and this time was passed by a vote of sixty-nine to thirty-two; in the process, Populist ranks were seriously shaken.

The issue pitted some leading Kansas Populists against one another. Annie Diggs and Stephen McLallin of the *Advocate,* now editors of the party's official state paper, were outspoken in their support of women's rights. Just as the issue was coming to a head in the house, the paper ran an article that declared that there was "no measure of greater importance before the Kansas legislature than the bill giving full suffrage to women." The measure's chief opponent was none other than the speaker of that Populist house, P. P. (Peter Percival) Elder, a longtime opponent of that particular reform. The sixty-eight-year-old farmer-banker-editor-politician was a formidable foe; few men could claim to have played a more active role than he in Kansas politics. After moving to the territory in 1857 from Maine, Elder had assisted in organizing Franklin County, the Republican party, and the first state government. He had been active in Kansas politics as a Republican for over twenty years, when he left the GOP in 1878 to become a Greenbacker. While a Republican, he had served in the legislature on a number of occasions, and as a Republican he had been house speaker, as well as lieutenant governor. In addition, he had been the Union Labor party's nominee for governor in 1888. But his views on sex roles more nearly mirrored the male chauvinism of the dominant culture, which was rather insidiously championed by the major parties.

During the house debate, Speaker Elder entered a special protest on the record setting forth his reasons for opposing the bill. It was, he said, "wholly unconstitutional" and contrary to public sentiment, and besides, women already enjoyed rights in Kansas "far in advance of any other state." Then came what was probably central to his stand: "This privilege conferred will bring to every primary, caucus and election—to our jury rooms, the bench, and the legislature—the ambitious and designing women only, to engage in all the tricks, intrigues and cunning incident to corrupt political campaigns, only to lower the moral standing of their sex; invites and creates jealousies and scandals, and jeopardizes their high moral standing; hurls women out from their central orb fixed by their Creator to an external place in the order of things." Elder went on to argue that the "demand for female suffrage is largely confined to the ambitious, office-seeking class; possessing an insatiable desire for the forum, and when allowed, will unfit this class for all the duties of domestic life and transfer them into politicians, and dangerous ones at that." He ended his protest by stating: "When the laws of nature shall so change the female organization as to make it possible for them to sing 'bass,' I shall then be quite willing for such a bill to become a law." In the meantime, he said, it would be "a grave mistake, an injury to both sexes and the party, to add another 'ism' to our political creed."

Four Republicans, an equal number of Democrats, and seven Populists in the house signed Elder's protest, which was appropriately labeled in the *Advocate*, "A Relic of the Dark Ages." Annie Diggs characterized the commentary as "coarse, boorish, ungentlemanly and entirely devoid of that dignity that should characterize the utterances of a representative of the people and especially of the speaker of the House." She asked, "who authorized Speaker Elder and his compatriots to define the particular 'central orb, fixed by their Creator' as the limit [with]in which woman shall move?" Diggs closed her critique by informing Elder that if he had "any future political aspirations he may as well abandon them. In a state where woman's influence in politics is as potent as it is in Kansas, it will be useless for any man who has so little respect for that influence, and whose allusions to the fair sex are characterized by the coarseness of this protest, to ever again become a candidate for office."

That most Populists supported the enfranchisement of women was a dubious victory. As expected, the Republican senate voted nay. In the process, the struggle had exposed a point of fundamental disagreement within the reform camp.

Another divisive issue, which had some linkage to women's suffrage, concerned the proscription of alcohol. Alcohol had been prohibited by constitutional proviso in Kansas since 1880. A resolution was now introduced into the house by a Republican to resubmit the state's prohibition amendment; the move was defeated rather decisively by a vote of seventy-two to twenty-six, but eighteen Populist representatives voted for resubmission. Prohibition and women's suffrage were supreme anathemas to many—if not most—Kansas Democrats. These two issues were bound to become only more troublesome. Embattled and increasingly desperate old-party leaders—Republicans, especially—were searching for openings into which they could drive wedges in the ranks of the less-than-monolithic reform coalition; they had found two rather quickly.

These issues were still only potentially explosive, even after the elections of 1892. Tension on these issues mounted only as direct overtures for concerted action were made with one or the other of the two old parties. Even before the Omaha convention, however, a debate developed in Kansas over the issue of fusion itself. Democratic leaders, state and national, who were confronting a presidential election were only too eager to work out an arrangement that promised to reduce Republican electoral votes. An element of the Populist leadership fully appreciated the fact that their party had won its legislative and congressional races in 1890, in part at least, because Democrats had not contested a number of those races and had openly cooperated in others. At the same time, their executive ticket had lost out in a three-way race. The 1891 local elections had again illustrated what was likely to happen when the new party battled both old ones. It was obvious that Populists still constituted a minority of the voters (39.4 percent at their 1894 high point); victory, many realized, required cooperation. But other elements of the Populist leadership, like Stephen McLallin, were convinced that fusion meant "a sacrifice of principle and an ultimate sacrifice of strength." Programmatic purists, or midroaders, opposed cooperation and accommodation with the old parties; in Kansas this specifically meant the Democratic party, because the GOP—the One-Party Dominant—was the target of the revolt and not a legitimate subject for cooperation or accommodation. That was simply intolerable to some Populist leaders, like Mary Lease, for whom opposition to fusion was less a matter of principle than of social pathology and prejudice, more often than not born of the Civil War.[5] To both types of extreme antifusionists, defeat was preferable to victory attained by fusion tactics. By June 1892, nonetheless, Populist and Democratic leaders were busy attempting to work out a strategy of cooperation in the campaign against their common Republican opposition.

The issue of cooperation carried over into the Populist state convention. Wichita, a city in Sedgwick County that was inhabited by about as many Democrats as could be found in any one spot in Kansas, was selected as the site. This in itself may well have signaled something about the predisposition of party leaders. Fusion was widely practiced in the county, and the city, with its labor vote, represented a potential base of support that the predominantly rural party needed to tap if it hoped to become a major force.

The Sedgwick County Populist chairman, Lorenzo D. Lewelling, was certainly willing to have Democratic support. He was known as an orator and was called upon to deliver what amounted to a keynote address. He used that opportunity very effectively. In a series of short and explosive paragraphs, he took the delegates by storm. "We are met today," he said, "to direct the movement of a greater and grander army than ever before went forward to victory." Let it be known, "Our battle is not for supremacy, but for equality. We demand no paternalism at the hands of the government, but we do demand protection from corporate vultures and legalized beasts of prey. We ask in God's name that the government shall be so administered that the humblest citizen shall have an equal chance." How can government "command the respect of the people," he asked, "when so large a portion are abandoned to become victims of superior cunning and insatiate greed?"

Populism is said to be merely a prelude to chaos, said Lewelling, "the ground work of anarchy, a sort of basement story of the edifice of destruction. But we don't believe it." People of goodwill know better. "No," he thundered, "the farmers and laborers of this country are not anarchists. They are earnestly seeking to avert the experiences of the old world and to subdue the spirit of anarchy with the milk of human kindness." But "God only knows what another generation of misrule may bring!"

Toward the end of the speech, the forty-five-year-old Wichita produce merchant, who had experienced an unusually diverse public and private career before moving to Kansas from Iowa only six years earlier, offered the delegates some significant advice: "While we are brave let us also we wise. Let us welcome honorable allies and we shall go forth to victory." At the finish, Lewelling received a wildly enthusiastic burst of applause and left the stage, having emerged from near obscurity as a prime prospect for the gubernatorial nomination, which he later received in a close contest with William D. Vincent, the party's state secretary and the pre-convention favorite of midroaders.

By late summer, with John Breidenthal, the party's young and highly capable state chairman, calling the shots, most Kansas Populists were convinced they had assured themselves of "honorable allies." Extreme antifusionists were of course outraged; at this stage their numbers were small, and a few may well have been, as charged, crypto-Republicans—those political Hessians John Ingalls had said it was permissible to hire. The immediate advantages of fusion were obvious, but the long-run consequences were not readily apparent. Democrats had endorsed the Wichita ticket, even though none of their colleagues had been nominated. Strategists from both parties worked to arrange it so that in most election contests, only one candidate—a Populist or a Democrat—was in the field against a Republican nominee.

One Kansas historian, although giving these events a rather peculiar conspiratorial spin, has aptly noted that Kansas Populists were "led under Breidenthal's skillful direction into an unwitting implicit endorsement of fusion."[6] The move undoubtedly placed additional strain on intraparty relations and tilted the balance of the reform coalition more strongly in favor of its component of former Democrats. It was, however, something of a chicken-or-egg question: since 1891, growing numbers of Alliancemen with Republican antecedents, like many southern Democrats, had simply been unable to bid their party farewell. They of course did not see the Republican party as an integral part of the problem nor as a principal target. On the other hand, many Kansas Populists of third-party and Democratic antecedents, and even a number of former Republicans who had truly burned their bridges, increasingly identified their cause as a struggle against what was called "modern Republicanism." One thing was certain: those Kansans who refused to follow the Alliance into politics or who later abandoned Populism in favor of the Republican party did not do so because they had concluded the GOP was more likely to implement the full radical Alliance–Populist program.

These circumstances and others that were related to the general collapse of the nation's economy in 1893—more than the influence of office seekers and the politics of compromise and expediency—pointed the way in Kansas to Populist–Democratic cooperation and accommodation, culminating ultimately in fusion. But personnel and programs did not mix to such an extent that it merited being called fusion until after the party's devastating defeat of 1894. Ironically, the 1894 campaign was the only

Kansas Populist campaign of the 1890s that lacked any Democratic support. It was, in fact, the only one in which Populists gave distinct signals to the Democratic party's remnant of conservative and reactionary loyalists (Grover Cleveland Democrats, for the most part) that no help was wanted. Purity exacted a high price.[7]

"A Protest against Corporate Aggression"

Not long after he was nominated for the presidency James Weaver began his personal effort to define and explain the party he represented. He told a gathering of Iowa friends and neighbors, "Men will pass away but principles are eternal." The maxim he highlighted that day was indeed old, one that had resonated among reformers since the Age of Jackson. "The whole movement," he said, "can be summed up in one sentence: 'Equal rights for all and special privileges to none.' It is simply a battle for liberty." Whose liberty? "The new movement proposes to take care of the men and women of the country and not of the corporations. This movement is a protest against corporate aggression."[8]

Weaver had promised that he would "visit every state," carrying the Populist banner into "the enemy's camp." Toward the end of July, accompanied by his wife Clara, Mary Lease, and several others, he headed west to launch the campaign officially from Denver. After eight days in Colorado the group traveled on to Reno. From Nevada they went to Los Angeles, then to Fresno, Oakland, and San Francisco. Enthusiastic and especially receptive crowds, ranging from four to twelve thousand, turned out for the meetings in California.

Then it was on the road again, north to Portland, Oregon, and from there to Tacoma and Seattle, Washington. A frenetic turnout awaited them in the Emerald City, so large and so rambunctious as to make it "almost dangerous to alight from the cars." Then it was over the Cascades, destination Spokane in eastern Washington. From there they traveled across the Idaho panhandle and into Montana, speaking in Butte and Helena. Then on to Cheyenne, with brief stops in between for speeches in Idaho and Wyoming. Altogether, they visited eight states and generated considerable enthusiasm for the cause.

Weaver had nothing but high praise for the performance of Mary Lease. She more than matched his speaking schedule, which on at least one day had them addressing eight separate meetings. Weaver reported: "Her hold upon the laboring people was something wonderful. They almost worshipped her from one end of the country to the other." This

Color + the South

was perhaps the inspiration for a later reference by Lease to herself as "Queen Mary," in describing how she was regarded by the masses.

It was back home, then on the road again by the third week of August. The itinerary next targeted Missouri and Arkansas, and the candidate spoke in those states until September. At that time Clara Weaver and Mary Lease rejoined the group for the great southern tour through Texas, Louisiana, Mississippi, Alabama, Florida, Georgia, Tennessee, the Carolinas, and the Virginias. The last three weeks of the campaign were devoted to the states of the old Northwest, closing in Des Moines where it had all begun.

The political climate in the South had grown even less receptive— downright hostile, in fact—as the move toward forming a third party became a reality. One South Carolina editor revealed how completely the lost cause and adherence to the Democratic party had blocked out some of the old party's more idealistic heritage. The Democratic party, he wrote, "is a white man's party, organized to maintain white supremacy and prevent a repetition of the destructive rule of ignorant negroes and unscrupulous whites. . . . The safety of the South . . . as well as the conservation of free institutions on these shores, depend upon the strength, unity and perpetuity of the [southern] Democratic party." In late August 1892 Tom Watson stated the case of the opposition more succinctly: "it may be boiled down into one word—*nigger.*"[9]

A short time later Watson elaborated on the subject in an article published in the *Arena.* Southern Populists, he wrote, faced this irrational roadblock:

> You might beseech a Southern white tenant to listen to you upon questions of finance, taxation, and transportation; you might demonstrate with mathematical precision that herein lay his way out of poverty into comfort; you might have him "almost persuaded" to the truth, but if the merchant who furnished his farm supplies (at tremendous usury) or the town politician (who never spoke to him excepting at election times) came along and cried "Negro rule!" the entire fabric of reason and common sense which you had patiently constructed would fall, and the poor tenant would joyously hug the chains of an actual wretchedness rather than do any experimenting on a question of mere sentiment.[10]

Watson

Despite all that, the fact that tens of thousands of white southerners did make the break demonstrates how desperate times were for the rural masses. Many Alliancemen had waited until the outcome of the 1892 national Democratic nominating convention before making their final de-

cision. The nomination of Grover Cleveland, who was diametrically opposed to Alliance monetary reforms and virtually all else, was the last
straw for many. Tillman's supporters in South Carolina had earlier described the prospect of the former president's third nomination "as a
prostitution of the principles of Democracy, as a repudiation of the demands of the Farmers' Alliance, which embody the true principles of Democracy, and a surrender of the rights of the people to the financial kings
of the country."[11]

After Polk's death, the national Alliance leadership had strongly favored the new party; however, state leaders and the rank and file began
to divide and move toward opposite poles. Many Alliancemen were convinced they could "remain at once good Democrats and good Alliancemen." Governor Ben Tillman, despite his apparent radicalism and
genuine chagrin, remained with the old party. In North Carolina, Elias
Carr, who had earlier been president of his state Alliance, repudiated the
new party and accepted the Democratic nomination for governor. In the
end, the Alliance became increasingly irrelevant as its former enthusiasts
abandoned the order to fight for or against Populism.

Most of the South's Alliance leaders probably remained with the Democrats. And those who made the break, as has aptly been said, "became
. . . not merely political apostates but traitors to [southern] civilization
itself, more to be reviled even than the Republicans into whose hands
they played."[12] Estimates indicate that approximately half the Alliance's
membership in the South became Populists. (One must emphasize here
that the agrarian sector in the West was likewise far from monolithic; the
rural community throughout the nation, in fact, produced more than its
share of bitter and dedicated anti-Populists. Historian Michael Rogin was
correct in connecting America's post–World War II reactionary right—
McCarthyism—to this anti-Populist segment of the rural community,
although the connections were not as exclusively rural as Rogin indicated.)[13] The remainder were simply unable or unwilling to jeopardize
their white-supremacist world for what might turn out to be a futile struggle to create a government more responsive to rural people—even if the
people were defined in narrow racist and sexist terms, which had a fatal
enervating effect in any case. This is that flawed or pseudocommitment
that I previously labeled the humane preference–limited. That race was
such a problem should not be surprising considering that even the supposedly more sophisticated editorial writers of the Atlanta *Constitution*
(one might with some risk assume theirs was not altogether a self-serv-
ing strategy) seemed to believe that white supremacy was of greater
consequence than "all the financial reform in the world."[14]

Populist strength in the South, as in the West, was heavily concentrated in the rural countryside; the towns and cities, for the most part, remained comfortably within the Democratic orbit. Quite frankly, radical economic reforms (greenback antimonopolism, in particular) had precious few rank-and-file supporters in the urban commercial centers; even mild financial reform was suspect within that domain. Inexorably, it seemed, urbanites in the South, as elsewhere, were emerging as the vanguard and storm centers of that ongoing economic revolution that was slowly but surely extending its reach from its northeastern stronghold, creating in the minds of many of those most estranged by the process, such as John Davis, a "new form of tyranny."

Populist strategists knew that breakthroughs in the South were critical to the party's future, and the national committee directed a number of its prominent speakers—some from outside the South—to the region. It soon became clear, however, that southerners themselves were most effective in appealing to those of their own region. Weaver's running mate, James Field, an ex-Confederate general who had sacrificed a leg for the cause, was readily accepted. According to one account, "he knew the oratorical language of the South and could speak it well; and he had little of the harshness and rancor in his system that characterized so many of the third-party speakers."[15]

Weaver and Lease began their journey into Dixie in early September. As it turned out, they might better have spent their time in the industrial Northeast (which was, incidentally, "enemy territory" that Weaver never visited). They would have made slight headway in that area, but the old-party attack that they surely would have elicited might well have generated some sympathy for them among the South's yankee-haters. The southern tour was not quite what they hoped it would be. Weaver had campaigned in the region a number of times before without incident but never as the candidate of a party that seriously threatened the South's One-Party Dominant. The effort proceeded reasonably well until the group reached Georgia. The Democratic press there, quite vicious in its attacks, worked up emotions and hatreds to a fever pitch by publishing false charges of "cruelty and oppression" Weaver had allegedly practiced on the people of Tennessee while he was a major in the Union Army. He was rotten-egged in Macon, where his wife bore the brunt of the attack. Anticipating the same or worse treatment down the line in Atlanta, Weaver canceled further public appearances in the state.

Mary Lease was also subjected to a bitter no-holds-barred verbal assault from the Democratic press. One southern editor spoke frankly when he declared that "the sight of a woman traveling around the country

making political speeches [was] . . . simply disgusting"; "Southern man-
hood," he wanted it known, "revolts at the idea of degrading womanhood
to the level of politics." Another Georgian wrote this after a Lease visit:

Well, boys, she is a plumb sight. If I had a hound dog that would bark at her as
she passed by the gate I'd kill him before night. She could set on a stump in the
shade and keep the cows out of a 100 acre corn field without a gun. She's got a
face that's harder and sharper than a butcher's cleaver. I could take her by the
heels and split an inch board with it. She's got a nose like an ant-eater, a voice
like a cat fight and a face that is rank poison to the naked eye.

Apparently, women simply had to remain down on the pedestal. As a
person already prone to hate Democrats per se, the southern tour did
nothing to cure Lease's particular psychological hangups. She reported
that General Weaver "was made a regular walking omelet by the Southern chivalry of Georgia."[16]

Weaver closed his southern tour in Pulaski, Tennessee, an area that
took some pride in being known as the birthplace of the Ku Klux Klan.
Threats were made against the candidate relating to his alleged role as
military commander at that site in 1863–64. It was broadcast that he had
better avoid the place. Weaver refused to be intimidated. He and Lease
spoke, under the watchful eyes of local supporters, and the meeting concluded without serious incident.

From Tennessee, Weaver journeyed to his party's national headquar-
ters in St. Louis. From there until the end of the campaign he labored to
fulfill engagements in Missouri, Illinois, Indiana, Minnesota, South Dakota, Nebraska, Kansas, and Iowa.

Toward the close of the canvass, several national figures—chief among
them Albion Tourgee, one of the last surviving and more genuine of the
radical Republicans—tried to get Weaver to withdraw his candidacy, fear-
ing that he would merely assure "the election of Grover Cleveland, with
the 'solid South,' as his controlling force." As Tourgee saw it, Cleveland's
election would be a threat to liberty and would likely result in "the permanent establishment and entrenchment in the most impregnable legal
forms, of that Southern spirit of intolerance and determination to rule or
ruin, of which you and I have in our own persons had more than one
exemplification."[17] Weaver apparently never gave that suggestion a serious second thought.

The Populists who were inclined toward cooperation and accommodation with the reform wing of the Democratic party, like Weaver, might

have been better served if the Republican party had had to take the blame for the collapse of the national economy that occurred not too many months after the Democrats assumed office in 1893. But that speculation gets one into the precarious historical area of what might have been. What is undeniable is that Grover Cleveland and the Democrats were assisted into office by Weaver's candidacy. The Populist ticket received just over one million votes (8.5 percent) and twenty-two electoral votes, becoming the first third party since 1860 to break into the electoral column. Cleveland's margin of victory over incumbent President Benjamin Harrison was just over 360,000 votes. More than 400,000 votes went to Weaver from states of the West that had once been strongly Republican.

As Weaver viewed the outcome, the election of Cleveland had resulted from a "violent reaction" and was not the result of "the deliberate judgment of the American people."[18] He understandably preferred to interpret the results as positively as possible—and the election definitely had a bright side. According to his overly optimistic calculations, Populists would "hold the balance of power in the Senate of the United States. We have doubled the number of our adherents in the House of Representatives, secured control of a number of State governments, hold the balance of power in a majority of the States . . . , and have succeeded in arousing a spirit of political independence among the people of the Northwest which cannot be disregarded in the future." The Cleveland administration, Weaver was certain, would fail because it had no "well-defined policy, except that of [a] contemptuous disregard for every element of reform." Populism, he said, had arrived none too soon, and its great work yet lay ahead: "Its mission is to restore to our government its original and only legitimate function, which has been well nigh lost by non-use, that of assuring to all its citizens—the weak as well as the mighty—the unmolested enjoyment of their inalienable rights."[19] Weaver's ability to articulate the meaning and purpose of Populism certainly had been refined in the crucible of the campaign; his postelection statement struck to the movement's core.

The candidate was most pleased with the vote in the far western states. The prizes were small, but the victory margins were large in Nevada, Colorado, and Idaho. Nine of Weaver's twenty-two electoral votes came from that area. Kansas was, however, recognized as "the banner Populist state." Populist–Democratic cooperation there had yielded just over 160,000 votes; Texas was second with nearly 100,000, followed by Alabama and Nebraska, both in the 80,000-plus range; Colorado came in with over 50,000; North Carolina, Georgia, and Missouri each topped 40,000; and Minnesota, Oregon, South Dakota, and California cast more than 20,000 votes each for the new party. These were the top twelve Populist states. Four were southern and six were western, excluding Minnesota and Missouri from the calculations. The performance of the party in the South and West encouraged the belief, in the minds of Weaver and others, that the creation of "a strong sectional party," such as had led to the creation of the Republican party back in the 1850s, was a real possibility. Untoward developments, however, would introduce a train of events that prevented that particular repetition of history.

Populists, with good cause, had expected more votes from the South than they received. The support was probably there; one will never know for sure. But the elections in the South were neither honest nor free. Homicides (African-Americans being the principal victims), assorted violent tactics, widespread intimidation, deviousness and deceit, blatant corruption, and massive vote frauds were all too common. This sorry situation was so well described by one southern Populist in a letter to Weaver that it merits extended treatment. A. M. West of Holly Springs, Mississippi, wrote that the Populists

have the country vote. The Democrats have the town vote *and the Count* and, I am persuaded, will use the same regardless of right or justice to perpetuate Democratic rule in this state. The cunningly devised provisions of our state constitution and statutory laws establishes an absolute Party despotism . . . as intolerant and tyrannical as human ingenuity can make it, under the supremacy of the constitution of the United States. It is truly fearful to contemplate the decay of patriotism and political honesty and the all-pervading corruption of the party leaders. They do not hesitate to adopt and execute any methods to accomplish their unholy purposes. They are oblivious to the sublime teachings and examples of the founders of the republic. They are unscrupulous in their defamation of human character. In their mad pursuit of power they ignore social and religious ties and make the supreme rule of their party the God of their worship. For these reasons we work, in this state, with no expectation that the vote, however cast, will be counted otherwise than for the Democratic party.[20]

In the aftermath, desperate, bloodied, and angry Populists formed at least two short-lived secret paramilitary organizations designed to fight fire with fire. The idea was to insure a fair count and honest elections. One, called The Industrial Legion of the United States, apparently got beyond the planning stage only in Kansas and Texas; the other, Gideon's

Band, was modeled explicitly on the old Videttes and operated briefly in Texas, possibly also in North Carolina. The early demise of these organizations was predictable, at least when under the command of genuine friends of liberty. How could a movement truly committed to democracy and a humane society adopt the undemocratic and inhumane practices of their mainstream opponents without succumbing to the very forces they were seeking to change? Contests are a bit too one-sided when one contending force refuses to be governed by a concern about humanity and the other does! Therein resides a dilemma historians should never lose sight of in treating the political battles of the late nineteenth century. Ultimately, the answer would be nonviolent resistance, but that approach requires a society and world community with at least an influential segment governed by a social conscience sufficiently elevated to make the approach effective rather than merely suicidal.

On the down side, there was a good deal more about the contest of 1892 to recommend pessimism than optimism. In spite of a tremendous effort at all levels, the outcome nearly everywhere was less than might have been expected. One Alliance historian reasoned that the party might well have fared better in the South solely as a national organization, leaving state and local offices to the Democrats. But that would have been out of the question, and rightly so. No national party could exist without vital grassroots support. Local organizations that challenged the South's One-Party Dominant naturally generated pressures toward cooperation with Republicans, the region's other pariahs, just as in the North and West, where Democrats had been the object of attention for possible cooperation.

Many southern Republicans, like many western Democrats, had been delighted to see the Populist party enter the contest. A number of them became Populists, as had Democrats outside the South, and they undoubtedly had no great reluctance about forming a league to combat the common foe. In North Carolina the Populists were always the least numerous of the three parties contending; they thus entered the contest hopeful that Republicans would endorse their nominees or join forces with them. North Carolina Republicans, however, named their own separate slate, anticipating that the split in the Democratic camp caused by the Populist revolt might be their big chance. In Georgia the Republican organization was not nearly as large as it was in the Tarheel State. Georgia Republicans endorsed the Populist nominee for governor while naming their own people for the remaining state offices.

South Carolina, the home of Tillmanism, was true to its maverick nature. Neither Populists nor Republicans nominated a slate for state offices. Governor Tillman ran in the primary as the regular nominee of the Democrats against the conservative Straight-Out Democrats, as he had in 1890, and drew votes from the two lesser challengers. In the general election, Populists put forward only their presidential and vice-presidential candidates. In Florida Republicans condemned rule by Democrats in the state as a systematic scheme designed "to rob the majority of its liberty." They assisted the Populist cause by nominating no one, leaving their people free to vote for Populists. Alabama Populists cooperated with Republicans from the outset, but before the campaign had run its course, cooperation gave way to a variety of fusion called by John Hicks "fairy complete and thoroughgoing." Based on the official but unreliable count, Alabamians subsequently cast a higher percentage of votes (36.6 percent) for Weaver than did the voters of any other southern state: Populists and Republicans in Louisiana waged a fusion effort from the start, dividing nominations between themselves. In Arkansas and Texas the two parties made no formal arrangements but reserved their fire for their mutual opponent. A significant number of Republicans in those two states became Populists; even more voted the Populist ticket.

Under attack and worried, southern Democratic loyalists, like Republicans in a number of western states, embraced various reforms. Florida Democrats, in effect, tacitly endorsed the Alliance monetary package. In North Carolina, South Carolina, Georgia, and Texas somewhat similar promises were made. Tillmanites in South Carolina simply incorporated the Ocala platform outright. In most southern states there were moves to endorse a number of the nonplatform, noneconomic, protoprogressive Populist reforms that were attached to the Omaha platform. When it was not simply a ploy, what these endorsements signified, unbeknownst at the time and later obscured by historians, was the simultaneous emergence of a more conservative and less fundamentally reconstructive economic approach to reform that would eventually be identified by its partisans as Progressivism, and still later as liberalism.[21]

Even the Populist heartland, the area once known as the Middle Border, provided far less support than enthusiasts had reason to expect. For the most part, it was only in those areas where Populists and Democrats cooperated or collaborated (fused) that significant victories were forthcoming. Kansas was the scene of the party's major triumph. There, Populist–Democratic cooperation was rewarded with the electoral vote for Weaver, five of seven congressional seats, election of the entire state ticket headed by Lewelling, undisputed control of the state senate, and o Hicks: genuine & free silver populists

a contested outcome in the lower house, in which Republicans were certified as the winners by a narrow but highly questionable margin. Following the election, Kansas Populists gleefully made preparations to inaugurate what they called "the first People's party government on earth."

Nebraska reformers found the election much less satisfying. Republicans captured the state's electoral votes for Harrison in a close contest and all the state offices even more decisively. Populists did fare somewhat better in the congressional races; with their help, Democrat William Jennings Bryan was reelected and Omer Kem and William McKeighan were returned to Congress—the latter as a result of Populist–Democratic fusion. Republicans won Nebraska's three other seats. The outcome of the legislative races was a special disappointment. No party won a majority in either house, which was quite a turnaround from 1890, when candidates representing the Alliance–Independent forces controlled both. Although the situation dimmed the prospect of passage of radical Populist measures, it would subsequently assist in bringing the Democrats and Populists together to send to the U.S. Senate William V. Allen, a forty-five-year-old former Republican lawyer and judge who would become, arguably, Populism's most talented and respected advocate on Capitol Hill.

North Dakotans proceeded much as had Kansans. Except for one minor office, their collaborative Populist–Democratic state ticket was successful, but Republicans retained control of the legislature and elected the state's one congressman. Minnesota Populists, following Donnelly's antifusionist lead, wound up in third place, winning balance-of-power leverage in the state senate and electing one congressman. South Dakota Populists and Democrats likewise rejected fusion, and there the Republicans ran away with all the prizes.

In his classic study historian John Hicks concluded that in the West o "genuine Populists, as distinguished from the free-silver Populists, were most numerous in Kansas, Nebraska, the Dakotas, and Minnesota." In the Mountain West and on the West Coast, he insisted, a silver hybrid predominated almost from the outset. A number of historians occupying different points on the interpretive spectrum have embraced this Hicksian view. More recently, however, several historians have insisted that western Populism was indeed the genuine article. So it would seem, and the debate appears to have resulted from the area's somewhat later involvement in the movement; it took firm hold at a time when the issue of gold versus silver was becoming a national obsession. Clearly, support for silver and bimetallism was strongest in the silver-mining areas of the Far West, and that element no doubt added a special flavor to the region's Populism. The Alliances and the Populist party included as a minor part of their multifaceted financial plank "the free and unlimited coinage of silver at the ratio of sixteen to one." In the West generally, support for silver was not a party issue—bimetallism was a Republican, Democratic, and Populist position. Consequently, as it became increasingly clear that the old parties, dominated by the industrial northeastern states, were unsympathetic to loosening up the monetary system, there was a strong tendency for Democrats and even many Republicans in certain areas to seek common ground with Populists on that issue. Fusion among these elements and competition over who was silver's best friend played a minor role in the 1892 campaigns.[22]

Election results encouraged the trend; fusionist state tickets won convincingly in Colorado and Wyoming, and in Nevada, Colorado, and Idaho Weaver electors won handily. The one Populist elector on the Democratic ticket polled the most votes in Oregon. In fact, in those states where fusion was arranged for presidential candidates, Weaver was successful in all except Wyoming. In a number of other states where fusion did not occur, Republicans won by virtue of pluralities rather than by the customary majorities, creating circumstances in various legislatures conducive to coalition tactics. It was clear, for example, that had Populists and Democrats cooperated in Montana, they would have won easily. In California, enough Republicans voted Populist that Democrats won all but one of that state's electoral votes.[23]

Viewed generally and historically, the new party's performance had been noteworthy, but there were some cold, harsh facts Populists needed to confront. For one, they failed to break the solid South. Nearly as significant, the victories along the Middle Border and in the Far West, including even the one in Kansas, had been less than complete. They had been too dependent on Democratic support and had been assisted and ultimately adulterated by silver sentiment and a less radical approach to reform than that of the Omaha platform.

Ominous also was the anemic support Populism generated in the industrial Northeast. From Iowa and Wisconsin east to Pennsylvania and New York and north to the New England states, Populist support was hardly evident. Nearly all those states contributed less than three percent of their votes. Even in Iowa, the most western and agricultural of this group and their presidential candidate's home state, Weaver's support was under five percent. Obviously, Populism had made no significant inroads among eastern farmers or workers, who constituted a very significant portion of the people.

Another consequence of the election was the accelerated dismantlement of the Alliances. Northern Republicans and southern Democrats left Alliance orders by the thousands. Many did so because of the Alliance decision to support the third party; others simply because they believed their association had been or should be superseded by the People's party. The orders continued to operate, but with each passing year membership dwindled and gradually their gatherings became, as they had begun, rather pathetic nonevents.

The last significant meeting of the southern Alliance occurred in Memphis shortly after the 1892 election. The issue of whether the order should resume its earlier nonpartisan posture or continue to support the People's party was fought out in the contest for leadership. C. W. Macune reemerged for the last time seeking the Alliance presidency and urging a return to the nonpartisan approach. The Alliance founder was by then under a dark cloud that had been created by charges of double-dealing, corruption, and political treachery in the campaign. H. L. Loucks of South Dakota, president of the NFA&IU and the primary advocate of Populist affiliation, won reelection by a large majority. So ended a debate that had gone on since the Ocala meeting. Shortly thereafter, Macune withdrew from the order and disappeared permanently from public view, residing in the East for a time and then returning to Texas, where he apparently lived until his death in 1940.[24]

Test in the West

Even though the People's party had failed to win full control of even one state government in the 1892 elections, in the West both it and its allies had done well enough to exercise considerable influence. In Kansas, and to a lesser extent in Nebraska, North Dakota, Colorado, and Minnesota, the party had made itself the object of special concern and scrutiny. Its friends and foes alike looked especially to those states to judge what might be forthcoming should the new party obtain the kind of control it desired. As 1893 approached, Populism was indeed "on trial in the West," and one would have had to look long and hard to find an impartial juror.

Kansas was the first state to go under the microscope. It all began jubilantly enough on 9 January 1893, which was Populism's triumphant moment. On that day Populist leaders and supporters from all over the state gathered in Topeka to celebrate the inauguration of what was proudly announced as "the first People's party government on earth." A procession down Kansas Avenue and the ribbons, flags, and flowers adorning the capitol's Representative Hall bore witness to the festive mood, but through it all there was a note of sobriety, an awareness that their party was on trial, and a realization that they had an important mission to complete.

More than others, Governor Lewelling felt the responsibilities of the moment. Having long prided himself on his ability to use the spoken and written word, Lewelling presented Kansans with an incomparable inaugural address. He asked that they put aside partisan differences to see that

political parties shall exist by reason of progressive principles rather than subsist upon the spoils of office. The "survival of the fittest" (or strongest) is the government of brutes and reptiles, and such philosophy must give place to a government which recognizes human brotherhood. It is the province of government to protect the weak, but the governments of to-day are resolved into a struggle of masses with classes for supremacy and bread, until business, home and personal integrity are trembling in the face of possible want in the family.

In this situation, said the Populist governor, "I appeal to the people of this great commonwealth to array themselves on the side of humanity and justice."

Still later Lewelling stated: "The problem of to-day is how to make the state subservient to the individual rather than to become his master. Government is a voluntary union for the common good. It guarantees to the individual life, liberty, and the pursuit of happiness. If the Government fails of these things, it fails in its mission. It ceases to be of advantage to the citizen; he is absolved from his allegiance, and is no longer held by the civil compact."

The governor then injected a bit of poetry: "'Talk to the winds, and reason with despair, / But tell not misery's sons that life is fair.'" After a discussion of the conditions confronting farmers, laborers, and businessmen, he concluded by asking whether government was capable of addressing these problems. His answer:

Government is not a failure, and the State has not been constructed in vain. This is the generation which has come to the rescue. . . . Conscience is in the saddle; we have leaped the bloody chasm, and entered a contest for the protection of home, humanity, and the dignity of labor. The grandeur of civilization shall be emphasized by the dawn of a new era, in which the people shall reign; and, if found necessary, they will "expand the powers of government to solve the enigmas of the times."

No mealy-mouthed words, those. For Populists they were at once an inspiration and a call to action—Populism distilled to its essence. For Republicans and not a few Democrats they were the worst kind of heresy. The editor of the state's major Republican daily referred to the speech as "his incendiary Haymarket inaugural" and an "old fashioned calamity howl," which was "well enough for the stump, but not so becoming in the executive of one of the most prosperous states on earth." Later, another Republican editor compared the inaugural with the governor's more innocuous message to the legislature and concluded that there was "a Doctor Jekyll and a Mr. Hyde in the executive office. . . . Doctor Jekyll wrote the governor's first message to the legislature; Hyde delivered the inaugural address."

The worst fears and exaggerations of Populism's opponents appeared to have been confirmed the day after the governor's inaugural, when the opening of the legislative session became at once a comic opera. Things went well enough in the senate, where the Populist majority managed to organize in routine fashion. But in the house chaos was the order of the day. Populist representatives were determined to prevent Republicans from organizing that body. Although Republicans held sixty-five certificates of election, Populists fifty-eight, and Democrats three, the Populists claimed that their party "had a majority of the *legally elected* representatives." One of these Republican certificates clearly belonged to a Populist, and Republicans and Populists had challenged each other's victories in a number of other cases. After the state supreme court refused to intervene on the ground that the legislature was the sole judge of its own elections, Populists took the position that all those representatives who had contests filed against their election victories should not be allowed to participate in the organization of the house. This was a sure way to insure a Populist majority, since ten Republicans had been challenged. But precedent was all on the side of Republicans in their contention that certificates of election—in this case, issued by a Republican election board—were prima facie evidence of eligibility and entitled them to organize the house before an investigation was conducted into the contested seats—a sure way of maintaining a Republican majority.

Both parties had sized up the situation and had mapped out their strategy before Secretary of State Russell Osborn called the session to order on the afternoon of 10 January. It was the secretary's responsibility to read the official list of members-elect. Populist strategists apparently hoped to have the secretary installed as temporary chairman so that he could assist in organizing the house for the Populists—presumably by helping to enforce the Populist position that all contested members-elect be omitted from the original organization. Apparently Osborn was not in accord with that plan, for he announced that he recognized that he had no legal right to serve as temporary chairman and would not do so unless he had the unanimous consent of the house. Immediately, Republicans voiced their opposition; Secretary Osborn, in turn, refused to read the names of the members-elect and left the hall with the official list. As soon as he had departed, both sides scrambled to elect a temporary chairman. Sixty-four Republicans on one side and sixty-eight Populists (fifty-eight with certificates and ten contestants) on the other proceeded, amidst utter pandemonium, to elect a dual set of officers. When they had completed this riotous maneuver, both sides notified the senate and the governor that the house was organized for action.

Adjournment was then in order. But the Douglass house (Republican) and the Dunsmore house (Populist), as they were immediately identified according to their speakers, were both afraid to vacate the hall for fear the other might bar their reentry. So both sides remained in the hall throughout a long, cold, and uncomfortable night. Midway through the next day a truce was arranged, according to which each would occupy the hall at alternate periods without attempting to prevent the other's reentry.

The following day, the Populist cause suffered a severe blow. The three Democrats joined the Douglass house, bringing its membership up to sixty-seven. Perhaps it was to counteract this move that the governor and the senate—in one of those we'll-be-damned-if-we-do-and-damned-if-we-don't situations—accorded their recognition to the Dunsmore house.

For the next thirty-one days the situation in the house remained unchanged. Populists and Republicans used the hall alternately, passing bills and making speeches, each attempting to be as oblivious as possible of the other. But the world outside, thanks to an extremely partisan press, was anything but oblivious to what was going on. Newsmen were having a field day with what was soon publicized throughout the nation as the Kansas Legislative War. From the opening blast, the battle of the press was won by Populism's opponents. Lacking a daily paper in the capital, the shaky Populist position was riddled through and through, and little could be done to offset the devastating attack. All kinds of advice and advisers descended on Topeka. Populists were waging their fight on Republican turf, and in the heat of the moment the city of Topeka became first of all the citadel of Republicanism and secondly the state's capital. Before long, the local Republican county sheriff had sworn in around "sixty Republican deputies," and Populists had recruited their own force of partisan "deputy adjutant generals." Each side prepared for the worst.

In the meantime both houses and the senate met in joint session, with Lieutenant Governor Daniels presiding, to elect a United States senator to fill the vacancy created by the death of Senator Preston Plumb the previous year. Republicans were outmaneuvered in that contest. Populists, reluctantly and not without causing irreparable damage within their party, supported John Martin, the Democratic leader who had promoted his party's endorsement of the Populist ticket. Republicans refused to respond to the call of the clerk of the Dunsmore house, which allowed Daniels, with the aid of parliamentary legerdemain, to muster a majority vote of duly elected members for Martin. Republicans protested, but the Democratic majority in the United States Senate, as expected, subsequently honored Martin's certificate of election.

This senatorial election took place on 26 January. The legislative session was being frittered away with no immediate prospect of solution, and feelings on both sides were becoming more inflamed. The leaders of the two factions professed their willingness to resolve the conflict, but each's term were completely unacceptable to the other. Then on 14 February Republicans decided to break the no-conflict agreement in hopes of precipitating a solution favorable to them. On that date the Douglass house adopted a resolution stating that if the duly elected representatives of the Dunsmore house did not join it by 21 February, their seats would be declared vacant. To expedite the matter, they ordered the arrest of the clerk of the Dunsmore house. With these decisive steps taken, the Douglass house adjourned until nine o'clock the next morning.

The Republican desire to force the situation to a conclusion was fulfilled: the Douglass house was called to order the next morning in a Topeka hotel. In the interval, Populists had "rescued" their clerk, taken possession of Representative Hall, and posted armed guards intent on admitting only those from the Douglass house whom they deemed eligible to membership. Republicans countered by marching en masse from the hotel to the hall. There they diverted the guards and took possession of the hall by battering down the door with a sledgehammer (which Populists later claimed bore rather appropriately the label of the Atchison, Topeka, and Santa Fe Railroad, whose main office was nearby). Populists then retired from the hall to regroup and to plan their next move; Republicans resumed business and issued an appeal to the outside for support in their battle to save, in their words, "constitutional government" from the "forces of anarchy and revolution."

By that afternoon the situation was critical. Republicans had recruited over six hundred assistant sergeants-at-arms, and the sheriff now had about four hundred deputies. With this force at their disposal, the refusal of the Republicans to allow the Populist house to take possession of the hall at its usual time appeared to indicate that a bloody battle was close at hand. Governor Lewelling at that point alerted the state militia; later that evening he appeared before the Douglass house and pleaded with Republicans to vacate the hall and wait for a decision through the courts. "As the matter now stands," said Lewelling, "it becomes my duty to use some method which I almost shrink from naming, to secure possession of this hall."

Republicans did not vacate the hall—they merely made preparations for additional barricades. Governor Lewelling need not have worried about having to use the militia against them, for the ill-equipped, undermanned, and outnumbered force that responded to his call was under the command of a Republican colonel by the name of Hughes, and it was no secret that Hughes had made up his mind not to use the troops to oust fellow Republicans from the hall. The next day, Thursday, 16 February, Colonel Hughes was ordered to clear the hall, but he refused to do it. By disobeying the governor's direct order, the colonel got himself relieved of command, eventually earning a court martial and dismissal from the militia; he may also have given both sides a little more time to work out a peaceful solution. The militia, under new command, took up its post around the capitol, but no second order was issued to clear the hall.

At this stage in the dispute Populism's journalistic opponents were taking full advantage of the situation to prove that everything they had ever written about Populism was true. The Kansas City *Mail* told its story under a banner headline that read "ANARCHY!"; the Wichita *Daily Eagle* preferred "ANARCHISTIC"; the Marion *Times* employed the headline "The JACOBINS"; and the Kansas City *Gazette* asked its readers the headline question: "Is the Kansas Trouble the Incipiency of a National Anarchist Uprising?" Similar headlines and articles flooded Kansas and the nation, no doubt delivering a devastating blow to whatever little goodwill the party may have accumulated since 1890.

Populist leaders were guilty of having made some egregious errors of judgment in their determination to control the house, but one would have to search long and hard to find any anarchists among them and even harder to find any Jacobins. Consequently, on the snowy winter night of 16–17 February, an overture by Governor Lewelling prompted a communication between the two sides that ended the conflict. The concessions were made by the Populists. The militia, assistant sergeants-at-arms, and deputy sheriffs were to be dismissed or discharged; and while both sides awaited the verdict of the courts as to which was the legal house, Republicans were to retain possession of the hall and Populists were to meet in other quarters. The agreement to resolve the issue in the state supreme court was crucial, for the decision of that Republican–dominated tribunal was a foregone conclusion.

On 28 February, after the court made the anticipated ruling, all those Populists who had the Republican stamp of approval (fifty-four, to be exact) pocketed their pride and claimed their seats in the Douglass house. The animosity generated by the dispute was not easily dispelled, however, and any real hope for cooperation between Populists and reform-minded Republicans had vanished. It was the situation of 1891 all over again, with the senate and house working at cross-purposes and only eleven legislative days left on the calendar. By the session's close, Republican and Populist legislators (all of whom had run on a reform platform, it should be noted) had little to show for their effort. Only two major reforms—an Australian ballot law and an act prohibiting corrupt practices in elections—and three minor ones were added to the statutes.

The most important item the session considered was the railroad regulatory measure, and it was beyond doubt a casualty of partisan animosity. Late in the session, Republicans in the house, with the aid of quite a few Populists, passed the so-called Greenlee railroad bill. This bill would have made the board of railroad commissioners an elective body with the necessary powers to carry into effect most of the regulations then desired. But in the original bill, Republicans had specified that the "present commissioners" (meaning Republicans) would serve until January 1894; in addition, the new commissioners were to be elected in 1893, an off-year election. Senate Populists objected to the first provision for obvious reasons and to the second because they believed their strength was diminished in off-year contests. The senate therefore amended the bill rather drastically before passing it with only three days left in the session; house Republicans refused to reconsider it as amended. Thus ended the work of the 1893 legislature.

What manner of people were these wagers of legislative war? In background, the 1893 house differed little from that of 1891. As a matter of fact, thirty-two of the 1893 legislators (twenty-one Populists and eleven Republicans) had served in the 1891 house. The typical Populist representative was a forty-five-year-old farmer or stock raiser, a native of Ohio, Illinois, Pennsylvania, or Indiana who had resided in Kansas since 1878. Twenty-three of the group were experienced legislators; half had attended or graduated from college; most of the remainder had only a common-school education. Roughly a third were former third-party men, while forty percent had come to the Populist party from the Republican party and a third from the Democratic party. The typical Republican representative, on the other hand, was a forty-six-year-old business or professional man, a native of Indiana, Pennsylvania, Ohio, New York, or Iowa, and a resident of Kansas since 1871. Slightly more than half had attended or graduated from college; the remainder, in approximately equal numbers, were recipients of only an academy or common-school education.

Like their colleagues in the house, the most significant difference between Populists and Republicans in the senate was their respective occupations. The Populist senator was in more than three of four cases a farmer or stock raiser, while the Republican senator was almost as frequently a business or professional man. At forty-four, the Populist senator was four years younger than his Republican counterpart, but both were most often natives of states like Illinois, Indiana, New York, or Pennsylvania, and both had come to Kansas in about the same year—the Populist in 1871 and the Republican in 1872. Republicans had more college-educated men in their ranks and more experienced legislators, but the majority on both sides had only a common-school education, and only three of the entire group had served in the previous senate.

These senators and representatives could now claim to have had some special legislative experiences that were not likely to be repeated—they were the veterans of the Kansas Legislative War. But the short biennial session made no allowances for the kind of campaign they had waged, nor were they likely to be decorated for their services. Populist legislators had failed in their purpose, and in addition, they had lost the war. Fate is not kind to losers—especially to those who were portrayed by opponents as determined and desperate men and who by their own admission represented a righteous cause but who had nevertheless surrendered to the enemy at the height of the battle. It made no difference that their foes had created a distorted and exaggerated image of them, or that they were well within the pattern of American democratic radicalism, which had long been more radical in rhetoric than in deed. Times had changed, and the cross-fertilization and the clash of urban and agrarian radicalism in the new industrial age had culminated, it would seem, in a literal-mindedness that was fatal to reasoned reform.

The Populist legislative defeat was also the Lewelling administration's defeat. Unlike the legislature, Governor Lewelling had time to soften his image in the public mind, but due to a combination of factors, he failed in that endeavor. His troubles began when he made some unfortunate appointments. The legislative war also had far-reaching effects on the administration not directly related to the controversy itself. After the 1893 session the worst that could possibly be said about the Lewelling administration was neither too outrageous to print nor too difficult to believe as far as the Republican press was concerned. Populism's Republican opponents were especially eager to exploit those issues that would hasten the demise of the Democratic–Populist coalition. The issues of women's suffrage and prohibition enforcement, linked to illegal gambling, proved especially useful in that endeavor.

Governor Lewelling and State Chairman Breidenthal were also guilty of attempting to maintain an effective Populist–Democratic coalition. Both men were realistic enough to know that Democratic support was crucial to the Populists if the latter were to maintain themselves in power. As part of that strategy, the administration and the Populist organization under Breidenthal's leadership tried to steer clear of the prohibition and women's suffrage issues, while at the same time attempting to strengthen the coalition by rewarding their Democratic supporters in the distribution of political offices. That could not be done without increasing their vulnerability to Republican attack, nor could it be accomplished without exacerbating party factionalism. Quite a few Populist leaders believed that the reform cause would flounder on the rock of fusion, and after the Democrats had abandoned them in the legislative war, and the Democratic Cleveland administration was saddled with the panic and depression of 1893 and had made itself extremely obnoxious by the repeal of the Silver Purchase Act, antifusion sentiment intensified sharply. While most antifusionists were not willing to destroy the Populist party to drive the Democrats out, a few favored that drastic remedy.

Beginning in November 1893 Mary Lease initiated a highly publicized quarrel with Governor Lewelling that led to his attempt to remove her from the state board of charities, to which she had been appointed. In February 1894 the state supreme court ruled that her position could not

socialism

be terminated "without cause and without notice." It then became a matter of preferring charges, and the administration wisely elected to drop
the whole matter.[25]

But the controversy in effect ended Mary Lease's role as a Populist
leader of consequence and caused irreparable damage in the process.
Just how great the damage was would be impossible to determine; it
undoubtedly contributed heavily to the party's 1894 defeat in Kansas.
Above all, the Lease revolt assisted the cause of antifusionists—both
irrational and rational types. An important assist also came from that
combination of circumstances that had burdened a Democratic president
with a national depression and by the policies adopted by President
Grover Cleveland in combating that calamity. As the depression deepened, furthermore, Kansas Populism, at least in its urban leadership,
became bolder, more radical in its rhetorical position. This combination
of developments virtually assured the termination of any effective coalition between Populists and Democrats.

Indeed, it was in 1893 that leading Populists began to discuss and to
endorse socialism with any degree of frequency. After the legislative war
Republicans had launched a concerted attack on the Populist party as a
foreign product led by socialists or worse. Populists, in turn, initiated a
discussion of socialism, partly in defense and partly to counter the growing popularity of watered-down financial reform, symbolized by silver.
Perhaps "Gas-and-Water" or Fabian, would be an appropriate prefix for
the brand of socialism espoused by most Populists; but whatever the
brand, socialism received a sympathetic hearing among many Kansas
Populists. Quite a few of them reasoned as Stephen McLallin did:

The best features of our government to-day, national, state, and municipal, are
those which are purely socialistic. We would refer especially to our public school
system and our postal system. There is not a feature of either that is not an
exemplification of pure socialism; and these meet with universal approval. Municipal ownership of waterworks, gas works, electric light plants, and other public
utilities by which the people receive the maximum of service for a minimum of
cost afford other examples of pure socialism, by which serious abuses are cor-
rected and great benefits secured to the public.

Such talk merely confirmed the worst fears and exaggerations of Republican leaders. It evoked extreme attacks, like that of J. G. Waters in the
1893 campaign, who told an audience in Newton that it was "the duty of
every Kansan to give this party a black eye, it is a foreign product, it has

Republican ideological attack

none of the sunlight of the state about it. It has the taint of steerage bilge-water that imported anarchists have brought ashore in their clothes. It is a bold pander to every bad element in society."

Having convinced themselves that the Populist party was led by people who were openly critical of capitalism and foes of the nation's "competitive system of government," Republicans began to employ all the weapons of the success myth and the folklore of capitalism in their continuing war against Populism. None were more effective in that variety of attack than a young Republican leader by the name of James H. Troutman. At the party's annual banquet in January 1894, he stated the Republican case against Populism with a clever combination of vitriol and exaggeration that was what likely won him his party's nomination for lieutenant governor a few months later. A party like the Populist party, he said, which was "conceived in iniquity, born in sin, rocked in the cradle of superstition and perfidy and nurtured in ignorance and hypocrisy must be of few days and full of trouble." In addition to "its contempt for the constitution and laws of the state," he said, "it has lived a life of duplicity and falsehood." The party had announced itself as the party of the laboring classes, but it

has crucified upon the altar of personal ambition and aggrandizement the distinctive claims of every form of industrial toil, and elevated to exalted places a class of nondescripts having no visible means of support. This party, organized as it maintains, to subserve the interest of the toiling masses, is dominated by lawyers without clients, by doctors without patients, by preachers without pulpits, by teachers without schools, by soldiers without courage, by editors without papers, by bankers without money, by financiers without credit, by moralists without morals, by farmers without farms, by women without husbands, and by statesmen out of jobs.

The people, Troutman said, had been fooled for a time by a Populist "elixir of moonshine," but they were now demanding "a more substantial diet" since they realized that the "entire creed" of the Populist party, "when reduced to its simplest form, is the sublimated quintessence of flapdoodle."

Troutman's assessment of Populism was severe but understandably so since the new party had challenged the conventional wisdom as never before. This was best illustrated by one of Governor Lewelling's executive orders. Early in December 1893, with the nation in the grips of its greatest depression, the governor appealed to local law enforcement officers to exercise restraint in applying the vagrancy statute that had been passed by the 1889 legislature. The governor predicated his action on the belief that

> the monopoly of labor saving machinery and its devotion to selfish instead of social use, [has] . . . rendered more and more human beings superfluous, until we have a standing army of the unemployed numbering even in the most prosperous times not less than one million able bodied men; yet, until recently it was the prevailing notion, as it is yet the notion of all but the work-people themselves and those of other classes given to thinking, that whosoever, being able bodied and willing to work can always find work to do.

Under the vagrancy law and similar city ordinances, wrote Lewelling, "thousands of men, guilty of no crime but that of seeking employment, have languished in the city prisons of Kansas or performed unrequited toil on 'rock piles' as municipal slaves, because ignorance of economic conditions had made us cruel."

Populism's opponents professed to be shocked that a message of this kind would be released by a Kansas governor; immediately the order was dubbed Lewelling's "Tramp Circular," and the opposition press rushed into print to heap abuse on the "disgraceful" message. The editor of the Cawker City *Record* wrote: "Bums, tramps, thugs, and wharf-rats come to Kansas. The right hand of fellowship is extended to you by our governor. Fear not the 'rock pile' or the 'bull pen,' they are banished. Walk right into the governor's office and occupy his chair; you are better qualified to fill it than the present incumbent." The Dighton *Herald* declared: "According to the suggestions of the Governor's letter, the safeguard of society has been torn down, idleness has been raised to the plain of pleasure and a premium placed on vagrancy. . . . This is some more of Lewelling's socialism and is an insult to society and civilization." And the Salina *Republican* told its readers: "Governor Lewelling has issued another semi-socialistic manifesto declaring that the social conditions under which we now live are responsible for tramps and intimates that the individual is not in any way responsible for his financial condition and that if he chose to be a lazy shiftless tramp he has a right to do so and that the people ought still to keep him in plenty of food and clothing." In their view the governor was "a disgrace to Anglo-Saxon civilization. A cowardly repulsive demagogue." Similar press comments were made by Republican editors throughout the state.

As governor, Lewelling was of course by no means as unconventional as Populist rhetoric and extremist attacks on his administration might lead one to believe. His options, after all, were limited, and he was determined that violence had to be avoided at all costs. Under the circumstances, his most effective avenue was, as he put it, to utilize the powers of moral suasion in behalf of "suffering humanity." But in the heated political atmosphere of 1893–94 that particular course merely encouraged Populism's opponents all the more to step up their campaign to insure that the first so-called People's party government on earth was also the last.

The administration of Colorado's Populist governor, Davis H. Waite, was probably even more controversial and drew especially heavy fire from anti-Populists. Much of the controversy resulted from the governor's determination to practice that which he preached. Already forty when the Civil War ended, Waite was as pure a product as there was of that old radical, neorepublican tradition that figured so prominently in Populism. (Only John R. Rogers, Washington state's later governor, it would seem, could compete with Waite for that distinction.) In 1893, reacting to the clamor for repeal of the Sherman Silver Purchase Act, Waite captured national headlines when he spoke of the possibility of revolution. "It is better, infinitely better," he added, "that blood should flow to the horses bridles rather than our national liberties should be destroyed." Thereafter, the opposition invariably referred to the man as "Bloody Bridles" Waite.

Waite's appointment troubles, his highly controversial effort to legalize the silver dollar by state action, and his strident pro-labor stand in the Cripple Creek miners' strike, among other things, convinced his foes, and even some later historians, that the man was a dangerous "fanatic." One old account concluded, "His public utterances were often intemperate, indiscreet, and harmful to the causes they were designed to serve. So many members of his own party and administration fell out with him as to make it clear that the governor was usually to blame."[26] The most recent study, however, contends that the man has been treated unfairly: "Waite was a social pioneer of his time, a courageous fighter for the rights of the people against powerful private interests, one of the best friends labor has ever had in any state governor's office, and a more genuine western hero than the outlaw types and the lucky strike-it-rich millionaire[s] . . . who have figured all too prominently in presentations of western and Colorado history."[27]

National / state dimensions

However, that may be, the test in the West was not particularly helpful in advancing party fortunes. Perhaps, as one basically sympathetic historian concluded long ago, Populist "genius lay in protest rather than in performance."[28] We should note, though, that never at any point did the Populists, on their own, gain full control of even one state government. We should also remind ourselves that Populism's agenda was, in the main, a national one that was incapable of fulfillment at the regional, state or local level. The party badly needed a national power base. The key questions were: Could that base be gained by adhering to the whole radical platform, or would it be necessary to shorten the list of demands in order to broaden support? Could the latter course even be attempted without betraying the essential meaning and mission of Populism?

Chapter Five

"No Middle Ground—
No Room to Tinker"

*The Gold and Silver Obsessions and Metamorphosis,
1893–1896*

*"You can't patch up this old social system so as to do any permanent
good," said he. "It's putting new cloth on an old garment. I've seen an
old grist mill that was all awry—twisted all out of shape, every which-
way—but every part of it shared in the twist and was adjusted to the
general snarled condition. Now, if some man had come in and said,
'This beam, or this upright, or this something or other is crooked, is out
of plumb,' and had fixed that particular part of the old mill just right,
the old thing would have been thrown all out of gear and wouldn't have
been fit to grind mud for a brick yard. Just so with the existing social
system. It's all out of whack, so if you straighten up any particular part
of it, the old thing will be all knocked out of gear, and we'll be worse off
bye and bye than we are now. You've got to overhaul the old mill all
through, or you'd better let it be as it is. Patch work won't do any good.
You've got to be satisfied with things as they are, or you've got to have
socialism, one or the other. There's no middle ground—no room to
tinker."*

—*Parable of the Old Grist Mill, G. C. Clemens*, The Dead Line,
Topeka, 1894

G. C. (Gaspar Christopher) Clemens was known as Topeka's Mark
Twain. Sad to say, the accomplished Kansas lawyer and quintessential
political gadfly had only a smidgen of the literary talent of the famous

Clemens' novel

writer whose surname and looks he fully shared. After 1889 he had become one of the most admirable and genuine of radicals among Populism's many leaders. Nearly four years into his Populist venture, he
became deeply worried about the cause to which he had committed himself; he then took time out from his political activities and legal practice
to write and publish, serially in Kansas's major Populist weekly, the novel
that included the prophetic parable of the old grist mill. His 1894 novel
seems to have been the only fictional work written by a Populist in the
period in question that specifically featured Populism.[1] Clemens's purpose in writing it was to help sustain and even to extend, if possible, his
party's commitment to fundamental reform.

That year his fellow Kansas Populists had forgone cooperation with
the state's more conservative Democrats, conducting their only middle-
of-the-road campaign; their reward in that 1894 election was a severe
thrashing at the hands of their Republican opponents. Thereafter, pressures in favor of moderating the party's platform and in favor of coalition
politics (fusion) steadily mounted. The search was on, in Kansas and
elsewhere, to identify and to emphasize the least-common-denominator
issue advocated by the various elements seeking reform—especially
among those that had become prominent after the national economic debacle of 1893. A monetary issue increasingly filled that bill, an issue the
party had advocated from the beginning but only as an aspect of a much
more fundamental reform of the economic system: free silver.

Free Silver

By 1896, the popularity of the silver issue and the move toward fusion
was outraging radical reformers like G. C. Clemens. In one of his pro-
tests Clemens wrote: "We can put silver back where it was in 1873, but
we cannot put the world back there. And, in the world of to-day, with its
gigantic trusts and combinations—none of which will our proposed allies
permit us to touch—would free silver restore the conditions of twenty-
three years ago? What folly to even dream!" Clemens wanted it understood that no Populists were "hostile to free silver. Our objection is to
preaching that free silver alone can work any great economic change."[2]
As the noted Chicago Populist Henry Demarest Lloyd observed at the
time, the free-silver issue had taken on the characteristics of a fledgling
cowbird[3] that was threatening to push all else from the reform nest.

How had that come about? It was complex; the debate involved the
proposition of whether silver, along with gold, should be utilized in back-

ing the monetary system. It had begun to emerge as an issue in the mid-1870s and became the key question of the pivotal presidential election of 1896. In that election free silver was defeated, along with its major advocate, William Jennings Bryan.

Although the United States did not officially commit to the gold standard until 1900, the nation had been on it de facto since 1879, as a result of silver's demonetization in 1873 and the implementation of the Resumption of Specie Payment Act in 1879. Gold thereby attained a preferential position. The dollar appreciated significantly throughout the period. (According to one study, deflation totaled 57.9 percent from 1870 to 1900. This is a national figure; undoubtedly the contraction was unevenly felt and was most severe in the agrarian South and West.) An ideal monetary arrangement—one most just to everyone concerned—would have maintained a stable dollar, that is, a dollar that retained a reasonably constant exchange value; in other words, one that neither appreciated nor depreciated in a significant manner. Ardent silver advocates, facing a severe and constant deflationary spiral, contended that silver would help bring about a stable dollar situation; gold-standard advocates, who had matters going their way, were convinced that results would be extreme in the opposite direction.

The issue cannot be explained in simple terms, and time has rendered the subject even more arcane. Decades after the great debate over the monetary system, the preferential position of gold was jettisoned during the Great Depression of the 1930s—happily, without the dreadful results prophesied by gold's partisans in the 1890s. This is not to suggest that the domestic and foreign monetary conditions in the two periods were the same, for they certainly were not; nor is it to suggest that the triumph of the silverites would have ushered in the millennium. It is to say, however, that both sides—the goldbugs and the silverites (as the combatants were popularly identified)—exaggerated the significance of the gold-versus-silver question. In their debates they obscured the thought of a number of individuals, sympathizers of financiers and their radical critics alike, who viewed the monetary needs of the nation in far more realistic terms.

The roots of the matter were intricately entangled in the controversial and far-reaching post–Civil War economic revolution. The dispute ultimately involved the whole question of what money is, how its value should be determined, and what the role of government should be in determining its value and quantity. Throughout American history there had been advocates of paper money backed merely by the credit of the government. The Civil War greenbacks had been money of that kind until 1879, when they became, literally, "as good as gold." In the face of an ever-worsening deflation, certain economic reformers viewed the resumption of specie payment in 1879 as unwarranted. The influential business community, on the other hand, bolstered by orthodox fiscal thought, insisted that true money was specie, which had intrinsic value and was therefore more readily acceptable in international exchange.

Until 1873, the government sanctioned a bimetallic standard. United States mints coined both silver and gold into dollars when bullion was presented. Before the Civil War the ratio between them had been set by law at approximately sixteen to one—that is, sixteen ounces of silver were recognized as equal in value to one ounce of gold, and the weight of a dollar in both metals was fixed accordingly. Because of its relative scarcity, silver was slightly undervalued at sixteen to one and was not carried to the mints for coinage. In 1873 in fairly routine fashion, Congress dropped the silver dollar from the list of coins—an act soon excoriated as the "Crime of '73."

Only a few key governmental leaders were aware of the timeliness of this action. It was timely because, between 1861 and 1873, silver output had increased, while at the same time gold production had entered a period of relative and absolute decline. Beginning in 1871, the major European financial powers, one after another, had also abandoned silver coinage. By 1874, as a result of vanishing governmental markets and a steadily declining silver price, it became profitable to sell silver at the legal ratio for coinage purposes, but at that point it was no longer possible. Studies have revealed that there was an element of "gold standard malice aforethought" in this maneuver, but it was not nearly as great as the determined opponents of a tight-money policy later contended.

Silver producers would have profited if the unlimited coinage of silver at the ratio of sixteen to one had remained in effect, and debt-burdened farmers and some small businessmen of the West and South also visualized advantages to themselves in the anticipated increase in the amount of circulating money—a prospect that was aggravated by a significant decline in the per capita circulation throughout the period.[4] As a result, from the middle 1870s to the middle 1890s, the silver issue assumed a prominent position on the list of reform demands, ultimately becoming the main one of the 1896 campaign.

By 1890, bimetallists had won several sops—halfway measures that satisfied neither the silver-mining interests nor the opponents of a tight-money policy. These were the Bland-Allison Act of 1878 and the Silver *free silver: coining @ 16:1 ratio*

Purchase Act of 1890. The former made provision for neither free silver (that is, coining it at the sixteen to one ratio) nor the unlimited coinage of silver; the latter virtually provided for the unlimited purchase of the domestic output, but at the current low market price, not at sixteen to one. Accordingly, the slumping price of silver in glutted world and domestic markets was not stemmed; nor was the deflationary spiral reversed.

Yet the silver agitation might never have grown as large as it did had it not been for a combination of circumstances set in motion by the 1892 elections. As we have seen, the new Populist party, despite an impressive showing, was confronted with the facts that it had virtually no following in the East or among urban laborers and that its comprehensive radical program had not been embraced by significant numbers of voters. Its national ticket had clearly been most successful in the bimetallic stronghold of the South and the West. Thereafter, the idea of cooperating with a disgruntled element of one or the other or both of the old parties on the basis of the money question generated an irresistible appeal, although the silver issue badly distorted the true Populist position on the money question.

As events would have it, the election of a Democratic president and Congress in 1892 ultimately intensified the move toward silver. Grover Cleveland was on record as determined to repeal the 1890 Silver Purchase Act, and after he was saddled with the depression that began in 1893, he called a special session of Congress for that purpose. In fact, Cleveland's shortsighted focus on the Silver Purchase Act as the cause of the downturn and its repeal as the cure assisted mightily in undermining Populism as a radical movement and in making silver a far more important issue than it merited. In seeking and winning a repeal of the act, the New York Democrat divided his party along sectional lines, and in the South and West, where silver sentiment knew no party bounds, the tendency of the disenchanted to seek common ground on that one issue was greatly exacerbated. The end result was an even greater polarization of the nation along sectional and rural-versus-urban lines; a repudiation of Cleveland's leadership by his own party and a declaration of Democratic support for silver; and the nomination of the Nebraska silverite William Jennings Bryan for president in 1896, first by his fellow Democrats and then by the Populists.

By the time Bryan was nominated, the market price of silver had fallen to about thirty-two to one. If government policy had been altered so as to open the mints to the unlimited purchase of the metal at sixteen to one internationally, the result would have produced a severe and probably unmanageable strain on the gold supply and a sharp dollar devaluation; on the other hand, bimetallism, implemented nationally, although it had potential problems, might have produced a salutary devaluation in the midst of a very serious depression. In the unfavorable political climate of the middle 1890s, however, the mere mention of such a course created an emotional fervor detrimental to reasoned consideration of the question.

The symbolism that attached itself to the monetary issue suggests its significance and helps to explain the defeat of silver. Reformers, especially western and southern agrarians, saw reflected in it their hopes for a better society, founded upon governmental concern for the welfare of all. This symbolism applies even though a return to bimetallism likely would not have had nearly as great an effect as was claimed. Insofar as free silver symbolized a commitment to governmental intervention in the economy for the purpose of achieving a stable dollar, it symbolized the quest for greater reforms. Conversely, to the business-creditor interests of the day, free silver epitomized all that was detestable. It controverted conventional economic standards by redefining the "proper role" of government, and given the international commitment to the gold standard, it threatened to isolate the United States from the European financial center. For these reasons the battle of the standards—gold versus silver—became a national obsession.[5]

It has been argued that Henry Lloyd's contention that silver was the "cowbird" of the Populist movement was false and that the issue grew in importance and emphasis quite naturally from having been an integral and distinct part of the Populist program. According to this view—advanced primarily on the basis of southern sources—socialism was "the real, late-coming 'cowbird' that tried to capture the nest."[6] In the sense that agitation both for public-ownership measures and for silver loomed larger from 1893 on, both were cowbirds; however, only silver claimed full title to the metaphor, as it grew to major proportions and ultimately pushed all else aside.

To assume that the silver issue represented the Populist position on the money question, one would have to badly misconceive the financial plank of the Omaha platform and the extent to which Populists advocated fundamental reform of the monetary system. As late as 1896 Senator Peffer defined his party's position quite clearly when he declared:

The money that the People's party demands is gold, silver, and paper. Populists believe in the unlimited and free coinage of both the metals, and if there is not enough of coin money in the country, supplement it with paper money. The difference between the Populists and the Democrats and the Republicans is this: That we do not believe in private notes of any kind to circulate as money; we do not believe in the Government of the United States or the Congress . . . delegating its authority "to coin money and to regulate the value thereof" to any class of people under heaven. We believe it is a function of government, and a sovereign function, to prepare and to issue its own money—its own gold money, its own silver money, its own paper money.[7]

Peffer and other Populists who served in Congress from 1891 to 1895 left no doubt where they stood on the monetary issue. In fact, the clearest indication of the party's national agenda was spelled out time and again on the floor of Congress—Populism's one and only truly national stage.

Congressional Populism, 1891–1895 (*Phase 1*)

Scholars have passionately debated the question of whether Populism was a backward-looking, reactionary movement or a forward-looking, radical-democratic one. Seen from the congressional angle, its proponents left little doubt that their movement was a democratic phenomenon. Although they were a vilified and "hopeless minority," as one of them put it, they nonetheless represented a missed opportunity of significant magnitude. At what was still a relatively early and crucial stage of America's industrialization, Populists spoke out loud and clear for changes that most would surely regard as democratic, or at least as conducive to the "greatest happiness of the greatest number." They called for fundamental changes that have not yet been achieved.

One can divide the Populist movement in Congress into two phases, although they were not as programmatically distinct as was once surmised. The first phase ran from 1890 to 1895; the second commenced in 1895, came to full maturity in the silver crusade of 1896, and gradually faded into insignificance as the twentieth century dawned. Phase one (with the important one-term exception of Georgia's Tom Watson) was a product of western Populism. By 1895, it had been greatly undermined by changes at the regional base—changes brought on by the frustrations of defeat, fusion, and national depression, and above all by the accentuation of the issue of gold versus silver. Phase two ushered onto the congressional scene a significant number of Populists from areas of the country previously not represented—most important, from the South. Attention here will be devoted to the first phase.

Eleven Populists were elected to the Fifty-second Congress (1891–93). Six of the eleven were Kansans—William Baker, Benjamin Clover, John Davis, John Otis, and Jerry Simpson to the House; William Peffer began his single term in the Senate and was joined there by James Kyle from South Dakota. The Populist contingent in the House also included Omer Kem and William McKeighan from Nebraska, Kittel Halvorson from Minnesota, and Thomas Watson from Georgia. Watson was the choice of his colleagues for speaker. Seven of these eleven were farmers.

Thirteen Populists participated in the Fifty-third Congress (1893–95). Nebraska elected William V. Allen to the Senate; the House delegation again included Baker, Davis, and Simpson, while Thomas J. Hudson and William A. Harris replaced Otis and Clover from Kansas. Kem and McKeighan returned to represent Nebraska; Haldor E. Boen replaced Halvorson from Minnesota; John Bell and Lafayette Pence from Colorado and Marion Cannon from California completed the delegation. Simpson replaced Watson as caucus leader in the Fifty-third Congress.

Honest-to-goodness farmers were slightly less prominent among the Populists of the Fifty-third Congress, since the replacements and new members were all lawyers except for Boen and Cannon. The change in composition was beneficial, however, because Halvorson and Clover had been inactive, and Otis, while involved, had been quite ineffectual. Their replacements were all more active and effective spokesmen. Watson's failure to return to Congress was a significant loss, but overall the Populist delegation to the Fifty-third Congress was stronger, more experienced, and more capable than that of the Fifty-second.

One need waste little space refuting the 1890s Neanderthal, "Uncle Hayseed" stereotype that was widely disseminated regarding these national leaders. It deserves about as much attention as the assertion that Jerry Simpson went about sockless or was a "Populist without principle." Suffice it to say that the stereotype is no more valid—probably less so—than most stereotypes. Historically, however, it is very important as a barometer of how serious a threat these radical agrarian leaders represented from the point of view of the powerful, procorporation spokesmen of the urban-industrial complex, whether those spokesmen resided in the manufacturing East or elsewhere in the nation. From the standpoint of

← Rural Stereotype

their most bitter opponents, Populist leaders were to be condemned unsparingly because of their unabashed readiness to identify with ordinary working people; their antagonism toward corporate oligarchy and their quasi-socialistic attitudes likewise figured prominently in justifying the opposition's extreme caricature.

The strength of the stereotype, especially its longevity, owes much to the powerful assumption, well established by 1890 and growing thereafter, that nothing "progressive" (that is, forward-looking) could possibly emanate from the ranks of the working classes, particularly from those who populated the rural hinterlands. "Everything" was seen as truly "up to date in Kansas City," or perhaps one should say New York City. Conversely, backwardness must reign elsewhere. The fact was, of course, that no village, farm, city, or region had a monopoly on greed or altruism. But the rural-urban dichotomy that had been exacerbated by post–Civil War economic development certainly encouraged contemporaries to believe that they had cornered the market on altruism and their opponents on greed. Images were greatly distorted. Populist congressmen, on the average, were as capable and qualified as their old-party opponents—if one injects the "soul supremacy" ingredient into the quotient, as Annie Diggs suggested should be done, they were even better qualified. They hailed from undercapitalized, underindustrialized, underurbanized, underprivileged, and therefore underco-opted areas of the nation. (These were not necessarily undercivilized areas, as some of their opponents were fond of suggesting.) Nonetheless, or possibly even because of this, they were, if anything, less inclined to seek scapegoats and more inclined to engage in fundamental analysis than were most of their congressional opponents.

Congressional Populism, as I have said, represented a missed opportunity of consequence, and Populists called for basic changes that have not yet been achieved. To support this judgment, and also to shed light on the issue of their alleged reactionary conservatism, what follows is a partial list of the changes that would have taken place had the Populists been able to work their will on the national government. At the top of the list, because it was basic to congressional Populist thought and *all* other reforms were clearly secondary to it, would be a system of public banking—one that completely divorced the banking and financial community from control over the nation's monetary system. Money would be no more than a medium of exchange, would be increased or decreased by the national government to adjust for deflation or inflation, and would be introduced directly into the stream of commerce, without the inter-

○ Congressional Pop. Agenda

vention of banks, at a minimal (cost of administration) rate of interest, to meet the changing needs of a growing industrial society. The subtreasury system was only one of several devices (albeit the first and most important) proposed by Populists to implement their idea of a truly just monetary system; it was, in other words, merely a means to a larger end, as the Omaha platform clearly indicated.

Railroads, at least those engaged in interstate commerce, would be owned and operated by the public. All institutions involved in the transmission of intelligence—in their day, the telephone and telegraph networks—would be managed in similar fashion, just as the postal service then was. During the Fifty-third Congress, midway through a severe depression we should remind ourselves, Senator Peffer even called for government ownership and operation of the coal industry in order to make that critical resource available at cost and to improve the lot of mine workers. Undoubtedly, the senator was merely extrapolating from his party's declaration that "all the natural sources of wealth" were "the heritage of the people." In fact, as Peffer plainly stated on 10 July 1894, bona fide Populists would eventually have "all public functions . . . exercised by and through public agencies." All government revenue would be derived without exemption, except for what was considered necessary for a bare standard of living, from a graduated income and/or land tax on the great wealth of the society. The president and vice president would be elected by a direct vote of the people. Subsidies to corporations (but not necessarily to individuals) would be strictly prohibited. Government bonded indebtedness, especially on terms favorable to monied interests, would be forbidden, and members of Congress would be required to divest themselves of corporate stock.

Populists also fought for a number of other changes that have since been implemented. But the failure to achieve their basic reforms—especially in the area of monetary policy—has rendered most of their *nonplatform* and generally noneconomic political reforms quite impotent, if not repugnant and counterproductive, over time. Beginning in 1893, the worst depression the country had experienced hit urban centers (it had already struck rural areas at least six years earlier) and more than 4 million men and women were unemployed by early 1894. At this time, in a still predominantly rural nation of about 63 million people, the Populists were the only politicos to sponsor, advocate, and defend legislation to put the unemployed to work. In fact, throughout the Fifty-third Congress they introduced and pleaded for quite a variety of emergency measures for that purpose—always coupled, of course, with their plan for reversing

o Socialism?

the financial contraction (deflation) that had been strangling sectors of the economy for years and that grew greatly in severity as the depression deepened. Perhaps of most interest is John Davis's proposal for the creation of a 500,000-man industrial army of the unemployed "to be put to work on authorized public improvements." The Kansan defended his measure by arguing that it was wiser "to furnish work for starving men in order to prevent the necessity of increasing 'the standing Army' to shoot them down."

Nearly all the Populists in Congress, at one time or another, proposed action to assist starving and destitute people in urban centers. Senator Peffer at one point endorsed a system of old-age assistance. In the Senate on 1 June 1894 he stated: "I would have every poor man have a home. And I would do more than that." For all the elderly people who have "passed through a lifetime of toil and have not saved anything for their old age I would pension the same as I would pension a soldier who . . . risked his life for the safety of the Republic. I would send the old people down to the grave in comfort instead of sending them to the almshouses and to the poor-houses." That certainly has a New Deal ring to it. Anti–New Dealers—Herbert Hoover and his "leave-it-alone liquidationist" advisers especially—would be shocked to learn that congressmen advocating such proposals would later be described as "conservatives" by at least one historian. But let us not be misled. Historians have been correct in divorcing Populism from twentieth-century liberalism, but they need to take greater care to insure that the separating is done for the correct reasons. The New Deal goal of accommodating some of the security features of socialism while at the same time saving capitalism seems to have been a bit too paradoxical. Lacking Populism's basic, structural national reforms, only the ghost, or pseudo-Populism, remained to haunt the house of liberalism.

To the list one could add a number of other measures, among them mortgage relief, women's suffrage, the advance payment of pensions due Civil War veterans in one lump sum (foreshadowing the Bonus payment demand of Hoover's day), direct election of senators, rural-free delivery, postal savings banks, and the Australian ballot.

In view of the programs they supported, were the Populists proponents of socialism? During the 1890s and ever since, that question has been debated with considerable passion. Since the 1950s historians have portrayed them as retrogressive capitalists, as cryptosocialists, and as neither capitalists nor socialists entirely. Their congressional opponents, on a number of occasions, accused them of being socialists; they

(anti-)
° Paternalism?   °°Agriculture

promptly denied that they were. And if they were, they were advocates
of a peculiar brand of socialism—the socialism of agrarianism or perhaps
what one person, in another context, has called "grass-roots socialism."
Public ownership, to their way of thinking, was to serve the interests of
millions of small-scale, land-owning farmers, businessmen, and wage-
earning laborers. Their basic, structural reforms in finance, land, and
transportation/communication, they sincerely—we might say naively—
believed would render unnecessary a wholesale change in the existing
arrangements regarding private property and private production.[8]

The argument has also been made that antipaternalism was a fundamental precept of Populism.[9] (Paternalism is defined as "a policy or practice of treating or governing people in a fatherly manner, especially by
providing for their needs without giving them responsibility." Virtually
any suggestion that government should concern itself with the general
welfare in the late nineteenth century encountered opposition on the basis of its being paternalistic and thus un-American.) Populist discussion
of paternalism always surfaced when their opponents charged them with
advocating it, a context that must be taken into account. If they were
antipaternalists, it was—like their socialism—a peculiar brand of antipaternalism. They themselves denied that they were paternalists. Nebraska's Omer Kem suggested that the Populist version of governmental
assistance ought to be called by a different name—"fraternalism." Paternalism in their eyes included *only* those governmental policies that favored corporate and monied interests at the expense of the masses.
Populists frequently defended themselves against the charge of paternalism by pointing to measures they regarded as evidence of the fact that
the country had experienced paternalism of the worst kind for decades—
paternalism for the rich.

The well-being and viability of small-scale agriculture was also a vital
component of their mind-set. They were unable to accept as compatible
with democracy and human freedom a vision of an American future composed of tenant farmers and large corporate farms, with a population
massed in urban centers and conspicuous for its pockets of destitute and
dependent workers. Jerry Simpson, who truly had a marvelous way with
words, may have expressed the Populist position best early in the Fifty-
second Congress. Speaking against the protective tariff, the former-
sailor-and-ship-captain-turned-rancher stated:

I regard agricultural labor as the great ocean, in accordance with which every
other form of labor must seek its level. If agriculture, more ancient than all other

forms of labor, is not profitable, so that men seek the cities in order that things may reach a level, you may dam up the rivers, you may back up the creeks, you may undertake to hold back the flood, but finally there will be an overflow, and labor, like water, will seek its level in this great ocean. All other trades and professions are the bays and rivers. To raise their level it is only necessary to raise the level of the ocean.

Populists were inclined to believe that agriculture was one of the basic (if not the most basic) industries, and much of their effort was aimed at enhancing the viability of the family farm, reversing the trend toward tenancy. Many, from their day forward, have seen this goal as unprogressive, inefficient, and not worth the price, and have easily dismissed it as a product of rural "fundamentalism" or "provincialism." That may be, but who can say that the ultimate price of the massive exodus of rural blacks and whites to urban centers and the gigantic farm programs since the 1930s have not been even more costly?

Special attention must be directed to two other criticisms that have been directed at congressional Populism. The first such generalization is that "legislative activity with a humane or 'liberal' rationale—child labor reform, the eight-hour day, woman suffrage—was exceedingly uncommon in Populist congressional circles." The second: "For the more qualitative aspects of social policy, such as the conditions of racial and ethnic minorities in America, they exhibited disinterest or disdain. On the few occasions in which they addressed themselves to Indian policy, for example, their attitudes were uncompromisingly reactionary." These issues mainly fall within the category of the nonplatform, protoprogressive, secondary concerns of the Populist national agenda. As regards Populists in the Fifty-second and Fifty-third congresses, nonetheless, these undocumented generalizations are prime examples of Alice-in-Wonderland history. Child labor, to my knowledge, had not emerged as a national issue, although Kansas Populists attempted to pass a state child-labor law in 1891. Populists supported the eight-hour day at every opportunity (Senator Peffer endorsed a six-hour limit in the Senate), and they seem to have been the only congressmen to speak in favor of women's suffrage and to introduce bills to accomplish that long-overdue reform. Their support of the vote for women, as a matter of fact, was one of the reasons a Connecticut Democrat in the Fifty-third Congress gave for why the nation should ostracize Populists.

As for racial and ethnic issues, the statement has also been made that Populist arguments for immigration restriction were based "largely upon racial and ethnic grounds." This important criticism was documented by quoting some unkind words by John Otis that were lifted nakedly from context. As was pointed out years ago, Otis, a Kansas Populist (with a Harvard degree, incidentally), had a nativist streak that was exacerbated by prohibitionist sentiment. He was defeated for reelection in 1892 and was ultimately isolated within the party itself when he linked up with a tiny lunatic-fringe element of extreme antifusionists. In an attempt to change a bill so as to require an appropriation for Indian schooling at home rather than in the eastern boarding schools (which Indians themselves hated), Otis stated that "Hiawatha and Minnehaha were creatures of fiction, and that the dirty degraded squaw and the poor, cruel, brutal Indian were very different creatures." But the assertion that Otis believed the Indian was, in the words of the critic, "manageable and educable only in the reservation context" seems a bit harsh. Otis's concern, apparently, was that the money be spent in the West. He followed the comment with this statement: "Now, do not misunderstand me. I am in favor of the education of the Indian, but I am in favor of educating him on the reservation at home; and when we come to the proper point, I shall be in favor of increasing the appropriation to help the home school, but I can not consistently aid and assist a school that is so far away from the theater of operation."

All other remarks by Populists on the Indian question leave no doubt concerning the positive nature of their attitudes. Simpson was particularly alert to prevent the agents of corporations from stealing Indian land and resources; Watson, Peffer, Kem, Davis, and others spoke out clearly for humane and fair treatment. In February 1892 Watson said:

I can not pretend that I am any great admirer of the policy which this Government has pursued with reference to the Indians. I can not see much beauty in taking from the Indian every dollar's worth of property he has got, pinning him down with a bayonet in one corner, and feeding him out of a spoon in the hands of an Indian agent. . . . When this Government chooses to go on another line and deal fairly, honorably, and liberally with these people, with a view to bettering their condition, righting wrongs of the past, recognizing the claims that they have upon us, I . . . shall not be deterred by the condition of my own people from giving my vote to such a policy.

Little the Populists had to say on either the Indian or the immigration question can compare with the negativity of their opponents. For example, Democratic congressman John Pendleton of West Virginia, a relatively young, college-educated lawyer, urged a draconian program, and when asked if his idea of an Indian policy was "to kill him or make him work?" his answer was straightforward: "Yes; one or the other."

The treatment of African-Americans, a disgraceful situation, was not prominently at issue except during the debate over the repeal of the federal election laws in the Fifty-third Congress. No Populist employed racist language, as did a number of southern and border-state Democrats (one of whom, Joel Bennett "Champ" Clark, would later become House speaker and a serious candidate for the presidency). Watson, in the Fifty-second Congress, courageously appealed for justice for the eight million oppressed black citizens as part of his eulogy for a fellow southern congressman. In the Senate during the Fifty-second Congress, Peffer presented a petition on behalf of the "colored people of Riley County, Kansas," who were protesting "mob or lynch law" throughout the nation. Peffer called the petition "very timely." He stated, "It is time for the American Congress to take prompt action in such cases."

All Populists in the House and Senate voted for the bill to repeal the federal election law in the Fifty-third Congress, in spite of an impassioned plea for continued support at the federal level by the only black congressman. George Washington Murray, a Republican from South Carolina who stood with the Populists and others against the repeal of the Silver Purchase Act, said, "I appeal to the Populists from the great West, who claim their mission to be the freedom of the human family, not only from financial but industrial and political slavery, to give no aid in untying the hands of the ballot-box stuffer and election conjurer." Populists, however, considered themselves bound by the following declaration of the Omaha platform: "We demand a free ballot and a fair count in all elections, and pledge ourselves to secure it to every legal voter without federal intervention, through the adoption by the states of the unperverted Australian or secret ballot system."

This particular proviso was apparently put into the platform at Omaha to appease the southern wing of the Alliance. Logic, consistency, and justice would certainly suggest that western Populists should have openly resisted the Democratic party's move to eliminate the last vestige of voter protection for blacks held over from the Reconstruction era. On this issue, especially, it would have been instructive to hear from Watson, who was not in this Congress. Judging from his article, "The Negro Question in the South," published in October 1892, the southern leader would have responded just as did Simpson, who pointed out that Populists meant what they said as regards no federal interference in this area but were just as determined to put an end to discriminatory procedures at the state level by instituting a truly free ballot.

Populist economic measures were unquestionably designed to aid poor blacks as well as poor whites. From 1891 to 1895, racial and ethnic arguments simply were not involved in the Populist call for immigration restriction—and this was in congresses whose members were not reluctant to make them openly.[10] Populist arguments were almost entirely economic, and their concern was directed at controlling the supply of exploited laborers that was used all too frequently to keep down wages and to frustrate the union movement. Simpson, a Canadian immigrant himself, called the Chinese exclusion measure a "disgrace to any civilized nation." When asked why he intended to vote for a measure he had thus described, he answered that he had no choice, until greater economic wrongs were righted, in order to protect the wages of labor.

Populists were prominent in opposing an anarchist exclusion provision that was favored by reactionaries and conservatives fearful of radicalism, because of the measure's vagueness and potential for political abuse. Even after they had been told that many dangerous anarchists were on the way to America and that the bill had been rewritten to define *anarchists* as only those who advocated violent overthrow of the government, one of them invoked parliamentary procedure to keep it from coming to a vote. (This 1894 definition, incidentally, parallels the definition that antiradical elements implemented in 1903 as regards immigration policy, and on the eve of the first Red Scare in 1918, it was broadened to have application to domestic politics.)

"Populist congressmen had little time, and apparently little inclination," it has been said, to promote "the specific causes of agrarian or labor interest groups"; moreover, "almost without exception the Populist approach to public spending was that of the meat-axe." It would be far more accurate to generalize in this area by saying that they continually endeavored to cut appropriations in areas that they regarded as wasteful or beneficial primarily to corporate interests. Populists were consistent foes of military spending, which they regarded as uncalled for in a time of "profound peace" when so many millions of unemployed and underemployed people were in need of assistance. They were warm friends of appropriations for education and for the destitute. Although they often called for cuts in spending, they constantly endeavored to increase appropriations for particular measures they saw as beneficial to the disadvantaged—and not only to rural Americans. In August 1894 one of their congressional opponents calculated, with much exaggeration made possible by double-counting their programs, that if all their measures were enacted, the cost would exceed $35 billion.

On the labor issue, Populists were strong defenders of labor's right to organize. Among other things, they insisted repeatedly that labor be granted as much protection by government as was management; they led a successful move to condemn the use of Pinkerton detectives in labor disputes, fought energetically to require automatic safety couplers on railroads, called for investigations into several labor-management disputes and industrial disasters, and they initiated the effort in Congress that led to the establishment of a national holiday for labor. At the behest of the Knights of Labor, they called for and obtained an investigation into the "slums of cities of more than 200,000 population," which they viewed as preliminary to doing something about improving the living conditions of all kinds of urban workers—unemployed, child, sweating, tenement house, and the like. In fact, on more than one occasion Senator Peffer earnestly tried to commit Congress to a thorough investigation of the whole range of relationships between management and labor. In the midst of a brutal depression, they were lonely defenders of the right of Jacob Coxey's unemployed "armies" to petition Congress for relief and employment in person at the nation's capitol. Most important, as indicated earlier, they alone brought forward measures designed to put unemployed laborers to work. Beyond that, they pioneeered the idea (not generally conceded until the depths of the 1930s depression) that in an advanced urban-industrial society the federal government has a role to play in cushioning the impact of economic collapse and in restoring and maintaining prosperity.

That congressional Populists were less inclined to seek scapegoats and more prone to engage in fundamental analysis than most of their congressional opponents was never more clearly illustrated than in the special session called by President Cleveland to repeal the Silver Purchase Act of 1890. The New York Democrat had simplistically singled this act out as the sole cause of (and its repeal as the sole cure for) the national depression that began in 1893. This important session, which ran from 7 August to 3 November 1893, merits closer study than it has received. Concerning the views of the Populists, it yet remains a missing chapter in the nation's history. A close examination of the debates that transpired therein renders laughable the view—fashionable during the 1950s—that the Populists were naive and ignorant about the industrial society that existed by the 1890s. The record abundantly demonstrates that they were among the few who were willing or able to get beyond absurd and superficial explanations for the nation's economic debacle. They in fact led the way in suggesting that it was time—indeed, long overdue—to be done with subterfuge and recrimination so that necessary changes could be made to avoid the boom-bust cycle, which most of their contemporaries considered inevitable and natural.

Considerable confusion and misrepresentation has persisted regarding the Populist position on the money question. Congressional Populists were not, to employ the words of one historian, "admitted and unabashed inflationists." As I have emphasized in the discussion of the silver issue, they were staunch foes of deflation, and they were determined to create a monetary system that was relatively stable and, above all, removed from private control. Because the dollar had been appreciating for a number of years, they advocated, logically enough, reflation in order to arrive at that point of stability. They frankly conceded the injustice of both inflationary and deflationary monetary systems. Congressman John Davis said in one of his articles:

There are two dishonest moneys. In a society where debts have been incurred on a given volume or basis, inflation cheats all creditors—it compels them to accept money of less value than they have agreed to take; and it may be added that the creditor classes have wearied the universe with their cries against inflation, against "dishonest money" and "cheap money"—money that is overissued. But, on the other hand, the contracted money—money that is too much limited—cheats all debtors, compelling them to pay all debts and taxes with money of greater value than what they agreed to pay. This is the money which the great creditors and fund holders call "honest money."

As Davis's remarks clearly indicate, Populists were not oblivious to the harmful consequences of injecting an unlimited quantity of money into the economy. Apparently, a number of congressional Populists gradually backed away from the subtreasury plan precisely because they came to view it as likely to create just that kind of money expansion (and because the land and commodity-loan plan was so immediately and so one-sidedly an agrarian relief proposal). And they were never fooled by the silver issue. It was for them only one of the milder reforms conducive to money expansion to counter the contraction (deflation) and to frustrate the intense and ultimately successful drive, then under way, to formally and "irrevocably" commit the nation to the gold standard. They opposed the Cleveland administration's bond and debt policies for that reason also. In their eyes the use of bonds and the creation of a national debt thereby were merely a means of maintaining and extending a financial system that enriched too few, impoverished the masses, and needlessly burdened future generations with a huge unearned-increment-due bill.

Such was the thrust of congressional Populism during phase one. Did it have a larger meaning? According to a recent general study, one of the preeminent values manifested in American culture is to insist that "a primary purpose of the law should be the furtherance of economic progress and social mobility, and that the maintenance of such progress and mobility is the best means for implementing democratic theory." Another, even more powerful preeminent value of the late nineteenth century that often contradicted the first was the notion that "the law ought to construct and maintain a large area for the functioning of *private enterprise* relatively immune from the incursions of public power." Populists and anti-Populists certainly could draw inspiration from both these propositions, but the Populists were more distinctly champions of the first and therefore were prime targets of those more partial to the second. Yet as we have seen, the Populist movement was by no means a monolith, and the elements it sought to unite were disparate. The fact that Populism was ultimately aborted owed much to that diversity. It owed much more, I am convinced, to the kind of society the nation was becoming by the 1890s. [11]

Populism in the States

G. C. Clemens's contention that there was "no middle ground—no room to tinker" may well stand the test of time. This verdict, for all we know, may require a century or more of unfolding events to confirm. Most Populists soon convinced themselves, nonetheless, that "half a loaf was better than none." Lacking real power to overhaul the nation's machinery in the three areas they had singled out for fundamental reform—the monetary system, the transportation and communication networks, and public land policy—it was not surprising that growing numbers of them were inclined to settle for what they could get. Increasingly, this meant tinkering with the system in the hope of making it more just. The tendency was especially apparent at the state level, particularly in the West, where Populism wielded its greatest influence.

Although women's suffrage was omitted from Populism's national platform in 1892 and again in 1896 (apparently for the purpose of wooing Democrats everywhere but especially in the South), western Populists waged a vigorous fight at the state and local levels to extend the voting privilege to women, often against the opposition of both major parties. Populist conventions in Kansas, Idaho, North Dakota, Oregon, and Washington came out in support of the reform. The issue was also hotly debated in a number of state legislatures. In 1869, Wyoming Territory, primarily for settlement-promotional reasons apparently, and Wyoming state in 1890, were first to grant women the vote. In 1893 Populist legislators in Colorado, with some Republican support, brought the issue before that state's male voters and it was passed. In 1891, as we have seen, Kansas Populist legislators attempted unsuccessfully to enfranchise women. In 1894 Kansas Populists made the vote for women their major issue. The proposition was voted down, however, despite strong support from the state's Populist rank-and-file minority, as was the Populist ticket in a three-way contest.[12]

Western Populists were generally more supportive of women's suffrage than were the old-party faithful. Republicans, for example, dominated North Dakota's legislature and were instrumental in twice defeating the measure, in 1893 and 1895. And in spite of strong Populist support, women's suffrage was voted down in the South Dakota legislature. Roll calls in Nebraska in 1891 and in Washington state four years later revealed that Populist legislators in significantly greater numbers than Republicans or Democrats supported women's suffrage. Probably reflecting their state party's atypical labor and urban orientation, Montana Populists were not as supportive of the vote for women, but as one historian has noted, "the immense popularity of Ella Knowles, the Populist candidate for state attorney general in 1892, indicates . . . broad acceptance of women in politics." Utah and Idaho also played important roles in franchise extension. Utah Territory, for reasons peculiar to Mormon settlement, granted the vote to women shortly after Wyoming had done so, and so did Washington Territory for four years beginning in 1883; in 1896 both Utah and Idaho did so as states. Apparently, only the Populists of Nevada, Arizona, and New Mexico were cool or indifferent to the reform. Overall, Populist support for women's suffrage in the West was such as to lend credence to a Kansas Populist editor's contention that "the cause of woman has been solely championed by Populism."[13]

Western Populists promoted a remarkable variety of reforms consistent with their belief that the time had arrived when government simply had to intervene to insure liberty and justice. One study of Populism at the legislative level, commenting on the 1897 Populist Kansas senate, even discovered what it saw as a rather surprising and avant-garde "social sensitivity." For example, Populist senators tried to create a system of kindergartens, sponsored a measure to levy taxes designed to "equal-ize educational opportunities," attempted to create a public defender's office to represent indigents and persons thought to be insane, and intro-duced a bill making it a felony for a male supervisor "to make improper advances to any woman working under his charge." They were also in-strumental in defeating a stringent capital-punishment measure. [14]

Kansas Populists were a substantial influence during four legislative sessions stretching from 1891 to 1897. But only during the legislature of 1897 were they in control of the state government in all its branches. By then, fusion politics and a significant split within the party between a more radical, "producer-oriented" majority and a less radical, coalition-building, "developer" minority had become quite evident. This split roughly foreshadowed the difference between original Populism and Democratic progressivism in Kansas. It should be emphasized, however, that even these fusionists of 1897 were significantly more reformist than their Republican opponents.

Over the course of these four legislatures and two Populist adminis-trations, Populists were responsible for a wide range of reforms. As for labor, they enacted laws against blacklisting and in favor of the eight-hour day for all government-related work, mandated the regulation and weigh-ing of coal at the mines, required the weekly payment of wages in lawful money as opposed to scrip, and enacted several measures relating to the health and safety of the state's mine workers. For the farmers, they placed restrictions on the alien-absentee ownership of land, provided for the regulation of warehouses and for the inspection, grading, weighing, and handling of grain, enacted a one-year real-estate redemption law, prohibited combinations designed to circumvent competition in the buy-ing and selling of livestock, regulated stockyards, and created a depart-ment for the inspection and weighing of grain, as well as a board of irrigation. As for the general interest, they created the office of bank commissioner, regulated insurance companies, created a school-text-book commission, enacted ballot-reform measures, promoted municipal ownership of public utilities, encouraged conservation, endeavored to minimize corrupt election practices, created a special court charged with the responsibility of regulating the railroads, and enacted antitrust laws.

While Populists pushed some of these measures through with a mea-sure of Republican support, they also brought forward a long list of sig-nificant reforms that were defeated by Republican opposition. Some of the reforms they enacted—the antitrust and alien-land ownership mea-sures, for example—proved ineffective or, like their special court to reg-

ulate the railroads, were invalidated by the judiciary. Considering the fact
that the party never constituted a majority of the Kansas electorate without Democratic support, their accomplishments at the state and local
levels were indeed remarkable. And the Populists' legacy, in Kansas and
elsewhere, went far beyond their legislative performance, which probably was not their most important contribution to American politics—a
judgment to be explained in the concluding chapter.[15]

Many of the same measures were championed by the Populists and
their Democratic allies throughout the West, although important regional
differences existed reflecting conditions peculiar to the locale and the
electorate. The battle between goldbugs and silverites predominated
there by 1896, as it did nearly everywhere, but the concerns of Populists
in the Mountain West and the Far West were more similar than dissimilar
to those in Kansas, Nebraska, and the Dakotas before and after the Panic
of 1893 and the intensification of the monetary debate. Populism west of
the Middle Border was apparently more antimonopoly than greenback in
orientation. The monopolistic targets also varied somewhat from state to
state. In certain areas it was the railroad monopoly; in others large irrigation companies or mining corporations became the targets; while in still
others land or cattle monopolies came in for special attention.[16]

No matter what their target, however, Populists everywhere—in the
North, South, East, and West—would no doubt have agreed with Populist senator George Turner of Spokane, Washington, who contended in
his first congressional speech that, in the years since the Civil War, government had operated "too much in the interest of moneyed corporations
and aggregations of capital and not sufficiently in the interest of the people of this country." It had been mistakenly assumed, said Turner, that
"the first duty of government" was "to concrete wealth and the instru-
mentalities which produce wealth. . . . But the truth is that the little
finger of one of our people is of more importance to Government [or at
least should be] than the wealth of a province."[17] The humane preference
was never more clearly stated.

Undoubtedly, Populists everywhere would also have responded affirmatively to the robber-baron metaphor Senator Turner set forth in the
same speech. Matthew Josephson later made the analogy a fixture of
historical interpretation in his 1934 book *The Robber Barons*. His thesis
came under heavy attack in the mid-1950s from the-end-justifies-the-
means school of historical interpretation, so Josephson added this comment to his preface to the 1962 edition: "It was not I, but the embattled
farmers of Kansas, who, in one of their anti-monopoly pamphlets of 1880,

first applied the nomenclature of Robber Barons to the masters of railway systems."[18] Perhaps, but Senator George Turner probably stated it most succinctly and gave it the kind of prominence that would elevate it from obscurity. After alluding to the injustice of having turned over a crucial public "function" to private interests, Turner stated:

The robber barons of the Middle Ages were not more ruthless in their forays upon the unwary traveler passing along the roads beneath their castles than these railroad barons of to-day are in their forays upon the general public. Their rule in the West has been to reach down into the pockets of the farmers as deep as they could and take therefrom every dollar and every penny left over and above the cost of production. The farming population of my State has been ground in the dust by the exactions of these great, monstrous railroad corporations, raised up by the voice of the law, without the proper safeguards to enforce a due respect for the rights and interests of the people.

One might reasonably conjecture that southerners could appreciate the westerner's imagery even more keenly than could other Americans—despite the fact that Turner was a former Reconstruction era "carpetbagger." Feelings engendered by the dependent, semicolonial economies of those areas where Populism flourished were nowhere more pervasive nor more acute than in the South. Desperate conditions, the tyranny of the furnishing merchants, and manipulation by distant, shadowy corporate oligarchies were all too real and far too familiar to the southern masses. The popular target below the Mason-Dixon line was not the transportation monopoly nearly so much as the monopoly of finance—what would come to be called, within a few years, the money trust.

That there were significant differences between the South and the West and that those differences extended into the Populist movement should surprise no one. Southern culture was still much influenced by traditional patterns of deference, most obviously in the areas of race and gender relationships. White racism and the cult of masculinity, a common affliction of American society and most of the world at the time, were quite strong in the South. Although the greater number of those belonging to that tiny minority of southerners who were relatively liberated from the two isms could be found among the Populists, the major thrust was clearly white racist and male dominant.[19] Women's suffrage and women's rights as such received little, if any, support from Dixie. Nearly all previous studies of southern Populism have been silent on the subject—a rather curious omission, it would seem, on the part of historians treating what purported to be a people's movement. To be sure, southern women actively participated in Alliance and Populist activities, as elsewhere, and there were some small breakthroughs. As one historian noted in a recent study of Georgia, the Populists "granted women very little. But when compared to Democrats, who conceded them virtually nothing, the Populists' tolerance was surprising. By allowing a few women to speak on the hustings and to participate in party business, the wool-hat boys demonstrated a reliance upon the opposite sex seldom seen in the late nineteenth-century South."[20]

Although Populists were more numerous in Texas and North Carolina and possibly even in Georgia and Alabama than any state in the West, they were, with the exception of the Tarheel State, less successful in winning elections. Corrupt practices, terror tactics, and a pronounced two-way split of the votes with the Populists on the losing end, severely limited their field of action. Even in North Carolina, where Populists and Republicans divided nominations and combined votes, their accomplishments would appear slight and definitely ephemeral. One historian, writing about 1950, concluded that the Populist–Republican coalition in North Carolina of "1894 and 1896 resulted in many fundamental changes." Among those cited as evidence: "the election [reform] law, the system of county and municipal government, more active Negro participation in politics, Negro office-holding, and the first and last Republican governor since 1876."[21] If that seems meager, as it does to me, perhaps it was due to the fact that North Carolina Populism emerges as a significant force only after the Panic of 1893 and the rise in importance of the silver issue. According to one study, by 1896 North Carolina Populists had "dropped their advocacy of a rudimentary class coalition of poor rural whites and blacks against an expanding industrial and financial capitalism . . . in exchange for a sectional alliance based on free silver, [with] the agricultural South and West [contending against] . . . the commercial and industrial North and East."[22] In the end, ironically enough, the primary outcome was to strengthen a growing "shadow" movement that would generate greater support by promoting the whites-only, less radical, and more capitalistically accommodative version of reform known as New South progressivism.

C. Vann Woodward, who has appropriately been called the "Godfather" of southern Populist historiography, long ago insisted that southern Populism was more genuinely radical than the western variety. With the possible exception of Texas, that interpretation is no longer tenable. To gauge radicalism simply by the strength of antifusionist sentiment directed at southern Democrats is a deceptive measurement. It overlooks the extreme revulsion and the murderous hostility and hatred that existed between southern Populists and the region's One-Party Dominant—the southern Democratic party. And as Bruce Palmer, one of Professor Woodward's many students, has pointed out regarding the research model that led Woodward to that interpretation: "Although Watson and the Georgia Populists in general arrived at a mid-road position in 1896, the logic of . . . radical analysis did not lead them there."[23]

Texas Populists clearly remained most solidly committed to the original program espoused by Populists (a product no doubt of the state's greater commitment to an ideology of greenback-antimonopolism, combined with that intense revulsion toward the state's One-Party Dominant). The recent tendency to put the Lone Star State in a special category, however, may have gone too far. Even in Texas the party's growth depended greatly on fusion with other factions—Republicans, especially.

All in all, Texas Populists battled courageously yet futilely. As elsewhere in the South, the opposition's use of terror tactics and corrupt election practices makes precise estimates of their real strength difficult if not impossible to assess. In 1892 and 1894, on the face of the returns, Populist Thomas L. Nugent was soundly defeated in both his races for governor. Only in 1896 did Populists manage to mount a significant challenge. In that election, Jerome Kearby, supported by "all consequential non-Democratic factions," polled more than a quarter of a million votes for governor but was still nearly 65,000 votes behind his Democratic opponent. Two years later, the Populist–Republican fusion candidate fared even worse. After that, the party gradually disintegrated, as did it everywhere.

The outcome for Texas Populists was only slightly better in their legislative races. In five contests from 1892 to 1900 the party managed to capture a total of only 41 out of approximately 640 house seats available. They did much worse in the senatorial races. Over the entire decade, in fact, they managed to elect only three of their people to Texas's upper house. In addition, not a single one of their nominees for Congress was victorious. Several of these congressional races, however, were closely contested and were likely stolen by the Democrats, as they were in Georgia. The party's most impressive victories came at the local level. County and precinct offices were within their reach, and they reaped their share of those offices. According to one study, they gave Texas "a real taste of Populism" at that level, yet "were but indifferently successful in the administration of their offices, though their shortcomings resulted ordinarily from lack of training and experience and not from malice or dishonesty."[24] The reforms sponsored by these Texas Populists, particularly in the legislature, were remarkably similar to those championed by Populists in Kansas and elsewhere.

Roscoe Martin's study of Texas Populism still contains much to recommend it as one of the more reliable guides to understanding the subject. Writing in the early 1930s, he seemed to anticipate, uncannily enough, a debate that would not reach full bloom for another twenty years. Said Martin, "Many professed that Populism had sprung from a single source and that it drew its strength from one group or party. Some supposed . . . [it] to be a latter day manifestation of Greenbackism; others insisted that it was merely a left wing branch of the Democratic Party; still others believed that its chief strength came from the Republican Party; and some zealots identified it with Socialism." Each of these "explanations" contained some "truth," wrote Martin, because "the People's Party commanded a considerable vote from each of the parties in question and from the Prohibition Party as well. The Reform movement therefore assumed a cosmopolitan political character, for it depended for its support not upon one party but upon all."[25] Texas and Oklahoma Territory, like Kansas and unlike most other areas in the South, however, were led by a high proportion of leaders who had been active since the Greenback–Labor battles of the 1870s. That made a difference with respect to substance, and that difference had occasionally confounded historians.

Martin's study of Texas also suggested a difference that may hold true for the South generally and set the region's Populist movement off somewhat from that of the West. Apparently the most prominent southern Populists, particularly those at the local and legislative levels, derived from a less privileged and thus less accomplished segment of society. Given the greater degree of deprivation that afflicted southern agriculture, that finding should come as no great surprise.[26]

For southern Populists who were victims of fraud and corruption, election reform understandably took on greater significance. In Georgia, Texas, and elsewhere Populists worked for a secret ballot, initiative, referendum, and the election of public officials generally. In the midst of a severe depression, everywhere they promoted economy in government by advocating reduction in salaries and by cutting appropriations for the state militias. Georgia Populists, in particular, worked for an end to the convict-lease system and supported the construction of a state prison as well as a reform school. Like Populists in other parts of the country, they advocated the expenditure of state money for the purchase of common-school textbooks. Antilynching laws likewise received their support, as did a measure expediting the appeal process and still another that assisted tenant farmers in disputes with landlords over cotton shares. There was at the same time considerable agreement between Democrats and Populists in Georgia. "With such harmony," wrote one historian, "some citizens wondered why the Populist party ever appeared. . . . They forgot that Populism had been founded as an answer to national issues."[27] Indeed it had.

Only North Carolina, among southern states, managed to send to Congress a significant Populist delegation. It was led impressively by Senator Marion Butler, a young, physically attractive, and relatively recent convert to Populism who seemed to undergo a gradual radicalization after arriving in the nation's capital. During the Fifty-fourth Congress (1895–97) North Carolina's group of five was the largest Populist state delegation in Congress, and in the one that followed (1897–99) the state's six-member delegation was second in size only to the one from Kansas. (The twenty-nine-member total of this Fifty-fifth Congress, by the way, was the largest of the five congresses that included a Populist faction.)

Populists in the entire South outside North Carolina managed to elect only two congressmen (three total, counting Tom Watson from the Fifty-second Congress, 1891–93). Both were from Alabama—Milford Howard, who served from 1895 to 1897, and Albert T. Goodwyn from 1896 to 1897. Howard served two terms and was a bona fide Populist; Goodwyn served only one year because of a contested election and while in the Congress voted with the Republican party. Goodwyn had been nominated by the Jeffersonian and People's party of Alabama's fifth district and was endorsed by the Republicans. It was said he ran on a platform whose principal planks called for "free coinage of silver, a protective tariff, and honest elections." The fusion effort in Alabama, concerning which Goodwyn was said to be the main proponent, succeeded in electing two New York–born Republican brothers to Congress—William Aldrich and Truman Aldrich in 1894 and William again in 1896. Most white southerners at the time (who, one suspects, had great satisfaction when these three left office) would likely identify the two brothers as the last of the carpetbaggers and Goodwyn at the last of the scalawags.[28]

These southerners were somewhat less inclined to speak out than Populists representing the West, but they seem to have been in tune with the Populist chorus. Although one might expect phase two of congressional Populism to have represented something of a departure from phase one, given the influence of fusion politics and the rise in importance of the gold-versus-silver question, the record suggests otherwise. Congressional Populists, during the fade-out, apparently did not retreat significantly from the doctrines that had been embodied in the Omaha platform.[29]

As the country entered 1896, it was obvious that a showdown of epic proportions was in the making. That February in the U.S. House, Alabama's Populist Milford Howard, who was never one to understate his case, announced in his first speech that it was his purpose to "appeal today for justice for those who sow that others may reap, for those who toil in poverty, hunger, and rags that the American plutocracy may revel in wealth and luxury beyond the dreams of avarice." He then quoted some famous lines from Shakespeare: "Mr. Speaker, 'There is a tide in the affairs of men, which, taken at the flood, leads on to fortune; omitted, all the voyage of their life is bound in shallows and in miseries.'" Make no mistake about it, said Howard, that "tide has come in the history of this country. The tide of protest, of popular indignation against the unlawful encroachments of the money power. . . . The masses of the country are like a great, troubled, restless, heaving ocean. . . . Wake up from your long sleep and stay the swiftly onrushing tide by just and wholesome laws ere it be too late."[30]

At that point the United States was nearly three years into a severe depression, and the nation continued to polarize. The Populists came under even heavier attack. Because of the public ownership aspects of their creed, congressional Populists increasingly felt called upon to defend their party. In one of his exchanges in the upper chamber, apparently presuming to speak for all, Senator Peffer stated:

We do believe that the Government of the United States should control by Government agencies; that all public functions ought to be exercised by public agencies in one way or another. That is the fundamental principle and the doctrine of the party to which I have the honor to belong; but we do not propose to go about and make a holocaust of this business; we do not propose to tear everything down, as anarchists would, to destroy. We are builders . . . ; we are not destroyers. In some respects, perhaps, we might be called iconoclasts, because we are breakers of images, but they are party images. We are not dangerous at all.[31]

Any party championing fundamental reform is bound to be attacked by those whose interests are threatened. Yet the fact that Senator Peffer felt compelled to make a disclaimer of that kind did not bode well for Populism; the defenders of the faith were clearly on the defensive.

The prophetic tide had definitely arrived. It remained to be seen whether the outcome would bring fortune or shallows and miseries.

Chapter Six

Shallows and Miseries

The Election of 1896 and the Decline, 1896–1900

> *The poor man is called a socialist if he believes that the wealth of the rich should be divided among the poor, but the rich man is called a financier if he devises a plan by which the pittance of the poor can be converted to his use.*
> —William Jennings Bryan, Congressional Speech against Repeal of the Silver Purchase Act, 16 August 1893

> *There are two ideas of government. There are those who believe that, if you will only legislate to make the well-to-do prosperous, their prosperity will leak through on those below. The Democratic idea, however, has been that if you legislate to make the masses prosperous, their prosperity will find its way up through every class which rests upon them.*
> —William Jennings Bryan, Cross of Gold Speech, Democratic National Convention, Chicago, 9 July 1896

By 1894, with an assist from Populism, the depression had set in motion a major realignment of American politics. Unrecognized at the time, the shift was heralded by the Republican party's recapture of the national House of Representatives that year. Ever since the end of Reconstruction the two major parties had battled to a virtual standoff. After 1894, for the first time legitimately since its creation four decades earlier, the Republican party became the nation's majority party, a position it would maintain for the next thirty-eight years (discounting the aberrant interregnum of the Progressive revolt and Woodrow Wilson's presidency,

1913–21). Following the economic collapse of 1929, Democrats would benefit from a similar seismic shift, creating another political realignment that is ongoing, despite some backing and filling and a tendency toward a Republican lock on the executive branch since the 1950s.

Could this 1890s realignment have turned out differently? Perhaps, if the election of 1892 had produced a Republican victory, thus saddling the Republicans with the depression. Undoubtedly, the economic debacle that began in 1893 would have wreaked as much havoc on the GOP as it did on the party of Grover Cleveland. Quite unintentionally, the Populist party had assisted in electing a Democrat by removing almost certain electoral votes from the Republican column. The Populists' task now was to recruit disaffected Democrats away from the conservative, gold-standard element of Cleveland's party, and to build a reform coalition that would lead to a different and more democratic realignment. Was that possible? To do all that, and to move beyond the myopia of blaming the party in power for all economic misfortune, was an enormous challenge.

Follow the Yellow Brick Road and the Cowardly Lion

Mountains of partisan literature accompanied the crusade to reestablish a bimetallic monetary standard. At the time a volume by Chicago writer William H. Harvey, *Coin's Financial School,* stood out like Pike's Peak. In the long run, however, another and quite improbable little book, a story for children written early in 1900 by another Chicagoan, had more enduring and decidedly more symbolic meaning. L. Frank Baum wrote the story, and he called it *The Wonderful Wizard of Oz.* Thanks to the 1939 movie version of the fairy tale, it eventually gained recognition from nearly every movie and television-era American—and quite a few people around the world. Surprisingly, more than six decades passed before scholars began to decipher the fairly obvious message ingeniously embedded within the story line of Baum's work—a classic parable on the silver crusade.

In 1964 Henry M. Littlefield, a public school teacher from New York state, first detected the hidden meaning of *Oz.*[1] Littlefield interpreted Dorothy as little Miss Innocent Everybody; the Scarecrow as the farmer (who has no brains but over and over again does the hard thinking for the group); the Tin Woodman as the worker (who has no heart but is so sensitive that he cries when he accidentally steps on a beetle); the Cowardly Lion as William Jennings Bryan or any major-party politico cowed by the money power (who has no courage but turns out to be quite brave indeed); the Wicked Witch of the East as the money power; and the Great Wizard of Oz as the confidence man-cum-agent of the money power. All that and more was accurately and eloquently interpreted by Littlefield.

But apparently because he was too much under the influence of the then-prevalent view of Populism—which simply collapsed two agrarianisms (the radical-liberal and conservative-reactionary variants) into one—Littlefield was unable to conceive of how Baum could possibly have been a pro-Bryan, prosilver Democrat and yet be opposed to Populism. Consequently, he and others have interpreted the Wicked Witch of the West as representing a "sentient and malign nature" or as "mortgage companies, heartless nature, and other things opposing progress there."[2]

Evidently, in Baum's mind, the evil western witch was none other than Populism—agrarian radicalism, socialism, or those on the left wing of the political spectrum generally. The western sorceress wore a silver whistle around her neck, symbolizing the silver plank of the Omaha platform. The original drawing of the western witch may even have been inspired by none other than "Pitchfork" Ben Tillman, the One-Eyed Plowboy who then as later symbolized in the minds of establishment types the worst side of the agrarian revolt. She (or he), as pictured, had only one good eye and wore a patch over the other. Dorothy, unknowingly assisted by the magic silver slippers (free silver) that she had taken from the evil Witch of the East, who had been killed when the Kansas tornado deposited Uncle Henry's house in Munchkin Country, eventually tossed a bucket of water on the western symbol of extremism, and the last remaining evil witch simply melted away. That was of course exactly what happened to Populism, once the Democratic party, behind Bryan, came out forthrightly for silver and reform.

Baum's story was an apt metaphor or parable of Progressivism, not Populism. It mirrored perfectly the middle-ground ideology that was fundamental among those who favored reform yet opposed Populism. Early in 1896, for example, Joseph Bristow, a young Kansas Republican newspaper editor (later, 1909–15, a U.S. senator), who fought the People's party from start to finish while championing a version of reform he characterized as "progressive," had already articulated the point of view that Baum later immortalized. Wrote Bristow:

We have a horror for the wild excesses of populistic doctrines. They are dangerous to a community, and demoralizing to the people. . . . There never has been a time in the history of this country when the people should be as careful and cautious in their selection of men for public position. . . . The Gormans, the Brices and the Platts [major-party tools of Wall Street, in his view] are the begetters of the Tillmans and Peffers. Between these two extremes [Baum's evil witches, East and West?] the great mass of the people suffer. The one represents the cool calculating selfishness of wealth and the desire for power. The other the wild fury of ignorance, envy and prejudice.[3]

Naturally, fervent Republican anti-Populists like Bristow, in the highly charged and polarized political atmosphere of the 1890s, were not inclined to make meaningful distinctions between Populism and Bryanism.

As historian David W. Noble recognized in his profound 1970 study *The Progressive Mind,* the 1890s "witnessed a terrible ideological division" among Americans that was indicative of the acute crisis the nation had reached in its runaway economic revolution. Populists, in urging a positive role for government, said Noble, had opened themselves up to the charge that they "were un-American; that it was they who were destroying the national covenant by advocating artificial patterns of government activity. . . . It was the Populist party, the defenders of laissez-faire thundered, which was the serpent threatening the purity and innocence of the American garden."[4]

Undoubtedly, genuine Populists and more conservative reformers like Bryan would not have been altogether in accord regarding the solutions, but a wide variety of dissidents had a fundamental area of agreement regarding who was responsible for the nation's predicament. This consensus had it that the serpent had been admitted to the garden by the partisans of finance capitalism and the proponents of a bastardized version of laissez-faire economics, insidiously confounded by an antisocial application of Darwinism; and it was they—plutocrats and goldbugs one and all, not their opponents—who endangered the society of free and equal producers that had characterized—or as some would have it, was meant to characterize—the republic. It was that kind of polarization and shared analysis, incidentally, that gave the silver issue its seductive appeal after 1893 (and that provided William Jennings Bryan with a long-lasting, reverential following), undermining, in the process, Populism's more radical and egalitarian producer-class approach in favor of what appears, certainly in retrospect, a self-defeating, rural-sectional alignment.

At the same time, one should be careful not to exaggerate the possibilities. The ongoing technological revolution was steadily separating people from their traditional producer roles and reshaping them in a more cosmopolitan and consumer-oriented mold. At the same time it was increasingly affirming by word and deed, contrary to a long tradition that insisted otherwise, that human rights were not universal and transcendent. Given this, who could say that Populism, in its time, was not doomed to fail no matter what? However that may be, by 1896 the proponents of the humane preference had become convinced the nation had arrived at Armageddon. It was now or never, do or die; nothing less than the American future, they devoutly believed, hung in the balance.[5]

Grover Cleveland's stubborn defense of the gold standard, intensified by his leave-it-alone-liquidationist approach to the depression, and the significant increase in votes for the People's party in the 1894 elections (more than a 40 percent increase over 1892, primarily from the Democratic South) gave Populists good reason to believe they might achieve major-party status in 1896. But this would be possible only if conservative financial elements retained control of both old parties. It was not an unlikely scenario in the case of the GOP, which had for years—and not with complete candor—identified with the cause of corporate America. But what about the Democrats? Would they stand by their man, or would they repudiate the policies of their one and only victorious candidate since 1856?

Cleveland's conservative financial stand brought forth a number of silver champions from all points on the political compass. Among them, a second-term Democratic congressman from Nebraska, William Jennings Bryan, stood head and shoulders above the rest. In August 1893, then only thirty-three, Bryan had delivered a speech in the special session called by Cleveland to repeal the Silver Purchase Act that registered for him, at that early date, a strong claim to the leadership of the silver cause and ultimately to the nomination of his party. So effective was that speech that members of the House made references to it for more than a year thereafter. This was no small accomplishment, among a group of politicians who were deluged with oratory day after day.[6]

Bryan continued to champion the silver cause and at the same time worked to build support across the country heading into the Chicago nominating convention of early July 1896. Another, even more spectacular speech that he made during the convention itself clinched the nomination for the Nebraskan. In his carefully crafted and powerfully delivered oration, Bryan simply overwhelmed his audience. He closed with this soon-to-be famous line: "we will answer their demand for a gold standard by saying to them: You shall not press down upon the brow of labor this crown of thorns, you shall not crucify mankind upon a cross of gold."

By nominating Bryan and by adopting a fairly comprehensive reform platform including silver, Democrats had done what more cautious and antifusionist Populists feared most. Their strategy was suddenly bankrupt, and their one great opportunity to achieve major-party status was torpedoed. The national committee, under Taubeneck's leadership, had purposely scheduled the Populist convention after those of the Republicans and Democrats, assuming both would embrace the gold standard. At St. Louis in June, Republicans obliged them with William McKinley, but Populists had underestimated the appeal of silver and Bryan among Democrats.

Bryan's nomination seriously complicated Populist politics. In Kansas, for example, the immediate reaction to Cleveland's repudiation was generally favorable. Only a few Populist leaders registered their dissent—most were Demophobes, to coin a term. One of those was Abe Steinberger, who raised some pertinent questions: "Is the Populist party," he asked, "ready to be dumped into the lap of Democracy? Are the men who have been fighting the battle of humanity in this country for twenty years willing to acknowledge all they wanted was a change in basic money? Are we ready to sacrifice all the demands of the Omaha platform on the cross of silver?"[7]

But what choice did they have? Populists nearly everywhere, outside the South especially, were now vulnerable to the logic of circumstances that suggested there must be only one silver candidate in the campaign lest the reform vote be split and the success of their gold-standard opponent assured. Even the highly principled, antifusionist editors of the Topeka *Advocate* were moved by the nomination of Bryan, and within a short time much of the Populist press began to urge his nomination at the upcoming Populist convention.

But could Populists support the Nebraska Democrat and still maintain party integrity? To extreme antifusionists, who existed everywhere but were most potent in the South where the Democrats were passionately—and for good reason—hated, especially in Georgia and Texas, the answer was a resounding no. Another, larger contingent of antifusionists, who were numerous wherever Populism existed, had doubts but recognized that the party had little choice. To fusionists and to those who had conceded everything to the silver issue, the question was really of no consequence.

Several prominent Kansas Populists, L. D. Lewelling and Frank Doster among them, suggested that the party endorse Bryan rather than nominate him. To do this, Populists would have to desist from naming a national ticket of their own. Two formidable stumbling blocks confronted that proposal. First was the determination of extreme antifusionists to carry on, come hell or high water; the other was the Democratic party's vice-presidential nominee, Arthur Sewall. A shipbuilder, a national banker, and a railway director from Maine, Sewall had nothing in common with Populists, except a less intense hostility to the single gold standard; he was in fact absolutely unacceptable to most Populists. As Ignatius Donnelly so aptly put it, Populists were "willing to swallow Democracy gilded with the genius of a Bryan," but they were unwilling to "stomach plutocracy in the body of Sewall."[8]

Under such circumstances, the decision of the Populist convention in St. Louis was understandable, albeit not altogether logical. After much maneuvering, no small amount of skullduggery, and considerable turmoil, the delegates nominated Tom Watson of Georgia—nearly as fervid an anti-Democrat antifusionist as existed in the Populist camp—for vice president; they then nominated Bryan for president.

With all the excitement generated by the repudiation of the Cleveland wing of the Democratic party and Bryan's nomination, historians have all but ignored the Populist platform of 1896. It was quite a remarkable document. The specific preamble of the Omaha platform was gone, but the sentiments expressed retained much of its flavor. It declared: "We realize that, while we have political independence, our financial and industrial independence is yet to be attained by restoring to our country the Constitutional control and exercise of the functions necessary to a people's government, which functions have been basely surrendered by our public servants to corporate monopolies."

The three main planks of Omaha headed the platform and were basically unchanged, except that the subtreasury system was omitted as a means of implementing their idea of a just banking and monetary system. As before, government ownership of the railroad and telegraph systems (except telephones) was included. This convention's platform also departed from Omaha's by incorporating within the core of the new document, rather than specifically excluding from the core, several other favored reforms, such as referendum, military pensions, economy in public salaries, and direct election of the president, vice president, and U.S. senators.

Several new and quite extraordinary planks were also included. The delegates endorsed the idea, which had consistently been advanced by their congressional delegations, that "in times of great industrial depression, idle labor should be employed on public works as far as practicable."

Even more remarkable, given the regressive course of history in that area, was their plank concerning voting rights: "Believing that the elective franchise and an untrammeled ballot are essential to a government of, for, and by the people, the People's party condemns the wholesale system of disfranchisement adopted in some States as unrepublican and undemocratic, and we declare it to be the duty of the several State legislatures to take such action as will secure a full, free and fair ballot and an honest count." (The use of the words *unrepublican* and *undemocratic* themselves suggest a significant evolution in terminology and in political thought.) The last segment made it clear that the entire platform represented what the party aimed to accomplish, yet conceded that the "financial question" (that is, bimetallism) was the "pressing issue" and welcomed the opportunity of joining with others in the campaign in support of that measure.[9]

Just the same, the arrangement worked out in St. Louis left few Populists entirely satisfied; in fact, it created new problems that had to be dealt with in order to manage a successful campaign and that continued to plague the reform effort throughout. Most Populists nonetheless reconciled themselves to the outcome, sensing that the proponents of silver and reform had a legitimate chance of capturing the presidency that November. With the Topeka *Advocate,* they could agree that Populists should go all out in their support of Bryan while endeavoring to maintain their independence and principles.[10]

It was a difficult, probably impossible, assignment. Fusion was the order of the day, especially outside the South. *Fusion,* not *coalition tactics* as before, was now the proper word for what occurred in that campaign—fusion involving Democrats, silver Republicans, and Populists.

Republicans, trapped by the quasi-gold plank of their national platform and painfully aware that the issue of silver appealed as strongly to a broad segment of western Republicans as it did to Populists and Democrats, had only ridicule left in their armory. For example, one prominent Kansas Republican leader and editor described the national Populist convention as

the most disgraceful aggregation that ever got together in America. Anarchists, howlers, tramps, highwayman, burglars, crazy men, wild-eyed men, men with unkempt and matted hair, men with long beards matted together with filth from their noses, men reeking with lice, men whose feet stank, and the odor from under whose arms would have knocked down a bull, brazen women, women with beards, women with voices like a gong, women with scrawny necks and dirty fingernails, women with their stockings out at the heels, women with snaggleteeth, strumpets, rips, and women possessed of devils, gathered there, and sweltered and stank for a whole week, making speeches, quarrelling, and fighting like cats in a back yard. Gray-haired, scrawny, yellow-skinned women appeared upon the stage dressed in hideous or indecent costumes, and gave performances that disgusted the most hardened Calamityites. . . . The gathering was so outlandish that each delegate imagined that the others were burlesquing him. To wind up the whole thing, delegates were brought up like the hogs they were.[11]

A young Republican journalist from Kansas by the name of William Allen White was also quick to perceive the threat building in his neck of the woods. A month *before* McKinley received the nomination of his party, White wrote an editorial for his *Emporia Gazette* stating that William McKinley, as the next president, had "a great opportunity before him." The question confronting the next president, wrote White, is: "Shall we have a new deal, or lose the deck one of these days?" Earlier in the same piece, he wrote: "The West has lots of labor; the East has lots of capital . . . Heretofore the capital end of the bargain has been given the best of it by the courts. It is time for the West to get a cinch. The farmer and his friends have paid the fiddler long enough to have a right to dance some."

It would be a mistake to imply that these thoughts were representative of the kind of campaign that White waged in his newspaper that year. In fact, he utilized the same line that his party had used against Populists practically from day one. The usual bill of fare featured ridicule and the cry of anarchy or socialism or communism, constructed around an antisocial Darwinian framework designed to depict Populist leaders—or farmers generally, by implication—as the misfits of society. On 6 August White declared: "The man who supports the Populists in this election[,] whether for road overseer or for President, is lending his vote and influence to the cause of anarchy." A week later he wrote: " 'Every man for himself and the devil take the hindermost' . . . is a fair statement of the idea of American government as it exists today. But during recent years, there has grown up in the West the un-American doctrine of state paternalism." Obviously, insisted White, "these two theories are violently antagonistic—one is American, Democratic, Saxon; the other is European, Socialist[ic], Celtic." Shortly before the election, White, never one to disguise his opinions, added this remark to his earlier revealing observations regarding Republican philosophy: "From time to time during this campaign the *Gazette* has charged that, while the rank and file of the Populists were honest, sincere but deluded men and women, the leaders

are the failures, the incompetent, the riffraff, the ragtag and bobtail of the community—in short the scum of the earth."

In the aftermath of such scurrility, it was small wonder that the feisty, sharp-tongued Republican editor was verbally accosted by angry Populists on the main street of Emporia one day in August 1896. This prompted him to write a more extensive, although not especially different, attack on Populism and Bryan that asked the question: "What's the Matter with Kansas?" His answer:

We all know; yet here we are at it again. We have an old mossback Jacksonian who snorts and howls because there is a bathtub in the state house; we are running that old jay for governor. We have another, shabby-wild-eyed, rattle-brained fanatic who has said openly in a dozen speeches that "the rights of the user are paramount to the rights of the owner"; we are running him for chief justice, so that capital will come tumbling over itself to get into the state. We have raked the old ash heap of failure . . . and found an old human hoop-skirt who has failed as a preacher, and we are going to run him for congressman-at-large. . . . Then we have discovered a kid without a law practice and have decided to run him for attorney general. Then, for fear some hint that the state had become respectable might percolate through the civilized portions of the nation, we have decided to send three or four harpies out lecturing, telling the people that Kansas is raising hell and letting the corn go to weeds.

There was more of the same, including epithets like "clodhoppers" and "gibbering idiots."

The article's only claim to originality was its pertinence to the 1896 presidential campaign and the clever manner in which White wrote it. The same kind of arguments had been used constantly since 1890, and so had some of White's satirical prose imperatives. Yet the editorial was picked up and copied by nearly every Republican newspaper in Kansas and in the larger cities outside Kansas, and it was used as campaign material by the Republican national committee. Why?

One reason was that White's editorial aptly represented the attitude of Republicans in the 1896 campaign against Bryan and his allies. Beyond that, White's view obviously struck a sympathetic chord at that precise moment throughout much of the nation. The response was all the more devastating because Populism—in its move toward silver and fusion—had been stripped of much of its protective ideological shield. Populists in the years from 1890 to 1894 seem not to have been greatly disturbed by the use of the success myth and a conservative rendition of Darwinism against them; many, perhaps most, of the Populists of 1896 were now sensitive to that attack. Perhaps this signaled the move toward a more accommodative reform persuasion soon to be known as Progressivism?[12]

White's solution to the problems confronting a nation in the midst of its second depression since entering a mature industrial epoch appealed to a fairly large and influential segment of American society. In addition to vanquishing Populists and Bryanites from governmental circles, his was an old solution candidly professed in that earlier editorial: "Every man for himself and the devil take the hindermost." Hard times must be resolved solely by means of economic growth and market forces under the guidance of business leaders. At best, the proper role of government was to condone policies aimed at funneling wealth into society from the top down, and the masses—farmers and laborers, above all—were supposed to leave government to those concerning whom White, apparently without even an atom of doubt, described as "decent, self-respecting men."

It was highly significant that White quoted a passage from Bryan's Cross of Gold speech to ridicule the Nebraskan and his supporters. Bryan had said, "There are two ideas of government. There are those who believe that, if you will only legislate to make the well-to-do prosperous, their prosperity will leak through on those below. The Democratic idea, however, has been that if you legislate to make the masses prosperous, their prosperity will find its way up through every class which rests upon them." This statement has not received nearly the attention it has deserved, not even from his most recent biographer, LeRoy Ashby.[13] Therein Bryan identified, without precisely naming them, two contending approaches regarding government and how it should go about restoring and maintaining prosperity. One would later come to be called "trickle down" ("supply-side economics," in the 1980s) and the other, "percolate up." Bryan was wrong about the Democratic party having been committed to the idea of legislating to make the masses prosperous. After the Civil War, third parties and Populism in particular pioneered that approach, and the fact that Bryan endorsed and championed the idea from within the Democratic party established his importance in American politics. Not until Franklin D. Roosevelt and the New Deal, in fact, would the "percolate-up" approach achieve a degree of legitimacy.

William Allen White's 1896 response to Populism's and William Jennings Bryan's idea of legislating to make the masses prosperous would resonate among conservatives and reactionaries from William McKinley to Herbert Hoover to Ronald Reagan—and no doubt beyond: "That's the stuff!" he wrote. "Give the prosperous man the dickens! . . . Whoop it up for the ragged trousers; put the lazy, greasy, fizzle . . . on the altar, and bow down and worship him. . . . What we need is not the respect of our fellow men, but the chance to get something for nothing." (It was little or no consolation to Bryan and his allies, but years later White conceded that he had been a political "reactionary" when he wrote this editorial, which made him virtually overnight a national Republican icon.)[14]

The vicious conservative counterattack, combined with Bryan's unrivaled inspirational campaign, soon converted many disgruntled Populists. Ignatius Donnelly, whose initial reaction to the Nebraskans' nomination was that the Democrats had "raped our convention while our own leaders held the struggling victim," was soon singing his praises. Midway through the campaign Donnelly met privately with Bryan, then noted in his diary: "His purposes are pure and noble. He is a great man; and if he is the choice of the people he will give the country an administration the greatest and best it has ever enjoyed. It seems to me he has been raised up by Providence to save the country from sinking into old world conditions."[15]

Bryan was endorsed by (among many others) Eugene Debs, Clarence Darrow, and Davis Waite—three individuals whose Populist bona fides were beyond reproach and who represented positions that cut across the party spectrum. Among prominent Populists outside the South, only Henry Demarest Lloyd, the movement's premier intellectual from Illinois, remained indifferent, no doubt because Lloyd recognized immediately that Bryan's nomination signified the demise of Populism. Another Illinois Populist, S. F. Norton, had been the choice of midroaders at the St. Louis convention, where he had been solidly backed by a large Texas delegation. By October, Norton too had publicly endorsed the Nebraskan and urged Populists to follow suit. It did not matter whether the man was or was not a genuine Populist, said Norton; it was enough "that every enemy reformers have encountered during the last twenty years [are] . . . today among Mr. Bryan's bitterest and most relentless opponents." That fact alone made him a soul brother.[16]

Nationally, Populism's big chance had gone by the wayside when conservative northeastern financial interests lost control of the Democratic party. It could be that Populism's contribution to that particular metamorphosis will stand as one of its more important achievements, as unintentional as that may have been. And as his most recent biographer

has said, "Bryan was far from a disastrous Populist candidate for president." He did indeed represent the reform cause "with distinction" and
"perhaps as well as anyone in 1896 could have."[17]

Despite the prodigious effort in Bryan's behalf, the end result added
up to defeat. Bryan and his supporters could console themselves only by
noting that their ticket had done well considering the enormous amount
of money that had been available to McKinley as compared with Bryan.
(Standard Oil and J. P. Morgan, by themselves, contributed more
money—$500,000 combined—to the Republican campaign than Bryan
managed to raise from all sources.) In their defense, Populists naturally
tended to overemphasize the role played by money, intimidation, and
corruption on the part of McKinley's supporters. They could point to the
fact that Bryan's losing popular vote constituted a higher total than any
previous presidential candidate. The electoral votes of twenty-two
states, encompassing the entire South and much of the West, belonged
to the Nebraskan. Yet McKinley's victory margin—over a half-million
popular and ninety-five electoral votes—was a decisive one for the
Republicans.[18]

For those who supported Bryan, the defeat was devastating beyond
description. Ignatius Donnelly probably came as close as anyone to capturing the feeling: "Alas and Alack!" he confided to his diary. "It seems
useless to contend against the money power. Every election marks another step downward into the abyss, from which there will be no return
save by fire and sword." Donnelly, the author of that famous dystopian
novel, *Caesar's Column,* was back in full force. The debacle even caused
the Minnesotan to question one of his more fundamental beliefs: "The
people are too shallow and too corrupt to conduct a republic." Donnelly
simply could not comprehend what had gone wrong. "We had a splendid
candidate and he . . . made a gigantic campaign; the elements of reform
were fairly united; and the depression of business universal, and yet in
spite of it all the bankrupt millions voted to keep the yoke on their own
necks. . . . I tremble for the future."[19]

People of course do not knowingly vote to keep their neck in a yoke.
Bryan lost because his candidacy did not appeal strongly enough to urban
America—urban-industrial labor, in particular. The myopic curse of laying
blame for the depression on the party in power was also a factor. Failure,
however, to carry even one of the states in that transition zone between
urban-industrial and agrarian America known as the Old Northwest
(Ohio, Illinois, Indiana, Michigan, Minnesota, and Wisconsin), the critical
area, was also the fatal shortcoming.

In the aftermath, William Allen White came up with the most profound assessment of what the election signified. "The fight came squarely," he said. "Mr. Bryan arrayed class against class. He appealed to the misery of the poor; he indexed [spotlighted] the luxurious appointments of the rich. He attempted to draw to his side all of those on the debt [*sic*] side of the ledger." McKinley and the Republicans, on the other hand, "fought out their fight on the principle of individual responsibility for individual failure or success." The GOP's position was that of "laissez faire" or "hands off." They "stood squarely for 'vested rights.'" They said, in effect, you cannot cut off the rich man's wealth without curtailing the poor man's income." Free silver was just a "dummy" issue, wrote White. "The issue went deeper. It permeated the political structure of the Nation. A change was a resolution—a resolution to a mild yet dangerous form of socialism." White was convinced that the issue had been "settled" for his "generation."[20]

The Emporia editor was on target with respect to the nation, especially if the challenge was seen as Populism rather than as Bryanism. But Bryan's election itself would have made a significant difference. Who can say how far the Great Commoner might have gone toward the position of Populism? He certainly would have gone as far as or farther than Woodrow Wilson's administration went nearly two decades later. We can be fairly confident that Bryan and his Populist allies would not have taken the imperialistic road, nor would they have encouraged the corporate-merger movement that occurred after McKinley and the Republicans took control in 1897. From that perspective one can easily visualize quite a different course for American history in the twentieth century.

Denouement: Co-optation and Petty Larceny, 1897–1900

Although defeated nationally, at the state and local levels the Populist-fusionist forces came out of the 1896 election stronger than ever—primarily in the West. In Kansas, for example, the party captured all three branches of the state government for the first and last time. But the fact that the victors had only the issue of bimetallism in common—concerning which nothing could be done at the state level—created a significant reform conundrum. What emerged from the new alignment, ultimately, was a brand of co-opted Populism that would energize the ranks of the Democratic party under the label Progressivism.[21]

American politics generally was greatly rejuvenated by the challenge of Populism and Bryanism. Gradually, Republicans in the West and Dem-

ocrats in the South adopted a number of Populism's nonradical demands
(a case of petty, as opposed to grand, larceny). Within a few years, former Populists themselves were losing sight of their party's original, fundamental reform demands. As they did so, they convinced themselves
that the insurgent reformers within both major parties had brazenly
stolen the very same Populist programs that these same anti-Populists
had fought so hard to defeat in the 1890s. To be sure, Populists generally
felt vindicated by Progressivism, but the Progressives—later claims to
the contrary notwithstanding—never embraced Populism's fundamental
economic reforms.

Early in 1898 an event Populists dearly supported administered the
coup de grace to their movement. As Tom Watson later said, "The Spanish War finished us. The blare of the bugle drowned the voice of the
Reformer." Watson saw more clearly than others the likely effect the
war would have on American society. Said Watson, "The privileged
classes all profit by this war. It takes the attention of the people off economic issues, and perpetuates the unjust system they have put upon us."
He asked, "What do the people get out of this war? The fighting and the
taxes." What would the country get out of the war? "Endless troubles,
complications, expense. Republics cannot go into the conquering business and remain republics."[22]

A minority of Populists became imperialists—more often than not, former Republicans like William Peffer and Mary Lease. But most Populists
were anti-imperialists, and contrary to Richard Hofstadter's prizewinning
study, they had no trouble distinguishing between wars of liberation and
wars of conquest.[23] Once it was clear that the McKinley administration
had taken the imperialist road, Populists everywhere, especially in the
West, became outspoken opponents of that foreign policy. The anti-im-
perialist movement found its strongest support in those areas where
agrarian radicalism had flourished. Having been one of the original punch-
ing bags, so to speak, of the imperialistically minded, along with the
American aborigines and African-Americans, it was only natural and logical that Populists would be among the most vocal foes of imperialism.
As Nebraska congressman William Neville recognized at the high point
of the debate: "The right to life, liberty, and the pursuit of happiness is
as . . . applicable to nations as to individuals." Those principles, as he
said, apply to the many wonderful varieties of human beings inhabiting
the earth, and they are "as precious to the poor as to the rich; as just to
the ignorant as to the educated; as sacred to the weak as to the strong."
Unfortunately, most of Neville's countrymen had taken a different road

from the one he was traveling, and as a result Populism remained somewhat inscrutable. The nation's most esteemed leaders at the turn of the century—such as Theodore Roosevelt—were telling Americans that their country was different, an historical exception, and that its activities and possessions abroad were not manifestations of imperialism but extentions of civilization and liberty. The nation would not seriously rethink that contention until nearly seven decades later, in the aftermath of an unnecessary and tragic war in Vietnam.

At about the same time, those principles inspired G. C. Clemens to challenge Kansas's segregated public school system in Topeka. By then an organizer and leader of the state's Democratic Socialists, Clemens utilized the arguments of John Marshall Harlan's famous 1896 dissent in *Plessy* v. *Ferguson* as part of his arguments against segregation, which had been authorized by Kansas law in 1879 for the state's larger cities. He lost, of course, but fifty years later, in another case involving the same school system, the Supreme Court under Chief Justice Earl Warren at long last vindicated Harlan and Clemens. That same Court also took the lead in a drive to resuscitate the nation's commitment to human rights. In the process the Warren Court became the focus of attack and controversy, and the proponents of the inhumane preference were mobilized once again, much as they had been mobilized by the earlier challenge of Populism. History may not repeat itself exactly. But at times, especially when lessons have been unlearned and problems left unresolved, the resemblance is so close as to be uncanny.

Epilogue

Somewhere over the Rainbow

An introduction to a 1960s volume of essays on Populism reads: "The glorious failure of the People's party as a political organization is today more sympathetically appreciated than it was in its own time. The problems which Populists sought to solve, and the prescription they offered, seem not so irrational as seen by their contemporaries."[1] This assessment is correct on all counts. If William Jennings Bryan was "America's most successful failure," the same can certainly be said of Populism. What made the movement historically interesting, even glorious, was the very same thing that guaranteed that it would fail as a political institution and be seen as irrational and un-American by an influential segment of American society—that portion already well accommodated to the culture of an urban-industrial and corporate-capitalistic society. Above all, these paradoxical characteristics were its producer-class ideology, its insistence on the humane preference, and its advocacy of a program designed to salvage an ideal world—a program that would selectively convert key segments of the economy to public ownership. As Jerry Simpson stated in 1891, most Populists believed that all "industrial enterprises" that were "essentially monopolistic . . . should be under government control, but everything else should be left in private hands."[2]

Such proposals were absolute anathema to the mainstream parties; they were even objectionable to a vocal minority within the Populist party itself, particularly in the South. This latter element was convinced that their society could somehow be saved without resorting to public ownership. In holding that belief they were probably much less realistic than others, but they were certainly a good deal less objectionable to mainstream Americans. Their approach would easily blend into that reform persuasion called Progressive.

Racism, sexism, possessive individualism, hypercapitalism, and imperialism were among the more important ingredients in the mind-set that frustrated and enervated the Populist movement. Perhaps they were all merely symptomatic of a more fundamental change at work within Western civilization—a change that increasingly confirmed and sanctioned the belief that human rights were after all not universal and transcendent and that capital accumulation was the sine qua non of progress. Most Americans, anti-Populists especially, would probably have agreed with their era's most acclaimed political economist-sociologist, William Graham Sumner, when he contended that society "cannot go outside of this alternative: liberty, inequality, survival of the fittest; not— liberty, equality, survival of the unfittest. The former carries society forward and favors all its best members; the latter carries society downwards and favors all its worst members."[3]

Some historians have argued that "the dominant imagination in America has been one that attempts to escape from the problem of community."[4] If that is true, the Populist phenomenon was an exception. For a brief moment in time hundreds of thousands of Americans, mainly but not exclusively ruralites, oblivious to Sumner's dire prophecy, joined hands and struggled to create their own special version of the cooperative commonwealth. That side of the movement was deeply religious and evangelical. As one historian has aptly noted, theirs "was a religious expression that rejected prevailing religious sentiments, for organized religion had failed its responsibilities." The Gospel of Wealth and competitive individualism having become orthodoxy among the town-based churches, Populists created "a Gospel of Populism" calculated to reshape the nation in such a way that human relationships would mirror "the Fatherhood of God and the Brotherhood of Man in the spirit, and according to the teaching, of Jesus Christ."[5]

This Gospel of Populism was inspired by a glaring discrepancy between that which America preached and that which it practiced. The Alliances and then the People's party became for a time the Populist church. Through them the Gospel of Populism was perfected and channeled. By such means a distraught population of rural people managed to briefly restore their self-esteem, as well as their sense of the possible.

The movement truly was a pentecost of politics. Throughout the South and West especially, farm families traveled miles and miles over primitive roads on horseback and in wagons and buggies to hear and practice the Gospel of Populism. The movement produced its own stores, newspapers, pamphleteers, cartoonists, poets, and a fairly elaborate folklore. It was common for Populists to address one another as Brother or Sister. Through the Alliances and the People's party, hundreds of thousands of rural Americans redesigned positive self-images for themselves at a time when the dominant society had begun to downgrade rural Americans in a thousand different ways. For a short time they were able to put aside the feeling of having become a "permanently underprivileged" class and substituted instead a sense of being part of a movement that was playing a vital role in moving America toward fulfillment of its betrayed promise. They were somebody. In a world increasingly driven by inhumane dictates, they were part of a grand movement to restore the humane preference.[6]

Quite a variety of discontents momentarily congealed in the 1890s, especially after the economic collapse of 1893, and Populism aptly reflected that development, not only in its appeal but in its internal dissensions. Because it was that kind of movement, one needs to be careful not to define the movement too exclusively. Certainly one must take note of its regional variations and internal polarities, and the term *populism* should be used generically, if at all, only after carefully defining what it is meant to be conveyed by its use. In its historic context, however, a leader of the Kansas Populists, John Dunsmore, speaker of the ill-fated Populist house of 1893, may well have captured its positive essence as succinctly as anyone:

Populism demands the enactment of new laws based on the natural rights of men, and not limited by precedents and accepted theories in relation to property, when such . . . do not meet the requirements of modern life. Populism does not necessarily mean "to nationalize all the essentials of existence. . . ." It does mean, however, that the power of law shall control and prohibit the centralization of land titles. That labor shall be provided with all necessary legal machinery to protect itself against the unjust demands of aggregated wealth. That not only the means of transportation, but all public utilities, shall be subject to public control, and when necessary, public ownership. That money of all kinds shall be issued direct by the government, and its legal tender value regulated by law, and not by foreign bankers and money-lenders.[7]

In the 1890s that bold philosophy and program of the Populists created much controversy, which has since been rivaled by the historiographical debate among their interpreters. Both are testimony to the complexity and dynamism of Populism, as well as an indication of the degree to which Populists challenged prevailing attitudes. Certainly there was much that was viable in the movement; above all, it contributed to an expansion of the conventional wisdom such as would eventually be conducive to a more creative social dialogue. Populism is sure to retain its fascination for students of history as long as people remain sensitive to questions of democracy and human rights in a world increasingly driven by the consequences of an ongoing technological-corporate revolution.

Perhaps *The Wonderful Wizard of Oz* holds the clue to why Populism retains its viability. In the final analysis, blue smoke and mirrors are still as effective in America in the 1990s as they were in the Land of Oz before Dorothy's arrival. Frank Baum's Progressive parable truly was a fairy tale. The Wicked Witch of the East (the money power) was not killed; nor was she even brought effectively under control, then or later. The Scarecrow (the farmer) did not go off to rule in the Emerald City (the nation's capital). The Tin Woodman (the laborer) did not go out West to rule benevolently over the Winkies (the area's primitives). The Cowardly Lion (William Jennings Bryan) may well have gone off to become King of the Beasts in a forest (of renowned political reformers), and Dorothy may have made it back to Kansas without her magic silver slippers. But ironically, the one really certain outcome was that the Wicked Witch of the West (Populism, agrarian radicalism, and socialism) was on her way to extinction. A noted former Populist, looking back from the 1920s, understood all too well why that was the case: "The plutocracy," he said, "would oppose the erection of a vigorous state until such time as it felt strong enough to control its activities."[8] Truer words were never spoken. The unfulfilled dream of Populists would remain somewhere over the rainbow.

Notes and References

Introduction

1. *Congressional Record,* 56th Cong., 1st sess., 6 February 1900, 1589–90. There were four other persons in the House who owed their election, in part, to Populism, but they thought of themselves as fusionists and were on their way to becoming Democrats. Neville alone identified himself as a member of the People's party. This assessment is based on the author's research for a study tentatively entitled "Congressional Populism and the Crisis of the 1890s."

2. This commitment was not without an element of exclusiveness and hypocrisy, which will be duly noted; but one must not lose sight of the fact that the blemish paled in comparison with the affliction of the mainstream parties. It was also complicated from beginning to end by a strong tendency to degenerate into agrarian-interest politics pure and simple—in other words, a politics of "give us more"—as in the case of the American Federation of Labor, the twentieth-century Farm Bureau, and business-industrial interests generally, from the old Gilded Age to the "New Gilded Age" of late-twentieth-century America.

3. Vernon L. Parrington, *The Beginnings of Critical Realism in America, 1860–1920,* vol. 3, *Main Currents in American Thought* (New York: Harcourt, 1958), 285–86.

4. On Parrington's Jeffersonianism and Populism, see E. H. Eby's excellent short essay in H. R. Lamar, ed., *The Reader's Encyclopedia of the American West* (New York: T. Y. Crowell, 1977). Thanks to Eby we now know that Parrington's magnum opus was, before the publishers ineptly intervened, originally and more appropriately entitled *The Democratic Spirit in American Literature.*

5. Garry Wills, *Inventing America: Jefferson's Declaration of Independence* (New York: Vintage, 1979), features this quote by Parrington and provides a treatment of the historiographical issues. Wills thoroughly agreed with those who had "demolished Parrington's thesis"; yet the thrust of Wills's book, as I read it, adds considerable weight to the contention that a more radical, non-Lockean

strain existed in the American heritage; so much for ideological blinders. See especially 352ff.

6. Worth Robert Miller, *Oklahoma Populism: A History of the People's Party in the Oklahoma Territory* (Norman: University of Oklahoma Press, 1987), 265.

7. Robert Fisher, *Let the People Decide: Neighborhood Organizing in America* (Boston: Twayne Publishers, 1984), xxiii–xxiv.

8. Regarding the influence of George and others, see these noteworthy recent studies: John L. Thomas, *Alternative America: Henry George, Edward Bellamy, Henry Demarest Lloyd and the Adversary Tradition* (Cambridge, Massachusetts: Harvard University Press, 1983); R. Jeffrey Lustig, *Corporate Liberalism: The Origins of Modern American Political Theory, 1890–1920* (Berkeley: University of California Press, 1982).

9. Chester McArthur Destler, *American Radicalism, 1865–1901: Essays and Documents* (New York: Octagon Books, 1963), viii.

10. Discussing Jefferson's politico-economic policies, Richard Hofstadter, *The American Political Tradition and the Men Who Made It* (New York: Vintage, 1961), 38, concluded that the thrust of it all was "not anti-capitalist but anti-mercantilist."

Chapter One

1. Lawrence Goodwyn, *Democratic Promise: The Populist Moment in America* (New York: Oxford University Press, 1976), 5.

2. Ibid. The "ramshackle welfare state" comparison was, I believe, coined by David Shannon years ago, but I have not been able to locate the article in which it appeared.

3. Ibid., 9.

4. The quote is from Parrington, *Critical Realism,* 309.

5. Garry Wills insists that "Adam Smith has been misinterpreted by those who base his economics on market *competition. . . .* Smith was conscripted to individualist uses by nineteenth-century liberalism [which was, I fear Wills would be surprised to learn, neoconservatism]; but he began as a good communitarian of the Scots school." Responsibility for this distorted view of Smith, Wills would appropriately lay at the doorstep of "America's plutocracy," which had come under "populist" attack. See *Inventing America,* especially 232, 353. For Rossiter's "Great Train Robbery," see *Conservatism in America: The Thankless Persuasion,* 2nd ed. (New York: Vintage, 1962), 130–31.

6. Sidney Fine has thoroughly treated the legal and judicial defense of the emerging industrial order, as well as late-nineteenth-century legislative efforts aimed at bringing corporate activities under control. See *Laissez Faire and the General-Welfare State* (Ann Arbor: The University of Michigan Press, 1966), especially chapters 5 and 10.

7. This commentary on reform is a much-revised version of a discussion, vintage 1966, first published in O. Gene Clanton, *Kansas Populism: Ideas and Men* (Lawrence: University Press of Kansas, 1969), 14–18.

8. Certainly in Kansas this was the case. See ibid., 65. Regarding that contrary argument, see Goodwyn, *Democratic Promise.*

9. The material contained in this section on pre-Populist Kansas third parties was researched and written for *Kansas Populism* but was ultimately excised; perhaps if it had been retained, several more recent treatments of the origin of Populism would have been a bit less Texanized.

10. William F. Zornow, "The Basis of Agrarian Unrest in Kansas," in John D. Bright, ed., *Kansas: The First Century,* vol. 1 (New York: Lewis Historical Publishing Co., 1956), 473–75.

11. Stefan Lorant, *The Presidency: A Pictorial History of Presidential Elections from Washington to Truman* (New York: Macmillan, 1952), 323.

12. *Topeka Commonwealth,* 13 June 1872.

13. Ibid., 12 September 1872.

14. Lorrant, *The Presidency,* 318.

15. Copies of all the platforms were reproduced in either the *Topeka Commonwealth* or the *Topeka Daily Capital.* Most of these were reprinted in Karl A. Svenson's "The Effect of Popular Dissent on Political Parties in Kansas" (Ph.D. diss., University of Iowa, 1948), 143–222.

16. Solon Justus Buck, *The Granger Movement: A Study of Agricultural Organization and Its Political, Economic, and Social Manifestations, 1870–1880* (Lincoln: University of Nebraska Press, 1965), 52ff.

17. John Davis, "Address to the Farmers of Kansas," in *Proceedings of the State Farmers' Convention* (Topeka: Farmers' Co-operative Association, 1873), 18.

18. *Topeka Commonwealth,* 30 March 1873.

19. Partly as a diversionary tactic, Democrats and Republican dissidents were frequently accused of wanting to undo the Civil War amendments.

20. *Topeka Commonwealth,* 7 August 1874.

21. Clarence J. Hein and Charles A. Sullivant, *Kansas Votes: Gubernatorial Elections, 1859–1956* (Lawrence: University Press of Kansas, 1958), 10–25.

22. See Svenson, "The Effect of Popular Dissent on Political Parties in Kansas," 143–222, for a convenient collection of the relevant platforms.

23. Republicans in the gubernatorial elections received these percentages and pluralities for these years: 1866, 70.4 percent, 11,219; 1876, 56.8 percent, 22,975; 1888, 53.5 percent, 73,259. See Hein and Sullivant, *Kansas Votes.*

24. Robert C. McMath, Jr., *Populist Vanguard: A History of the Southern Farmers' Alliance* (Chapel Hill: University of North Carolina Press, 1975), 77; Goodwyn, *Democratic Promise,* chapters 2 and 3, especially.

25. Buck, *Granger Movement,* especially chapter 6.

26. John D. Hicks, *The Populist Revolt: A History of the Farmers' Alliance*

and the People's Party (Minneapolis: University of Minnesota Press, 1931), 96ff; Clanton, *Kansas Populism,* 54.

27. Hicks, *Populist Revolt,* 104–5; Goodwyn, *Democratic Promise,* 33ff.

28. Roy V. Scott, *The Agrarian Movement in Illinois, 1880–1896* (Urbana: University of Illinois Press, 1962), 22ff; Hicks, *Populist Revolt,* 98–104; Goodwyn, *Democratic Promise,* 160–61.

29. Goodwyn, *Democratic Promise,* 28.

30. Quoted in ibid., 27.

31. Ibid., 36–40.

32. Ibid., 50.

33. Ibid., 81.

34. Ibid., 82–83.

35. Hicks, *Populist Revolt,* 107.

36. Goodwyn, *Democratic Promise,* 147.

37. Hicks, *Populist Revolt,* 106–8; Goodwyn, *Democratic Promise,* 83–86.

38. Hicks, *Populist Revolt,* 124.

39. It is possible that Macune derived his ideas from a Kansas source, and indirectly from a Russian example. See the series of articles by G. Campbell in the *Advocate,* Topeka, beginning with the 25 February 1891 issue. Campbell's 4 March 1891 article contained this: "In 1882 I published in the Mound Valley *Herald,* under the caption 'Russia and America,' the following article, which will be observed embraces all the features of the sub-treasury bill, a measure which has become famous." Here is an excerpt, supposedly from the 1882 article:

According to a letter of recent date from our consul at Russia, one of the demands of the nihilists is the loan of money from their government on their grain. It is claimed that their money loaners charge them, not only exorbitant rates of interest, but as soon as the crop is thrashed, they demand payment and force the peasant to sell his grain at much less than it costs to produce it. To prevent this injustice to the farmer, the nihilists want the government to construct warehouses and receive the grain, and loan them rubles to the amount of 80 per cent. of its value, and then when the crop is sold the government shall reimburse itself for interest and storage, and the balance of the proceeds of the sale goes to the peasant.

This would not be a bad system for the farmers of the United States. Suppose the government would construct a warehouse in each county at a central location, or in the cities for that matter, and would receive the grain of the farmers at the warehouse or at the nearest railroad station and advance them loans to the extent of 80 per cent. of the market value. This would enable the farmer to hold his grain, and when the grain shall have been sold at prices to justify production, then let the government reimburse itself for transportation, storage and interest on the loan of money upon the grain at a low rate, and the balance remaining of the proceeds of the sale, be returned to the farmer producing the grain.

Campbell also wrote: "This article, with some modifications, was published in *United Labor* of 1887 in No. 24 of the series on file in the office of the historical society at Topeka, Kansas." Could Macune have acquired his ideas from this source? Incidentally, no one challenged this series of articles, entitled "The Early History of the Farmers' Alliance." They were either a fairly elaborate fraud or the real McCoy; if the latter, historians would need to drastically revise their history of the subtreasury plan.

Incidentally, the ideas of Thomas Mendenhall were popularized by Edward Kellogg. Mendenhall published works in 1816 and 1834 that contained virtually all the ideas later put forward by Kellogg in works of 1837 and 1842. My forthcoming study of congressional Populism will include a more extensive treatment of the roots of Populism, part of which includes the influence of Mendenhall and Kellogg.

40. Clanton, *Kansas Populism,* 142–46; also "Intolerant Populist? The Disaffection of Mary Elizabeth Lease," *Kansas Historical Quarterly* (Summer 1968), 189–200.

41. Hicks, *Populist Revolt,* 187–88.

42. Quoted in ibid., 192.

43. For a greatly extended discussion of the subtreasury idea, see Hicks, *Populist Revolt,* and Goodwyn, *Democratic Promise;* both historians devote long chapters to the plan. Goodwyn's book also includes an independent analysis, in the appendix, by an economist.

Chapter Two

1. Goodwyn, *Democratic Promise,* 195.

2. James C. Malin, *A Concern About Humanity: Notes on Reform, 1872–1912 at the National and Kansas Levels of Thought* (Lawrence, Kansas: Author, 1964), 155–65.

3. Raymond Miller interviewed Rightmire in July 1927 for his study of Kansas Populism. Rightmire told Miller he had never been a member of the Farmers' Alliance. Miller does not tell us whether he then asked Rightmire about his claim to having been sworn in in Texas. Miller also contended all three of the editors were ineligible for membership in the Texas order. I cannot resolve this problem, but it does seem likely that Rightmire was never a member of the Farmers' Alliance. It is possible, of course, that the three went to Texas and arranged for someone else who was eligible for membership to be sworn in as an organizer. See Raymond Miller, "The Populist Party in Kansas" (Ph.D. diss., University of Chicago, 1928), 94.

4. W. F. Rightmire, "The Alliance Movement in Kansas—Origin of the People's Party," *Transactions of the Kansas State Historical Society, 1905–1906,* 1–8.

5. McMath, *Populist Vanguard,* 80.

6. Goodwyn, *Democratic Promise,* 630.

7. Rightmire, "The Alliance Movement," 1–8.

8. Clanton, *Kansas Populism,* 50–51; Robert C. McMath, "Preface to Populism: The Origin and Economic Development of the 'Southern' Farmers' Alliance in Kansas," *Kansas Historical Quarterly* (Spring 1976), 55–65.

Only research buffs should read the remainder of this note. Because so many historians have debated this matter, I have devoted the space here and in the text to what will surely not be as pertinent to casual students. It is nonetheless important and questions yet remain, especially regarding B. H. Clover's Alliance activities. Rightmire asserted Clover was first elected president of the northern branch of the state Alliance on 20 December 1888 in Topeka. This was apparently one of a number of verifiable errors in his account. As indicated, I. M. Morris was its president. Another Alliance—probably one with a southern affiliation—met in Augusta on 22 December, when the state organization was created and Clover was elected president. Some of this confusion probably resulted from the secrecy involved and also from the use of a common name—Farmers' Alliance—by both orders. Although matters have since been clarified somewhat, apparently no one has clearly documented Clover's rise to leadership. Did he begin as president of a northern suballiance affiliate—perhaps in *"Cloverdale"* (wherever that was, or was it Cedar Vale or Silverdale)? Suballiances generally constituted an immediate neighborhood (comfortable horse-and-buggy distance)—fifty or fewer members. Was Clover persuaded to make the switch by the Videttes or their agent—possibly W. P. Brush? Was Clover one of those disgruntled Republicans? Several historians—Lawrence Goodwyn and Worth Miller, for example—have identified him as a former Greenbacker and Union Laborite (as did Rightmire, which probably was where it originated). But the record does not suggest a third-party background for the Cowley County farmer, and the state Alliance newspaper insisted he had always been a Republican (*Advocate,* Topeka, 3 September 1890, 5). Clover abandoned the Populist party early in 1894, throwing his support to the Republicans; a few years later he committed suicide.

Incidentally, the *Cambridge News* (Cambridge was Clover's home base), 8 February 1889, printed this note: Clover "is president of the Farmers' Alliance in this part of Kansas, and is making things lively in the interest of the Alliance." John Rogers, who was in the thick of all these organizational moves and also one of the editors Rightmire said had gone to Dallas with him to be initiated into the southern order, *first* listed Clover as president of the Kansas State Alliance and Co-operative Union on 19 April 1889. The two previous weekly issues listed the officers of the "Kansas State Alliance (Northern Branch)." But the whole affair may have been complicated by a deliberate strategy. Rightmire put it this way: "Through the channels of the old Vidette organization instructions were sent to the members of the Union Labor party [Rogers was chairman of the Harvey

County Union Labor party] to hold back from membership and to denounce the Alliance as a move on the part of the old parties to steal the Union Labor party, until all their Republican and Democratic neighbors had been initiated, then to allow themselves to be coaxed to join, and . . . to begin applying the tenets of the platform to the condition of the farmers and laborers of Kansas. "

More obviously needs to be done by future researchers. One should start with a very careful reading of the *Kansas Commoner* and the *Nonconformist,* from about September 1887 through early 1889. Surely some evidence will appear of at least a trip to Texas if one indeed occurred. It may turn out that Rightmire revealed more truth than some have been willing to concede.

9. Stanley Parsons et al., "The Role of Cooperatives in the Development of the Movement Culture of Populism," *Journal of American History* 69 (March 1983), 881.

10. All the material in this chapter, unless otherwise indicated, has been drawn from Clanton, *Kansas Populism,* where documentation will be found.

11. *Advocate,* Meriden, 17 August 1889.

12. Goodwyn, *Democratic Promise,* 214. Goodwyn has written (646), "The phrase 'Alliance ticket' was employed in Kansas in 1890, though many have subsequently used 'Populist ticket' to describe the politics of that campaign." Early on, the official Alliance state newspaper countered that very argument by saying: "The people's party is no more an Alliance party than it is a Knights of Labor party, a F.M.B.A. party or a grange party, for all participated by their several delegations in its organization." *Advocate,* Topeka, 24 September 1890.

13. Malin, *Concern About Humanity,* 35–36.

14. Robert W. Larson, *Populism in the Mountain West* (Albuquerque: University of New Mexico Press, 1986), passim.

15. Bruce Palmer, *"Man Over Money": The Southern Populist Critique of American Capitalism* (Chapel Hill: University of North Carolina Press, 1980).

16. See Goodwyn, *Democratic Promise,* 210, for Nebraska Populism as a "shadow movement"; Hicks, *Populist Revolt,* 156–57.

17. Hicks, *Populist Revolt,* 156–58.

18. Goodwyn, *Democratic Promise.*

19. C. Vann Woodward, *Tom Watson: Agrarian Rebel* (New York: Macmillan, 1938), is the classic study of this subject.

20. Hicks, *Populist Revolt,* and Goodwyn, *Democratic Promise,* both contain objective and penetrating treatments of Ben Tillman.

21. The name Mary Ellen stuck so well that some historians, taking their cue from opposition sources, continued to refer to her as Mary Ellen six and seven decades later.

22. Mary Lease also edited the *Wichita Independent* from 17 November 1888 to 16 March 1889. She actually contributed few editorials to the weekly during the short time she was listed as editor. Not long after taking on the task,

her home in Wichita burned to the ground, and apparently she became more active in her law practice and/or lecturing to assist herself financially.

23. Those interested in pursuing this dragon to its den might determine whether and when Lease spoke in Harvey County in 1891; they should also examine the *Kansas City Star* closely for the days and weeks immediately before 7 August 1891. See also Katherine B. Clinton, "What Did You Say, Mrs. Lease?" *Kansas Quarterly* (Fall 1969), 52–59.

24. This judgment is based on the fact that the author has read virtually every word Jerry Simpson uttered for the record during his six-year tenure.

25. In an earlier interview Simpson said this:

I never made a speech without stockings on in my life and I never pulled up my pants to show what kind of stockings I wore. The story was sent out by an anti-Alliance newspaper correspondent to a paper in my district. It was made out of whole cloth and it was instigated, I suppose, by the remarks that I made concerning my opponent who was noted for his fine dressing and his expensive and aristocratic airs. I called him "Silkstocking Hal," and may have said that farmers could not afford to wear stockings of that kind.

You people don't understand the farmers of Kansas. They are the pick of the East. The most enterprising of the young men of the country went from New York, New England and Ohio and other states to Kansas and we have the best of this element in our party.

Goodland *Republic,* 25 December 1891, quoting an interview with the Chicago *Sentinel.*

26. Hicks, *Populist Revolt,* 178–79; Goodwyn, *Democratic Promise,* 222.

27. Hicks, *Populist Revolt,* 178–80; Gene Clanton, "'Hayseed Socialism' on the Hill: Congressional Populism, 1891–1895," *Western Historical Quarterly* (April 1984), 142–43.

28. Hicks, *Populist Revolt,* 180–85; LeRoy Ashby, *William Jennings Bryan: Champion of Democracy* (Boston: Twayne Publishers, 1987).

Chapter Three

1. *Advocate,* Topeka, 23 July 1890. On this trip Polk spoke in two other southeastern Kansas towns; in Columbus, to eight thousand, and in Emporia, to fifteen thousand. Describing the turnout in Emporia one local newspaper pictured the size of the parade as follows: "When the head of the procession was under the equator the tail was just coming round the north pole." See ibid., 9 July 1892.

2. Quoted in Hicks, *Populist Revolt,* 206.

3. Pronounced *O-cow-la.*

4. As Lawrence Goodwyn has noted, "A party that seriously hoped to challenge the dominant Republicans of the North simply could not be tainted with the stain of rebellion." That course would likely send thousands of Alliance farmers from the north and west of Texas back to their original Republican home, which apparently explained, more than the move into the third-party arena or fusion between Democrats and Republicans, Populist losses in Kansas a year later. As a matter of fact, Frank McGrath, Kansas Alliance president, caused quite a stir a few months after the Ocala conference when he announced that "the Farmers' Alliance in the northwestern states will either be in union with the south, 'in the middle of the road in 1892,' or the northwestern states will return their old-time majorities for their old party, and the union of the west and south for the protection of their homogeneous interests will be deferred for another generation." Goodwyn, *Democratic Promise*, 226, and *Advocate*, Topeka, 22 April 1891.

5. Goodwyn (*Democratic Promise*, 230) writes: "While Macune maneuvered desperately to . . . prevent [third-party action], Southern radicals like [W. L.] Lamb, [J. M.] Perdue, and W. Scott Morgan of Arkansas worked closely with the Kansans on the call for the Cincinnati convention." Whether this was at Ocala or later, Goodwyn does not make clear. The original call was published in the *Advocate*, 24 December 1890, and of those mentioned by Goodwyn, only Scott Morgan signed it. Texans who signed were H. J. Spencer, Weldon; A. E. Bailey, Palestine; and R. M. Humphrey, Houston. Apparently all were associated with the Colored Farmers' Alliance and Cooperative Union (CFA&CU). As in the case of Texas, the few who signed from the southern states appear to have been associated with the CFA&CU. Apparently only Arkansas, with Morgan, L. P. Featherston, and Isom P. Langley signing, was ready for radical action. At least two of Arkansas's signers were whites.

6. A recent study also somewhat obfuscates the nearly complete absence, at this point, of southern white support for a new party by focusing on the conference's vote relative to Henry Cabot Lodge's diversionary federal "election bill," known in the South as "the force bill." All eight Texas and Alabama delegates, along with two from Arkansas and one from Florida, joined eighteen colleagues from the North and West in voting to table a resolution condemning Lodge's bill. The resolution passed by a vote of forty-eight to twenty-nine. The thirteen votes from the North and West against the Lodge bill, however, would suggest that more than race was involved. The threat to enforce that portion of the Fourteenth Amendment mandating the vote for adult male citizens or a reduction in congressional representation equivalent, proportionately, to the number of such citizens denied the franchise proved highly serviceable to those who stood to gain by a strategy of divide and conquer in both old parties. But the intensity of emotion and near unanimity of the southern delegations on the matter of votes for black male citizens was truly ominous. See Goodwyn, *Democratic Promise*, 227–28.

7. In January 1891 the Kansas Citizens' Alliance was also organized nationally as the National Citizens' Industrial Alliance (NCIA) in Topeka. Both organizations, especially the NRPA, would play a national role that was remarkably similar to that played by the Kansas State Reform Association until the Kansas People's party was created.

8. According to Robert McMath, "The Associated Press accounts that appeared in the [*New York*] *Times* were written by William S. McAllister of Mississippi." Goodwyn describes McAllister as "an anti-third party, anti-Macune, anti-subtreasurite segregationist." Perhaps this explains some of the confusion. McMath, *Populist Vanguard,* 189; Goodwyn, *Democratic Promise,* 227.

9. Hicks, *Populist Revolt,* 208; McMath, *Populist Vanguard,* 107ff; Goodwyn, *Democratic Promise,* 225–27.

10. All the major platforms except that of 1896 and later are in Hicks, *Populist Revolt,* 427–44. Regarding the possible effect of the subtreasury system, see William P. Yohe, "An Economic Appraisal of the Sub-Treasury Plan," in Goodwyn, *Democratic Promise,* 571–81.

11. Perhaps because of the involvement of the Citizens' Alliance with this Confederation, Rightmire and others created the NCIA that same month (see note 7). Both these organizations originated in Kansas, and Rightmire was designated secretary for both. Rightmire claimed (and it rings true) that the NCIA was formed to provide an organization "somewhat similar to the Farmers' Alliance, and yet upon the plan of the old Videttes, to pledge its members against voting for any person nominated for any office by a convention of either the Democratic or Republican parties." Rightmire, "The Alliance Movement in Kansas," 1–8.

12. Hicks, *Populist Revolt,* 210–11; Goodwyn, *Democratic Promise,* 231–32.

13. McMath, *Populist Vanguard,* 110–12; Goodwyn, *Democratic Promise,* 230–31, 239–40.

14. On 31 December 1890 through the *Advocate,* Stephen McLallin, who had participated in these events, made this announcement: "The proposed conference of delegates of the various reform organizations that was to convene at Cincinnati on the 23d of February, 1891, has been postponed to a later date. This is the result of a conference held at Jacksonville, Florida, on Saturday evening, December 13, at which Mr. Powderly, John Davis and other prominent Knights of Labor, and the leading men of the FA&IU were present."

15. Whereas aspects of Rightmire's account concerning the early years are suspect and clearly in error at points, what he had to say about his activities from 1890 on are substantially documented by the contemporary record. See especially the *Advocate* for 1 April and 6 May 1891. See also Clanton, *Kansas Populism.*

16. Goodwyn, *Democratic Promise,* 242–43.

17. The original call included the Independent party, the People's party,

the Union Labor party, "the late Federal and Confederate Soldiers," the Farmers' Alliance, the Farmers' Mutual Benefit Association, the Citizens' Alliance, the Knights of Labor, and the Colored Farmers' Alliance. The supplemental call added the American Federation of Labor, Trades Unions and Trades Assemblies, the Federation of Railway Employees, and the Nationalists.

18. Unless otherwise indicated, information concerning the conference has been derived from the *Cincinnati Enquirer,* 18–21 May 1891.

19. A cynic would surely conclude that Rightmire's primary objective was to benefit his legal practice. Throughout the period involved, he was busy with his profession and increasing his caseload. In fact, during 1890 and 1891 he advertised for business in the *Advocate.*

20. Apparently, Rightmire overestimated the number of African slaves by nearly two million; he also exaggerated the number of Americans oppressed by the industrial system.

21. John Hicks mistakenly identified Sarah Emery as a "Kansas woman"; Richard Hofstadter later repeated Hicks's error, and a number of others followed suit.

22. The reporter was not clear about what kind of flag Davis was carrying; it could have been a Texas flag or even a Confederate flag. It seems unlikely, however, that either of these would have produced the demonstration that occurred.

23. Hicks, *Populist Revolt,* 214.

24. Rightmire, "The Alliance Movement in Kansas," 1–8.

25. Quoted in Hicks, *Populist Revolt,* 216.

26. *Kansas City Star,* 12 April 1931; Hicks, *Populist Revolt,* 238–39; George B. Tindall, "Populism: A Semantic Identity Crisis," *Virginia Quarterly Review* (Autumn 1972), 507–8.

27. Quoted in Hicks, *Populist Revolt,* 217.

28. Ibid., 218.

29. Goodland *Republic,* Kansas, 4 September 1891. Ely was a Johns Hopkins and University of Wisconsin economist. He was one of the more important scholarly pioneers of the new school of political economy. To the extent that Populism is to be placed somewhere between extreme individualism and complete socialism, Ely was its primary scholarly champion, for that was the essence of his new economics. See Fine, *Laissez Faire and the General-Welfare State,* 229–41. Apparently the Ely work Simpson alluded to was *Problems of To-day: A Discussion of Protective Tariffs, Taxation, and Monopolies,* published in 1890. One historian has argued that when the Populists "found themselves in need of economic authorities upon whom to rely they chose Adam Smith and David Ricardo, not Richard T. Ely or the other young, reformist economists." See Karel D. Bicha, *Western Populism: Studies in an Ambivalent Conservatism* (Lawrence, Kansas: Coronado Press, 1976), 128.

30. For interpretations that place greater emphasis on the silver panacea

and fusion politics see, Goodwyn, *Democratic Promise,* and Peter H. Argersinger, *Populism and Politics: William Alfred Peffer and the People's Party* (Lexington: University of Kentucky Press, 1974).

31. Goodwyn, *Democratic Promise,* 289–90.

32. Hicks (*Populist Revolt,* 221), working from a confused Kansas source, referred to this document as the party's "famous manifesto." Actually, the People's party manifesto was issued by the Kansas Populist legislators in early March 1891. It contained no significant rhetorical flourishes. See the "Address of the State Central Committee of the People's Party to the People of Kansas," *Advocate,* Topeka, 2 December 1891.

33. Populist chairman Levi Dumbauld and secretary W. D. Vincent signed this address. The portion quoted here was most likely written by William Davis Vincent, a thirty-nine-year-old former Greenbacker and merchant from Clay Center, who served as railroad commissioner and congressman. Apparently, he was not related to the Winfield Vincents.

34. There is some confusion about how many congressmen were involved in this meeting. Woodward (*Tom Watson,* 191) indicates fifteen; Hicks (*Populist Revolt,* 222) says twenty-five. The latter figure is probably correct.

35. *Advocate,* Topeka, 23 December 1891.

36. Letter from Macune to McLallin, ibid., 18 March 1891, 7.

37. The quoted phrase belongs to Hicks, *Populist Revolt,* 223, but my use of it departs somewhat from the earlier study.

38. Quoted in Goodwyn, *Democratic Promise,* 264–65.

39. Quoted in Argersinger, *Populism and Politics,* 109–10.

40. This is the slightly edited and improved version adopted at Omaha.

41. Woodward, *Tom Watson,* 202.

42. Quoted in Hicks, *Populist Revolt,* 228.

43. Hicks, *Populist Revolt,* 223–30; Woodward, *Tom Watson,* 201–2; Argersinger, *Politics and Populism,* 109–10; Goodwyn, *Democratic Promise,* 264–67.

44. *Advocate,* Topeka, 2 March 1892, 5.

45. Woodward, *Tom Watson,* 202. Woodward, incidentally, used the word *Negro* and did not put it in quotes. I suspect, however, that Livingston would not have hesitated to use the word inserted here—to whites in any case.

46. Argersinger, *Populism and Politics,* 111; Goodwyn, *Democratic Promise,* 270.

47. Quoted in Hicks, *Populist Revolt,* 232; Goodwyn, *Democratic Promise,* 271.

48. *Advocate,* Topeka, 6 July 1892.

49. Fred Emory Haynes, *James Baird Weaver* (Iowa City: State Historical Society of Iowa, 1919), 345.

50. *Advocate,* Topeka, 6 July 1892; Hicks, *Populist Revolt,* 231–37; Gene Clanton, "James Baird Weaver," in Lamar, ed., *American West,* 1246–47.

Chapter Four

1. Thomas E. Watson, "Why the People's Party Should Elect the Next President," *Arena* (July 1892), 204.

2. Martin Ridge, *Ignatius Donnelly: The Portrait of a Politician* (Chicago: University of Chicago Press, 1962), 284, 293.

3. Eva McDonald-Valesh, "The Strength and Weakness of the People's Movement," *Arena* (March 1892), 727–28.

4. Material pertaining to Kansas in this chapter, unless otherwise indicated, has been drawn from Clanton, *Kansas Populism,* where it is fully documented. The author retains a number of copies of this 1969 study, which will be given to serious researchers on request.

5. For a treatment of Lease's behavior in this affair, see my "Intolerant Populist? The Disaffection of Mary Elizabeth Lease," *Kansas Historical Quarterly* (Summer 1968), 189–200.

6. Argersinger, *Populism and Politics,* 134.

7. Argersinger (ibid., 128ff), viewing these developments from the perspective of Senator Peffer and an even more extreme and quite small (at least before 1893) fringe element of midroad Populists, classified the Kansas campaign of 1892 as a fusion campaign. I rather think that distorts the picture, albeit in a subtle and sophisticated manner.

8. Quoted in Haynes, *Weaver,* 317.

9. Quoted in Hicks, *Populist Revolt,* 238–39.

10. Thomas E. Watson, "The Negro Question in the South," *Arena,* (October 1892), 541.

11. Hicks, *Populist Revolt,* 241.

12. Ibid., 243.

13. See Michael Paul Rogin, *The Intellectuals and McCarthy: The Radical Specter* (Cambridge, Massachusetts: MIT Press, 1967).

14. Quoted in Woodward, *Tom Watson,* 223.

15. Hicks, *Populist Revolt,* 243–44.

16. Quoted in ibid., 244; the comment on Lease is attributed to a person by the name of Horn. See *Salina Weekly Republican,* 28 October 1892.

17. Quoted in Haynes, *Weaver,* 330–31.

18. Quoted in ibid., 339.

19. Quoted in ibid., 340.

20. Quoted in ibid., 336–37.

21. Hicks, *Populist Revolt,* 245ff; Haynes, *Weaver,* 335–38; Goodwyn, *Democratic Promise,* 309ff.

22. Hicks, *Populist Revolt,* 255. On western Populism and the silver issue, see especially Thomas A. Clinch's *Urban Populism and Free Silver in Montana* (Missoula: University of Montana Press, 1970), and Larson, *Populism in the Mountain West.*

23. Hicks, *Populist Revolt,* 265ff., and Larson, *Populism in the Mountain West,* 95.

24. Hicks, *Populist Revolt,* 272–73, and Goodwyn, *Democratic Promise,* 344–46.

25. For a full treatment of this affair see Clanton, "Intolerant Populist?" 189–200.

26. Hicks, *Populist Revolt,* 298–99.

27. John R. Morris, *Davis H. Waite: The Ideology of a Western Populist* (Washington, D.C.: University Press of America, 1982), vii; and Thomas W. Riddle, "The Old Radicalism in America: John R. Rogers and the Populist Movement in Washington, 1891–1900" (Ph.D. diss., Washington State University, 1976).

28. Hicks, *Populist Revolt,* 299.

Chapter Five

1. Michael J. Brodhead and O. Gene Clanton, "G. C. Clemens: 'Sociable Socialist,'" *Kansas Historical Quarterly* (Winter 1974), 475–502.

2. Clanton, *Kansas Populism,* 193.

3. The cowbird is notorious for laying its eggs in the nest of another bird, to be hatched and fed by its unsuspecting host; frequently, it grows to larger size and crowds out the host's own young.

4. Milton Friedman and Anna Jacobson Schwartz, *A Monetary History of the United States, 1867–1960* (Princeton, New Jersey: Princeton University Press, 1963), 134, insist that if silver had been restored in 1879, the nation could have avoided the disastrous deflationary spiral of 1879–97.

5. I first wrote much of the material in this chapter regarding the silver issue for Lamar, ed., *American West;* it is republished here with permission.

6. Robert F. Durden, "The 'Cow-bird' Grounded: The Populist Nomination of Bryan and Tom Watson in 1896," *Mississippi Valley Historical Review* (December 1963), 397–423.

7. *Congressional Record,* 54th Cong., 1st sess., 2479.

8. Before rushing too quickly to disassociate Populism from socialism, however, perhaps one should note that even Karl Marx made some significant distinctions between types of property: "Political economy," wrote Marx, "confuses on principle two very different kinds of private property, of which one rests on the producers' own labour, the other on the employment of the labour of others. It forgets that the latter not only is the direct antithesis of the former, but absolutely grows on its tomb alone." At another point he wrote: "We know that the means of production and subsistence, while they remain the property of the immediate producer, are not capital. They become capital, only under circum-

stances in which they serve at the same time as means of exploitation and subjection of the labourer." *Capital* (Encyclopaedia Britannica, 1952), 379–80.

9. On Populism and antipaternalism, see Bicha, *Western Populism,* 114–15.

10. Immigration restriction was advocated by Populists in the interest of organized labor. Those who are prone to view the issue in a strictly racist context, overlooking its economic, social, and political potential, would be well advised to try a counterfactual exercise. Ask yourself what would have been the impact on American history had there been no immigration to the United States after 1865.

Senator George Turner, in his first speech wherein he utilized the robber baron metaphor treated later in this chapter, spoke primarily to oppose an immigration restriction bill that was then under consideration. In this speech Turner included a remarkable number of liberal arguments against the measure. As he saw it those who supported restriction were merely scapegoating. Said Turner, "It is much better that we should endeavor to remedy the disease rather than attempt to combat the symptoms." As he saw it, "A better remedy . . . would be to put the people of this country to work. Give us a wise and a just economic system which will insure labor its fair reward, not only in the factory but on the farm. Do that, and the engorged population of our great centers will soon be remedied, and those centers will reach a normal and healthy condition." *Congressional Record,* Senate, 7 January 1898, 429.

11. Much of the material in this chapter regarding Congress first appeared in Clanton, "'Hayseed Socialism' on the Hill" and is reproduced with permission.

12. Morris, *Davis H. Waite,* 100ff; Peter H. Argersinger, "Ideology and Behavior: Legislative Politics and Western Populism," *Agricultural History* 58 (1984), 45–46; T. A. Larson, "Woman Suffrage," in Lamar, ed., *American West,* 1282–85; Clanton, *Kansas Populism,* 92–95, 100–101, 168.

13. Larson, *Populism in the Mountain West,* 125, 143, 155, 186 n. 34; T. A. Larson, "Woman Suffrage," 1282–85.

14. Argersinger, "Ideology and Behavior," 53; see also Argersinger's "Populists in Power: Public Policy and Legislative Behavior," *Journal of Interdisciplinary History* 18 (Summer 1987), 81–105, for additional documentation of western Populism's greater propensity toward reform than either of the two old parties.

15. Clanton, *Kansas Populism,* 232–33, and passim.

16. Larson, *Populism in the Mountain West,* passim.

17. *Congressional Record,* 55th Cong., 2nd sess., 7 January 1898, 429.

18. Ibid.

19. Gerald H. Gaither's *Blacks and the Populist Revolt: Ballots and Bigotry in the "New South"* (University: University of Alabama Press, 1977) is by far the most thorough treatment of the subject named in the title.

20. Barton C. Shaw, *The Wool-Hat Boys: Georgia's Populist Party* (Baton Rouge: Louisiana State University Press, 1984), 178.

21. Helen G. Edmonds, *The Negro and Fusion Politics in North Carolina, 1894–1901* (Chapel Hill: University of North Carolina Press, 1951), 219.

22. Palmer, *"Man Over Money"*, 144.

23. Ibid., 182.

24. Ibid., 70.

25. Ibid., 70.

26. More work is needed in this area, and researchers ought to take care to note merited distinctions that exist between the region's major leaders and lower-level functionaries. Barton Shaw's careful examination of Georgia Populism was an excellent beginning; Shaw has effectively documented what a number of others only guessed at or asserted from insufficient data. See *Wool-Hat Boys*, 130ff.

27. Ibid., 127, 139.

28. William Warren Rogers, *The One-Gallused Rebellion: Agrarianism in Alabama, 1865–1896* (Baton Rouge: Louisiana State University Press, 1970), 287–89, 296, 326–27.

29. I have completed research on the three congresses of 1895–1901 but have not systematically explored that evidence. Although I am fairly confident regarding the generalization above, it is of course advanced tentatively.

30. *Congressional Record*, 54th Cong., 1st sess., 10 February 1896, 1566.

31. Ibid., 25 April 1896, 4412.

Chapter Six

1. Henry M. Littlefield, "The Wizard of Oz: Parable on Populism," *American Quarterly* (Spring 1964), 48–58.

2. Ibid., 55; R. Hal Williams, *Years of Decision: American Politics in the 1890s* (New York: John Wiley & Sons, 1978), 105–6.

3. *Ottawa Weekly Herald,* Kansas, 6 February 1896.

4. David W. Noble, *The Progressive Mind, 1890–1917* (Chicago: Rand McNally & Co., 1970), 9.

5. Ibid., 9–14; Bruce Palmer, *"Man Over Money"*, is excellent in identifying this shared critique among southerners.

6. Paolo E. Coletta, *William Jennings Bryan: Political Evangelist 1860–1908* (Lincoln: University of Nebraska Press, 1964), 83–87; Paul Glad, *McKinley, Bryan, and the People* (Philadelphia: J. B. Lippincott Co., 1964), 81–83.

7. Clanton, *Kansas Populism*, 185–86.

8. Ibid., 186–87.

9. Melvin I. Urofsky, ed., *Documents of American Constitutional and Legal History,* vol. 2 (New York: Alfred A. Knopf, 1989), 28–32.

10. Clanton, *Kansas Populism*, 186.

11. Quoted in ibid., 189–90.

12. Ibid., 190–92.

13. Coletta notes this similarity to "New Deal Democracy" but does not develop the point. See *Political Evangelist,* 140.

14. Clanton, *Kansas Populism,* 192.

15. Quoted in Robert F. Durden, *Climax of Populism: The Election of 1896* (Lexington: University of Kentucky Press, 1965), 80.

16. Ibid., 114.

17. Ashby, *William Jennings Bryan,* 65.

18. Ibid., 67–71; Durden, *Climax of Populism,* 126ff.

19. Quoted in Durden, *Climax of Populism,* 162–63.

20. *Emporia Gazette,* Kansas, 5 November 1896.

21. For an extended treatment of the relationship between Progressivism and Populism, see O. Gene Clanton, "Populism, Progressivism, and Equality: The Kansas Paradigm," *Agricultural History* (July 1977), 559–81. This article was researched and written for delivery at the 1973 meeting of the Organization of American Historians; one should note its revisionist approach as compared to *Kansas Populism.*

22. Quoted in Woodward, *Tom Watson,* 334–35.

23. Richard Hofstadter, *The Age of Reform: From Bryan to F.D.R.* (New York: Vintage, 1955), 85–88.

Epilogue

1. Homer E. Socolofsky, Editor's Introduction to "Populism," *Kansas Quarterly* (Fall 1969), 5.

2. Interview with Simpson reported in Goodland *Republic,* Kansas, 4 September 1891.

3. Sumner quote from McCloskey, *American Conservatism,* 49.

4. Noble, *Progressive Mind,* ix.

5. Peter H. Argersinger, "Pentecostal Politics in Kansas: Religion, the Farmers' Alliance, and the Gospel of Populism," *Kansas Quarterly* (Fall 1969), 35.

6. Ibid., passim.

7. Clanton, *Kansas Populism,* 216–17.

8. Parrington, *Critical Realism,* 117.

Bibliographic Essay

What follows is a short list of works I consider most useful in understanding the Populist movement. Affirmatively and otherwise, the best indication of materials considered pertinent will be found in the Notes and References. For those seeking more comprehensive coverage, essays contained within the following works, spanning nearly three decades of discussion and debate, are strongly recommended: Walter T. K. Nugent, *The Tolerant Populists: Kansas, Populism, and Nativism* (Chicago: University of Chicago Press, 1963); Norman Pollack, *The Populist Mind* (Indianapolis: Bobbs-Merrill Co., 1967); and Worth Robert Miller, *Oklahoma Populism: A History of the People's Party in the Oklahoma Territory* (Norman: University of Oklahoma Press, 1987). Miller's historiographical essay is the best discussion of the literature to appear recently.

Those interested in identifying the primary sources should refer to the many references and bibliographies included with this and other state, regional, and general studies.

First- and Second-Generation Literature, 1896–1940

The earliest treatments of Populism appeared while the movement was still under way. Two contemporary, nonacademic, and conflicting interpretations by anti-Populists were those of Charles S. Gleed, "The True Significance of Western Unrest," *Forum* 16 (October 1893), 251–60, and Frank Basil Tracy, "Rise and Doom of the Populist Party," *Forum* 16 (October 1893), 240–50. The first scholarly treatments were those of Frederick Emory Haynes, "The New Sectionalism," *Quarterly Journal of Economics* 10 (April 1896), and Frank McVey, "The Populist Movement," *Economic Studies* 1 (August 1896). McVey's was the more extensive of the two and viewed Populism as socialistic and a product of ill-advised "paternalistic" policies practiced in the West. Haynes dealt with the movement in a much larger and less polemical context, as an aspect of a worldwide political awakening of the working classes.

Much influenced by Frederick Jackson Turner and the voguish frontier thesis, within a generation, a number of younger historians undertook monographic studies of Populism at the local and state levels that would eventually provide much of the raw material necessary for a general study. Solon Justus Buck, who along with McVey taught at the University of Minnesota, wrote the first general study, entitled *The Agrarian Crusade: A Chronicle of the Farmer in Politics* (New Haven, Connecticut: Yale University Press, 1920). Buck's history was sketchy, rather pedestrian, and contained little that was new or different. In light of what was to follow, it is noteworthy that Buck, even though a Turnerian, did not employ the frontier thesis as an integral part of his interpretation. Perhaps that was because he had dealt with earlier agrarian movements and was cognizant of the southern component. In 1913 Buck had published *The Granger Movement,* his most noteworthy study.

As seen through Buck's eyes, the twenty-four years that had elapsed since the earliest treatments had not altered the view of Populism appreciably. That would change in the decade following the appearance of *The Agrarian Crusade,* as the impact of the Progressive Era took hold. Among others, Francis B. Simkins, Alex M. Arnett, John D. Barnhard, Raymond C. Miller, Hallie Farmer, Herman C. Nixon, Ernest D. Stewart, and John D. Hicks wrote numerous articles and monographs on various aspects of the movement. All that was lacking was an overall treatment, solidly grounded in the sources.

In 1931 John D. Hicks filled that need by publishing *The Populist Revolt: A History of the Farmers' Alliance and the People's Party* (Minneapolis: University of Minnesota Press). Almost immediately, *The Populist Revolt* became the standard. Hicks provided a more exhaustive and penetrating history fashioned on essentially the same framework, and in much the same style, as Buck, except that Hicks made the Turner thesis a central part of his explanation for the movement.

Third- and Fourth-Generation Literature, 1940–1980

While Hicks's study dominated the field, several scholars soon were raising questions regarding his general interpretative framework. Chester McArthur Destler, early on, and Fred Shannon, later, both took issue with aspects of Hicks's study. In 1946 Destler published *American Radicalism, 1865–1901: Essays and Documents* (New London: Connecticut College Press), and in 1945 Shannon published *The Farmer's Last Frontier: Agriculture, 1860–1897* (New York: Farrar & Rinehart). Destler and Shannon were part of a growing revolt against the Turner thesis that had begun at about the same time Hicks published his volume. Increasingly, the Turner thesis was discounted as a way of making sense out of late-nineteenth-century agrarian movements. As that happened, another view of

Populism began to emerge suggesting the movement was a premodernist, even atavist and retrogressive, phenomenon. Apparently Richard Hofstadter pioneered that point of view in "Parrington and the Jeffersonian Tradition," *Journal of the History of Ideas* (October 1941), 391–400. Eric Goldman took the same approach in a more influential study published in 1952 entitled *Rendezvous with Destiny: A History of Modern American Reform* (New York: Alfred A. Knopf).

The same year Goldman's book appeared, C. Vann Woodward published his monumental study, *Origins of the New South, 1877–1913* (Baton Rouge: Louisiana State University Press). Woodward's treatment followed interpretatively the position he had established in 1938 with his highly acclaimed biography, *Tom Watson: Agrarian Rebel* (New York: Macmillan). His roots and his subject being southern, Woodward was not under the spell of the Turner thesis; his treatment placed Populism more effectively within a class and economic framework, portraying a movement that was forward looking and, in comparison with the forces against which it was contending, democratic. Because he was neither a Turnerian nor a proponent of the retrogressive thesis created in the vacuum produced by the debunking of the frontier thesis, Woodward's studies retained a degree of viability and influence beyond that of all other historians of Populism.

Ideologically, elimination of the frontier explanation created a serious gap in Populist historiography. It would seem that the void was filled, unconsciously perhaps, by a view of Populism as a case of retrogressive utopianism—a view that was, in a sense, a mid-twentieth-century variation on the Turner thesis. However that may be, once the frontier explanation was dropped, historians were faced with two logical possibilities. One, they could picture the movement as retrogressive and recreate the frontier explanation in the form of an "agrarian myth" or some other device, thereby placing the accent on harmony and unity and nostalgia. On the other hand, they could adopt an economic approach, stressing class conflict and interpreting the Populist movement as a product of abuses inherent in industrial capitalism, ahead of its time in advancing proposals to cope with the problems of industrial America. Both approaches were prominently represented in treatments of the Populist movement beginning with third-generation literature.

In 1955 Richard Hofstadter elaborated on his earlier insistence that Populism was a retrogressive movement. This he did with a work that was awarded the Pulitzer prize for history: *The Age of Reform: Bryan to F.D.R.* (New York: Vintage). As regards Populism, the book was a splendid example of history as non sequitur, but it was enormously influential and added considerable support to a number of other writers who were portraying Populism in an even more unsavory light. Hofstadter's *Age of Reform* was, nonetheless, instrumental in rejuvenating Populist studies. Quite a number of works soon appeared putting the new views to the test.

In 1959 C. Vann Woodward joined the debate with a prominent article taking issue with the various negative interpretations. Shortly thereafter, Norman Pollack launched his career with a spirited challenge to Hofstadter et al. Pollack mounted what constituted a counterrevisionist defense of Populism. In 1962 he published *The Populist Response to Industrial America: Midwestern Populist Thought* (Cambridge, Massachusetts: Harvard University Press). In that work, Populism emerged as a movement even more avant-garde and radical than earlier accounts had contended.

In 1963 Walter T. K. Nugent published his carefully researched study of a key Populist state. The title of his book, *The Tolerant Populists: Kansas, Populism, and Nativism,* indicated clearly what his research had demonstrated. In 1969 O. Gene Clanton, in *Kansas Populism: Ideas and Men* (Lawrence: University Press of Kansas), also focused on that state in an effort to determine, more systematically than had previously been done, who the Populists were and what their movement signified historically. Both Kansas studies pointed to a more balanced view than had been presented in either Hofstadter's or Pollack's interpretations. The same may be said of these: Sheldon Hackney, *Populism to Progressivism in Alabama* (Princeton, New Jersey: Princeton University Press, 1969); William Warren Rogers, *The One-Gallused Rebellion: Agrarianism in Alabama, 1865–1896* (Baton Rouge: Louisiana State University Press, 1970); Stanley B. Parsons, *The Populist Context: Rural Versus Urban Power on a Great Plains Frontier* (Westport, Connecticut: Greenwood Press, 1973); Thomas A. Clinch, *Urban Populism and Free Silver in Montana* (Helena: University of Montana Press, 1970); Robert W. Larson, *New Mexico Populism* (Boulder: Colorado Associated University Press, 1974), and *Populism in the Mountain West* (Albuquerque: University of New Mexico Press, 1986); Peter H. Argersinger, *Populism and Politics: William Alfred Peffer and the People's Party* (Lexington: University of Kentucky Press, 1974); James Edward Wright, *The Politics of Populism: Dissent in Colorado* (New Haven, Connecticut: Yale University Press, 1974); and Robert W. Cherney, *Populism, Progressivism, and the Transformation of Nebraska Politics, 1885–1912* (Lincoln: University of Nebraska Press, 1981).

Michael Paul Rogin, *The Intellectuals and McCarthy: The Radical Specter* (Cambridge, Massachusetts: MIT Press, 1967), represented "a tour de force of historical criticism" concerning the 1950s contention that the reactionary right in the years after World War II grew out of an old left. Rogin's book, in addition to being a thorough critique of the pluralist or consensus school of interpretation, made a compelling case that the New Right grew out of an Old Right—the same elements, ironically, that had opposed Populism with such extreme vigor. With this study Rogin added his name to that of Pollack as a so-called New Left critic of consensus history as applied to Populism.

The climax of fourth-generation Populist studies came in 1976 with Lawrence Goodwyn's *Democratic Promise: The Populist Moment in America* (New York: Oxford University Press, 1976). Goodwyn's general study was an extended treatment of his earlier work on Texas Populism—based primarily on rather selective use of secondary sources. As a result, the movement beyond that base either bore an uncanny resemblance to Texas Populism or was found wanting by what amounts to an incredible orthodoxy test. That was unfortunate because Goodwyn had a number of important things to say about Populism and American culture generally. *Democratic Promise* and the smaller paperback version of the study, as a result, rather than being viewed as replacements for Hicks's *Populist Revolt,* will likely be remembered more for their provocative critiques of the hypercapitalistic and "progressive" society that emerged supreme as Populism was defeated.

For an impressively researched and balanced study of southern Populism, with relevance outside Dixie, see Bruce Palmer, *"Man Over Money": The Southern Populist Critique of American Capitalism* (Chapel Hill: University of North Carolina Press, 1980). Indispensable also for the crucial but still underresearched topic of southern race relations and the role African-Americans played in the Alliances and the Populist movement is Gerald A. Gaither, *Blacks and the Populist Revolt: Ballots and Bigotry in the "New South"* (University of Alabama Press, 1977).

On the origins of Populism, particularly as regards its old radical, producer-class, or neorepublican roots, see Thomas W. Riddle's soon-to-be published study, "The Old Radicalism in America: John R. Rogers and the Populist Movement in Washington, 1891–1900" (Ph.D. diss., Washington State University, 1976); Steven Hahn, *The Roots of Southern Populism: Yeoman Farmers and the Transformation of the Georgia Upcountry, 1850–1890* (New York: Oxford University Press, 1983); Barton C. Shaw, *The Wool-Hat Boys: Georgia's Populist Party* (Baton Rouge: Louisiana State University Press, 1984); Worth Robert Miller, *Oklahoma Populism: A History of the People's Party in the Oklahoma Territory* (Norman: University of Oklahoma Press, 1987); and Scott G. McNall, *The Road to Rebellion: Class Formation and Kansas Populism, 1865–1900* (Chicago: University of Chicago Press, 1988).

Norman Pollack's latest book, *The Just Polity: Populism, Law, and Human Welfare* (Urbana: University of Illinois Press, 1987), would seem to confirm that on the issue of Populism's place on a capitalism-to-socialism continuum, there now exists a consensus placing it somewhere between the two, encompassing, among others, Clanton, Goodwyn, Palmer, and now Pollack.

As regards Populism and the larger context, these studies are especially important: Chester McArthur Destler's study noted earlier; V. L. Parrington, *The Beginnings of Critical Realism in America: 1860–1920* (Norman: University of Oklahoma Press, 1987); Robert McCloskey, *American Conservatism in the Age of Enterprise, 1865–1910* (New York: Harper Torchbooks, 1964); Sidney Fine, *Laissez Faire and the General-Welfare State: A Study of Conflict in American Thought, 1865–1901* (Ann Arbor: University of Michigan Press, 1966); Clinton Rossiter, *Conservatism in America: The Thankless Persuasion* (New York: Vintage, 1962); Garry Wills, *Inventing America: Jefferson's Declaration of Independence* (New York: Vintage, 1979); Richard K. Matthews, *The Radical Politics of*

Thomas Jefferson: A Revisionist View (Lawrence: University Press of Kansas, 1986); R. Jeffrey Lustig. *Corporate Liberalism: The Origins of Modern American Political Theory, 1890–1920* (Berkeley: University of California Press, 1982); and John L. Thomas, *Alternative America: Henry George, Edward Bellamy, Henry Demarest Lloyd and the Adversary Tradition* (Cambridge, Massachusetts: Harvard University Press, 1983).

Index

Style 98

The Author

Gene Clanton earned his bachelor's and master's degrees from Kansas State Teacher's College of Pittsburg, his hometown, in 1959 and 1961, respectively. In 1967 he earned his Ph.D. in history from the University of Kansas. He has been a public school teacher in Lamar, Colorado, visiting professor at Georgia State College in Atlanta, and on the faculty of Texas A&M University. He has been teaching at Washington State University since 1968.

He is the author of *Kansas Populism: Ideas and Men* (1969) and numerous essays and reviews relating to Populism, Progressivism, and related topics. He is at work on a study of congressional Populism and the 1890s.

Ignores religious dimension of Populism?